FROM GOLD
TO GOLD JA

FROM GOLD TEETH TO GOLD JACKET

MY LIFE IN FOOTBALL AND BUSINESS

EDGERRIN JAMES
with JOHN HARRIS

FOREWORD BY PEYTON MANNING

SPORTS
PUBLISHING

Sports Publishing books may be purchased in bulk at special discounts for sales promotion, corporate gifts, fund-raising, or educational purposes. Special editions can also be created to specifications. For details, contact the Special Sales Department, Sports Publishing, 307 West 36th Street, 11th Floor, New York, NY 10018 or sportspubbooks@skyhorsepublishing.com.

Sports Publishing® is a registered trademark of Skyhorse Publishing, Inc.®, a Delaware corporation.

Visit our website at www.sportspubbooks.com.

10 9 8 7 6 5 4 3 2 1

Library of Congress Cataloging-in-Publication Data is available on file.

Jacket design by Brian Peterson
Front jacket photo courtesy of the Indianapolis Colts
Back jacket and spine photos courtesy of the Pro Football Hall of Fame

Print ISBN: 978-1-68358-432-2
Ebook ISBN: 978-1-68358-433-9

Printed in the United States of America

CONTENTS

FOREWORD

BY PEYTON MANNING

I REALLY enjoyed getting to know Edgerrin and being his teammate. He was an unbelievable talent. I liked him from the get-go. To me, one of the best things players can say about you when you stop playing is: He was a great teammate. I remember telling my father, Archie Manning, that Edgerrin James was the best teammate I ever had. I really meant that and still do to this day. He was dependable. He always played. He always practiced. He didn't miss practice because his back was hurting. He was a quiet guy who didn't say a lot, but instead spoke with his actions. He didn't boast about what he was going to do. He just did the work. And he was unselfish. Edgerrin took a lot of pride in his pass-blocking and he took a lot of pride in his ability to catch the ball. He always picked up the blitz. He was a great runner but, to me, he was equally as great of a pass protector and he knew who to block. You didn't have to worry about him being in there on a pivotal play. He was an every-down back who never came out of the game. There are a lot of great players who do this well or that better, but as an overall teammate, he just had it. He's a guy you liked having in your huddle with you. I liked having him behind me.

I have good memories being Edgerrin's teammate. You watched him score a touchdown, and he was like Barry Sanders.

He'd hand the ball to the referee, or he'd keep it and give it to the equipment guy if it was special. He acted like this is what I'm supposed to do. Some guys spike it and celebrate. There was no dancing, no spiking the ball. He didn't bring attention to himself. I always appreciated that.

I still remember the first time I saw him run with the ball after we drafted him out of Miami. We played the Saints in a preseason game. I knew who Edgerrin was, that great game he had against UCLA when he rushed for 299 yards. When I heard Edgerrin's name called on draft day, I was excited because he was a special running back who was coming to the Colts. He held out for a few weeks and missed training camp, but I saw him in minicamps so I knew what he could do in practice. But you always want to see it up close and personal on the field in a game. He didn't come in boasting about what he was going to do. He just came in and went to work. We ran a draw play against the Saints and our line didn't block anybody. This defensive tackle had him right in his grasp. He spun out for a nice gain and later ran for a touchdown in the same drive. I remember saying, "Wow. This is gonna be fun."

The biggest compliment I can give Edgerrin James is that I took so much pride in faking and carrying out my fake after handing him the ball. It's not a rest play for the quarterback. Faking is about discipline and effort. That all changed with Edgerrin. You would call me the biggest hypocrite if you watched film of me and Edgerrin. A lot of times I wasn't carrying out my fakes because I wanted to watch him run the ball. If I handed off to him, I didn't want to run to the other side and carry out the fake. I wanted to see. I had the best view of anybody in that stadium. Nobody had a better view because I was right behind No.

32. My coaches would say, 'Peyton, come on.' I couldn't help it. It was too good of a view to miss.

I think somehow it had gotten in the narrative that the reason Edgerrin had such great success with the Colts was because we had great receivers and we threw the ball so well and that allowed him to be a great running back because teams wanted to stop the pass. I'm saying no, no no, it worked the other way. The reason we threw the ball so well is because we knew we were going to get one-on-one coverage outside on our receivers because the defense was keying on the run. Edgerrin took a lot of pride in knowing that defenses had to put an extra defender down there close to the line of scrimmage to stop him. He allowed us to throw the ball because teams were trying to stop him. Our offense started with him and his ability to run the ball.

Edgerrin helped establish a winning culture in Indianapolis. After he arrived, free agents wanted to come and play in Indy. The Colts had some good teams through the years, but there were a lot of years when they were considered an easy win. Edgerrin James helped change that. For us to win 12 games seven seasons in a row, he was a big part of that. Indiana is a football state now. When Edgerrin and I got there, it was a basketball state, it was a car racing state. It was a combination of people who helped change that perception. Edgerrin will always be remembered as one of the pillars who transformed the Indianapolis Colts.

INTRODUCTION

BY JOHN HARRIS

THE night before the UCLA game, the most important game of his life, University of Miami running back Edgerrin James, sans a crystal ball, boldly and correctly predicted his future.

It was a heartfelt, business-driven prognosis based on years of not only enduring but overcoming the slings and arrows of living a hard knock life circa 1998.

Among the greatest offensive players in the storied history of Hurricanes football, James bet on himself, and won—big. A well-balanced running back, James was deceptively fast and possessed the speed to burst through holes and locate daylight (he was timed in a blazing 4.38 seconds in the 40-yard dash at UM's pro day), with the raw power to break tackles and create his own holes. In his three years at The U, he averaged an astronomical six yards per carry.

With the NFL draft only a few months away, James set his sights squarely on securing the bag of cold hard cash that would forever lift his family out of poverty and guarantee generational wealth.

"I just needed one time to get the money," James said. "I get the money one time, and I'm not worried about it anymore. I'm not worried about the money because I can live without doing all the things that a lot of people try to do with money. I never cared about money, as far as I've got to use it. I just wanted money for the safety and to be able to provide for my family."

This book is about James's rise to prominence, as a football phenom from the Deep South who didn't permit himself to be shackled by life's circumstances and evolved into a college legend on his way to becoming an NFL superstar, culminating in the rarified air of the Pro Football Hall of Fame in Canton, Ohio. The book's title, *From Gold Teeth to Gold Jacket*, identifies James as a unique personality whose nontraditional appearance countered societal norms—from his gold teeth to the long dreadlocks dangling outside his helmet. To be blunt, some segments of society prejudged him without really knowing him. This book traces James's roots as a young entrepreneur who played football to satisfy his deep-seated business instincts, creating remarkable riches.

From Gold Teeth to Gold Jacket reveals that James, despite his humble beginnings, was ahead of the curve financially among his NFL peers, prompting legendary sports agent Leigh Steinberg to marvel about James's "steel-trap mind." An early example of James's astute financial acumen emerged when he chose not to hire representation until after he was drafted. "There were two sides to Edgerrin," said Steinberg, who, along with eventual MLB team owner Jeff Moorad, negotiated James's first pro deal in 1999. "There was the superficial Edgerrin who had dreadlocks and interesting teeth that would tend to give people a perception about who he was. The real Edgerrin was extremely bright . . . and incredibly organized in how he went about things."

* * *

Edgerrin's story is meant to both entertain and educate, and put his vast accomplishments and contributions into historical perspective. To wit: He's second on the NFL's all-time list of money earned by running backs. He's unofficially the first NFL player to be selected as high as No. 4 in the draft without an agent. At the time of his signing, his rookie contract was the largest ever for an NFL running back, and his money grab during the 1999 season was the highest single total for a rookie. He is one of only four players in NFL history to compile four 1,500-yard rushing seasons. In college, he was the first running back at the University of Miami to post two consecutive seasons with 1,000-plus rushing yards, and he's tied for first in school history with 14 career 100- yard rushing games. He holds the two best single-game rushing performances at Miami. He's also the first former Miami student-athlete to make a major financial contribution to the school's athletic department.

Growing up dirt poor in rural Immokalee, a little over an hour's drive from tony Coral Gables, his home away from home for three years, James learned, for better or worse, how to do without.

As a youngster, he once slept three to a bed with his brothers in his grandmother's house when his mother worked three jobs to support them. He paid for his college education with a football scholarship and Pell Grants. He became a teenage father.

In other words, he grew up thinking fast on his feet.

At Miami, he chose an academic major that provided him with enough free time to learn the team playbook and hone his football skills, while keeping him academically eligible.

His path to the promised land was clear from the beginning.

No grades meant no football, and no football meant no NFL, which, of course, meant no big-time money for the James household. Keeping it real, James's aptitude for football and the lifetime financial security it could provide him and his family is why he repped Miami Hurricanes gear so fiercely on Saturday afternoons.

"I totally committed to football, even adjusted my school schedule," James said. "Everything was based around football because I found a love that I can attack and take my family to a whole new level.

"I didn't drink. I didn't smoke. I totally locked in. And then I had my daughter. That's another thing that got me focused: my daughter. My mom. My daughter's momma. I've got to make sure they're all good."

He loved playing football, of course. One of his fondest memories about playing Pop Warner as a kid was that the first day of practice always fell on his birthday (August 1). Since his family didn't celebrate birthdays, due to the fact that he was raised as a Jehovah's Witness (who do not celebrate birthdays and holidays), the opening of Pop Warner season each summer became, in essence, his birthday gift.

James was confident he would perform spectacularly against UCLA, telling teammate Santana Moss of his lofty goal to rush for 300 yards against an opponent some viewed as the best college football team in the country, and use that performance as a springboard to the NFL.

So what if the Hurricanes, recovering from the effects of NCAA probation, were embarrassed the previous week at Syracuse, 66–13? Or that unbeaten UCLA was in national championship contention and flaunting a 20-game winning streak?

Didn't James always say that football came easy to him—so easy that he chose football over his beloved basketball because running to daylight and scoring touchdowns was ingrained in his DNA?

None of it mattered because James bought into his own hype; that the stars were perfectly aligned for him to live in the moment and ride the wave of good fortune that would surely come his way as a result of him doing what he was destined to do.

Damned if he didn't do precisely that.

In what became his watershed moment at Miami—and a career-defining moment overall—James tied a school record with 39 carries. He rushed for a school-record 299 yards and scored three touchdowns in the Hurricanes' 49–45 upset victory over UCLA at the Orange Bowl on December 5, 1998. In doing so, James broke his own single-game rushing mark of 271 yards, set the previous season against Boston College.

At one point in the fourth quarter, James made good on his prediction to Moss when he crossed the 300-yard milestone, but he was later stopped in the backfield for a loss. His third and final touchdown of the game—a 1-yard bolt around left end in the waning seconds—fueled a furious comeback and provided the winning margin.

More than two decades later, UCLA linebacker Ramogi Huma recalled James's performance with reverence.

"Edgerrin was extremely hard to tackle. He should probably be the biggest UCLA supporter of all time because we put him so far on the map," Huma said.

"On the national stage in a very significant game, he ran through us. Most of those yards were after contact. He was the real deal.

"There's some big guys that can move. But what stood out to me was his balance. His balance was impeccable."

Soon after the regular season ended, James, emboldened by his breakout game against UCLA, a 156-yard, two-touchdown follow-up performance against North Carolina State in the Micron PC Bowl, and a pressing need to provide for his family, bypassed his final year of college eligibility to enter the 1999 NFL Draft.

Despite languishing below the national radar and performing in the shadows of Heisman Trophy winner and fellow running back Ricky Williams, James was the surprise and unpopular No. 4 overall selection by the Indianapolis Colts—one pick ahead of Williams, his college albatross. Not only did the Colts, who targeted a running back in the draft, pass over Williams to grab James (to the dismay of their fans and local media covering the team), but rewarded him with a seven-year, $49.5 million contract—the highest pact given to a rookie running back in NFL history. In his first year alone, James netted $14.8 million, a rookie record regardless of position.

James was worth every dollar. He joined Eric Dickerson and Earl Campbell as the only players since the 1970 merger to lead the NFL in rushing in each of their first two seasons.

With James cracking the starting lineup as a rookie, Indianapolis improved from 3–13 to 13–3 for the greatest one-year turnaround in league history, won the AFC East, and hosted their first-ever playoff game since the franchise had moved to Indy in 1984.

The UCLA game was James's inspiration for everything that followed.

"Everything was lined up the right way," James said. "I was aware of what was at stake. The UCLA game gave me the opportunity to show what I could do."

James made his bold prediction to Moss, his roommate for the UCLA game, the night before the clash at the Orange Bowl.

Miami's football players were traditionally paired up the night before a game. On the occasion of the Hurricanes' final regular season contest, James roomed with Moss, the flashy wide receiver. Though normally rooming with fellow running back James Jackson, he was paired up with Moss, as Jackson was sidelined with an injury.

Moss usually roomed with fellow wide receiver Reggie Wayne, who was out for the season with a knee injury. It was the first time James and Moss had roomed together. The players discussed their individual goals for the game when James dropped his bombshell.

"EJ shared some things with me before the UCLA game," Moss said. "He told me he was going to rush for 300 yards. He also said, 'If I go out here and do what I plan on doing, I'm out of here. Between me and you.'"

"My confidence, my belief, comes from a person that's prepared, a person that's ready," James said. "People want to follow people that bring something to the table. Nobody wants to get behind a person that don't know nothing, that don't bring nothing to the table. I've always been a real quiet, positive leader."

James's confidence and belief rubbed off on his teammates. The Hurricanes couldn't have beaten UCLA without him.

"We were always all ears when EJ opened his mouth," said Moss, who caught a long touchdown pass in the UCLA game. "He was a big reason why we were so successful because we actually got a chance to play alongside him. Just seeing how he went about his business motivated everybody.

"I'm looking at him as a young buck like, I know that's something he's keeping to himself. But to actually share these words with him before the game, and he went out and did exactly what he said he was going to do, I never saw it done in my life like he did it.

"All I could do was shake my head."

The uncertain buildup to the UCLA game was fraught with challenges. The game, originally scheduled for September, was postponed because of Hurricane Georges blowing through the Florida Keys. It was later canceled due to the incompatibility of both teams' schedules. The on-again, off-again cross-country matchup was eventually rescheduled and finalized for the first weekend in December.

For James, the UCLA game provided a second chance, a welcome opportunity to not only prove to the college football world that the Miami Hurricanes were indeed back, but also to validate his own legitimacy as a special running back with high-end NFL potential.

"No one really knew who we were. We knew we were good. Everybody in the locker room, anybody around our team, knew we were good. We were on our way to getting our program back, but we were coming off probation so we didn't play a lot of games on national TV. We didn't normally get to play against a top-ranked team like UCLA in the Orange Bowl. All eyes were on this game. We had nothing to lose.

INTRODUCTION

"James Jackson, the guy I split carries with, didn't play. That meant a bigger workload for me. I think that game told people on the national scene this kid right here can play, he's the real deal. My last carry in the Orange Bowl was the game-winning touchdown. UCLA had a national championship on the line that was stopped by an underdog. You can't write it any better than that."

Wayne recalled the exact moment he knew James was leaving Miami for the NFL

"Something got into him that day against UCLA," Wayne said. "As he's running up and down the field, you could see those gold teeth flashing in between his facemask. He's just lit up.

"He was our offense. He was everything we needed. I'll never forget this one time he came to the sideline. He was already well over 200 yards.

"I'm like, 'Damn, bro, what's next? You hit 'em with the long run. You hit 'em with the short game. You hit 'em with the pass out of the backfield.'

"EJ looked at me and said, 'The NFL is next.' That's when I knew we done lost EJ.

"In the next couple weeks, EJ declared for the draft. As teammates, everybody knew he was gone and all the backups were glad that he was gone because then they got a chance to play. That's Clinton Portis and Najeh Davenport and James Jackson. These dudes are some of Miami's greats. They were excited for his opportunity but happy to see him go."

PART I:
IMMOKALEE (1978–1993)

1

THE EARLY YEARS

Edgerrin got his business sense from my mom. He would leave school and go and get on her couch. One thing about my mom, m-o-n-e-y meant a lot to her, okay? She drilled that into his head about making money. She said there's so many ways you can make money legal. He listened to her.

He had a grind in him that was unreal. It was an eat, sleep, and grind mentality . . . and our entire family is grateful for that.

—Julie James, Edgerrin's mother

IMMOKALEE is a special place to me. It's unique. It shapes you.

To give you a better understanding, Immokalee was a small town, one of the poorest cities in the whole state of Florida, if not the entire country. It has one high school. You grew up there, hung out there, went to school there, so it becomes all you know. The way we look at things, the way things go for people who live there, it's just real tough.

With everything going on there, the hardest thing to do is make it out. You're living below the poverty line; there are so many things that work against you. There's other places, bigger cities where there's bigger opportunities. But if you make it out, you can make it anywhere.

With all that said, we're still in the richest county in the state. You got a chance to actually see things, see the dream. Twenty minutes away in the same county, Collier County, you have people that actually live good. Naples was predominately white. Naples represented the wealthy, the upper echelon of the area. I grew up around a bunch of minorities. Blacks. Mexicans. Haitians. Migrant workers. There weren't a lot of whites around. When you see that, you start understanding why a person moves the way they move, why they think the way they think. For me and my family, it was a whole different world.

Those are things that stand out when you're young.

It was definitely motivation for me because when you can see it, you realize you can be it. It's a matter of if you're going to do what it takes.

I was always determined to do more. You don't have nobody to give you nothing; the only way you can get something is you've got to do what it takes. Whatever it takes.

For me, it was always how can I get the advantage, how can I get the upper hand? I'm always looking for an advantage—even to this day. To get the advantage, you have to do more. The bare minimum, that's what everybody else does. I had to ask myself, how can I push myself so that I'm not in the same category as everybody else? That's always been my mindset. I made sure that

I'm always going to do more just to give myself a chance to be successful.

But it all comes back to the beginning. All the things I'm able to do and accomplish is because I know where I came from. It gives you a greater appreciation for things other people take for granted.

I come from a tight-knit group. Everybody knows everybody. Outsiders, we look at them like, "Hold up. I just met this guy. I don't have to trust you. I don't have to do nothing with you. I don't know you. I've been going my whole life without you. You're not important to me."

It's instinct, personality, and upbringing.

When you're out of your comfort zone, you usually stay in your shell. It worked perfect for me because I'm not used to talking to everybody or knowing everybody. I'd rather stay over here.

When I played for the Colts I was up for an ESPY award. I was sitting in the projects back home. We were watching the ESPYs on TV. Someone said, "Why aren't you at the ESPYs?" I said, "The season is over. I'm not interested in going to that. That's not my bag." Any time you live in areas where there's poverty, all those areas are the same. They all run parallel. Immokalee was a typical Florida town. If you're there, you look at it one way. If you come from another situation, you look at it another way. I've never been afraid to say where I'm from because that was all part of my ammo. That's what drove me. It's how you represent where your feet are. You can put me in any city, any place, and I'm always going to be me. It's just the way we look at things. The way we do things. Making the most out of every-thing, and then outlasting everybody.

When I got older, I would go back to Immokalee or go through there, just to get that fight, just to get that hunger. It brings that realness out in me.

It's like, "Everybody else is soft. Everybody else is spoiled. We're real grit."

When I go back through there now, I'm like "Dang, we really used to live like this?"

It makes you understand that anybody that's complaining, whining . . . well, you guys are trippin'. When I go back home, I try to get refocused. Sometimes I go through there just because. Just to get that perspective that says, "Don't get too comfortable. Don't relax. They're not like you. They can't be like you. Nobody else is going through this."

That's why I'm driven. What shaped you? What made you? You have to know where you're coming from.

If you ever go to a Third World country and see the way they're living, you get a greater appreciation for the ones that made it out and why they're willing to work so hard. Why they're willing to work in the hot fields and do hard labor.

You wonder why, until you go over there.

When you go over there, you get a greater appreciation for them. You come to understand. "I see why they're willing to do all these things just to come to America."

For me, it's the same thing. Immokalee felt like being from one of those Third World countries, because it kinda is. When people would ask, "Was Immokalee really that bad?" all I would says is, "Go live there."

I can truly say sometimes when I went to a Third World country, I didn't feel out of place or out of touch. It wasn't foreign to me. I could relate.

We had trailers in Immokalee. There were huts. The way people actually lived, it was a bunch of migrants that came to live there. Mexicans and a bunch of hard-working people. Haitians came over there to live. There were a lot of immigrants. It wasn't high end.

Looking back on one of the buildings me and my brothers lived in with my momma, I remember that it had a flat roof. The rain would come pouring in. There were rats. It was an American version of a Third World country.

When it was time to take a shower, you got your towel. You walk barefoot or you walk on the back of your shoes to the shower and leave your shoes right at the door. You walked to the bathroom because we didn't have our own bathroom. That's where we took our showers. It was a little community area with showers. It was like a locker room shower. You go in there, turn the water on, take your soap, take your shower. There's no privacy. Everybody knows you're taking a shower. They know when you're going to the bathroom. After I took my shower, I went back to the house, and I'm happy. People don't really know what happiness is.

Years later, after I made it to the NFL, I bought that building where we lived. We made every improvement that we could under the codes. You had to tear stuff down to bring it up to the new building codes. After I bought it, that building doesn't look nothing like it used to. And it still looks bad.

I'm quite sure there's a lot of people that can't relate. We were living place to place, but it was cool.

FROM GOLD TEETH TO GOLD JACKET

> ## *JULIE JAMES SAID IT WAS A CONSTANT STRUGGLE RAISING HER YOUNG SONS BY HERSELF*

My kids came up tough. Being a single parent was no joke. I don't wish that on anybody; to raise children by themselves, as it was overwhelming. I reminisce a lot about how I even made it.

I walked to work a lot of the time. I finally got an advance and bought a bicycle and started riding it to work. Sometimes I worked three jobs. Two of them would be temporary. I did cafeteria work, but I also cleaned a lady's house on Saturdays. There were certain things that you needed to know how to do. I did tax work; I found a way to do somebody's books. Side jobs like that. We had to maintain for three or four months until watermelon season. We would leave in June and not come back until November or December. We could actually live off that money we made those six months.

Me and the boys lived in a roach- and rat-infested apartment with the lowest of the low kind of people. We stayed there for a while before we moved into a house and stayed there for eight months. I was trying to see if I could handle such a big change, but I couldn't. Me and my two youngest sons went to Tallahassee for three months. At the time, EJ was staying with his father. We were back within three months. Each time we made a move, it was better than the last place we stayed.

Growing up, Edgerrin was the oldest one in the house. I had two older sons, but they didn't live with me. Edgerrin was the oldest one over my other two sons. He was the man of the house. I trusted him.

We had a bond. I used to sit him down and cry on his shoulder as if he was an adult. I put him up there. He was the one that I nurtured and believed in.

We would go up the street and stay there until two in the morning. There was a store where people hung out, and I'd

(Continued on next page)

just be there talking with different people. I allowed my kids up there with me because I didn't have a babysitter. That was our form of entertainment. They had a good time with me.

When you come from a small environment like Immokalee, there were so many things to drag you down.

Everybody knows what everybody's doing.

The only thing that was going on was illegal stuff.

Some gravitated to that. Some of them actually got on drugs. It was a wave that went through Immokalee like a bad storm.

Edgerrin was nine or ten. He saw all this stuff. It was nothing hidden from the eye.

It was just a fortunate thing. He could have easily succumbed to that environment, he really could have, because it was right in our family. It was a blessing, because when it's that close to home, it's only a matter of time before it penetrates one of the kids.

Praying is a good word for what I did. Prayer does help.

Edgerrin got his business sense from my mom. He would leave school and go and get on her couch. One thing about my mom, m-o-n-e-y meant a lot to her, okay? She drilled that into his head about making money. She said there's so many ways you can make money legal. He listened to her.

He had a grind in him that was unreal. It was an eat, sleep, and grind mentality . . . and our entire family is grateful for that.

You gotta understand. Kids. Racism. Material things. None of that matters until you make them matter. A Black kid and a white kid will play together, but if you make it a point of emphasis to divide them, what do you think it's going to do to those kids?

If I'm eating, I'm eating good. It ain't, "Oh, you're eating welfare food." No. My Momma cooked this food. It tastes good. Then you get introduced to some new or fancy food. It tastes good, but it looks better. It's presented better. Now your thoughts change.

We lived in a lot of different places, so we never got settled in any one place. After we moved out of the efficiency with the flat roof, we moved to another house and stayed there for a little while. When we left there, we moved to a Habitat for Humanity house. With Habitat for Humanity, you were required to physically put in hours of work to help build houses. We lived in a three-bedroom house and I finally got my own room.

I ended up buying that house and we still have it today.

The crazy part about it is when things are embedded in you, they're embedded in you.

My momma still goes to that house. I bought her a half-million dollar house, but she goes to the Habitat For Humanity house more than she goes to the half-million dollar house.

When you start putting things in perspective, it's like, "We really lived like this. And I'm not going back."

That's how I feel. I promised my momma we're not going back ever again.

That tells you how bad I am. I'm a bad motherfucker because I made it out of this shit. You have to take that approach.

That's why I don't beg and I don't lean on anybody. I'm off the muscle. I had to train my mind to say, 'I'm built different because I didn't have those opportunities.' I had to figure things out with little to no help. I had to put in a lot of work. I had to earn mine because I'm not the son of this person who can help me or that person who has all these connections. No. I'm the son of a man that has twenty-some kids—that's who I am. You can't make me flinch. I came out of a situation that you're not supposed to come out of.

* * *

I have a big family. My childhood was built around my family.

My grandma had thirteen kids. All of her sons had kids. And a lot of them had double-digit kids. I don't want to put a number to it, but that paints a pretty good picture right there.

My momma had me when she was eighteen. I didn't live with my father. Me and my brothers grew up in a single-parent home. I don't like painting this picture that we were just so down, that it was so bad–which it wasn't. It was just the norm.

Was it a happy childhood? I mean, we made the best out of what we had. When you're surrounded by people that come from the same situation, it's not so much that it's bad, but rather just the norm.

At a young age, I knew I had to work to help my family. That's the first thing I learned. Nowadays, kids learn if you just beg or cry, if you whine, you can get things. You can complain and get things. You can bullshit people and get things. That's their approach. I realized that my approach had to be that if I wanted something, I had to work for it.

That's one of the things I look at with my kids now. The kids that don't have, they're so creative. Creativity comes from not having, so they use creative resources. And they'll kind of trick your kids. These kids will make you think it's cool to live in the projects, saying things like, "We had a ball last night. We were playing cards."

First of all, there ain't that much space where they live, but they'll make it seem like it's so fun. And it'll have your kids saying, "I live a terrible life." Trying to be thuggin' and doing all kinds of crazy stuff.

They think that it's better over there when, in reality, these people are making the best out of their situation. And they're making it fun.

I was one of those kids.

The only time you realize you don't have is when you see what other people have. They let you know that you don't have. The world tells you those things.

You sit back and say, "I wish I had more than one pair of shoes." My kids have twenty pair of shoes and it's like, "It's not good enough." Get out of here. You crazy? The stuff I had to go through, my kids couldn't care less about it. They're not even aware it exists. They're not conditioned to think how we used to think. As a parent, you have to find that balance. I want my kids to want nicer things, have nicer things—the best of the best. At the same time, I want them to appreciate those things, to understand that what they have I didn't, and most don't.

My momma, Julie James, raised me and my brothers Jeff, and GMan (Gerren) by herself. Me and my brothers shared a bed. If there wasn't enough room in the bed, someone slept on the floor. No big deal, that's just how it was.

Momma was always working. She worked in a school cafeteria and held other jobs to make ends meet. That was no easy task. They called her a single mom, but she was so much more to us.

She instilled in me a sense of pride and purpose. Thanks to her, I learned the importance of being true to myself no matter the circumstances, as well as being grounded. As I grew older, I really didn't give space to newcomers and outsiders. I always surrounded myself with my people, my family. As a result, I've always been able to keep it real and live in my element. I never left my element and never forgot where I came from. A lot of people go outside their element, but that was never my style.

In terms of our family, we had each other—and that was good enough. We didn't spend time thinking about what we didn't have, or how good other people had it. There was always something for us to do, there was always family around. We had our friends, but we spent most of our time with family. We were always there for each other. We had a big family with lots of cousins and aunts and uncles. Even when we got older, we still spent a lot of our time with family when we weren't at school or playing sports and hanging out.

We spent a lot of time at my grandma's house. My grandma's house was the center of my world.

Some of my brothers lived in different places, but we spent a lot of time at my grandma's house. We were there every day. It's where everything was happening. All of our cousins were there. We did everything there. We had fun. We played there. We ate there. We slept there.

Everything came full circle after I got to the pros. I was able to buy the building I grew up in. My grandparents were going to lose the property. It was a 16-unit building. I learned a lot from that situation.

One of my uncles came into some money and was able to save the property, and then, later on, I was able to buy it and keep it. It taught me a lot about deeds and taxes and how easily you can lose real estate. There's so much more than people realize and understand. You can be a victim or you can be somebody that capitalizes on it.

* * *

Every day after school, from the time I was little up until high school, I'd come home, take a nap, and lay on my grandma's couch. My grandma would always talk to me. She'd tell me about getting money, having money, having your own. She kept pounding that stuff into my head, even at a young age. She instilled in me the "get your own" mentality. Even though I was young, she knew it was important that I understand this, and she made sure I did.

Everybody in my family hustled in some shape or form. My granddaddy didn't go to school for it, but he knew business. He was a contractor, as did my Uncle Ike and Uncle Johnny. As contractors, my uncles worked in Georgia, harvesting watermelons. When I was finally old enough to travel with them, I was able to make my own money and make my own decisions, learning and understanding the value of a dollar. I spent my summers working next to crackheads at twenty dollars a truckload. Hauling watermelons in the hot sun toughened me up for football.

Hauling watermelons at fourteen was my way to show people that I was a man. Grownups are doing this, I can do this, too. I can make the same money they're making.

Kids back home were making five dollars an hour, while I was making $100, $200 a day. I had a chance to do what adults do. I'm younger and I'm holding my own. That was the initial motivation.

It wasn't easy money. Far from it. You're in the hot sun. After picking the watermelons, you gotta load them onto the truck.

That ain't no easy feat. Now you're on the truck, and gotta drive to the next stop. Once there, you gotta pick them up again, and now throw them from the truck to the belt. Neither one of my teenage son's can do that. Hell, I'm not letting them do that. One of my son's said, "Daddy, I want to try doing the watermelons." I said the only way you're going out there is if I own the watermelon field. It's hot as hell. I worked from seven in the morning to seven at night, seven days a week during the summer months right up until the start of school

Other kids would try it because they saw all the money you were making, but it will break you down physically. It makes a man out of you. There's no way you want to do something like that. But when you're got a mission and things you're trying to accomplish—like needing clothes for school—that was my best shot at doing it without getting in trouble.

You got paid by the truck. Two people worked on a truck. If you did ten trucks a day, you made $100. And then I figured, why not do a whole truck by myself? That was $200 a day.

Hauling watermelons gave you grown-man strength. Grown-man strength was a different kind of strength. You're not lifting weights, but nobody's going to push you around. You're throwing those watermelons. You're using your legs, your back, and your arms.

When I was thirteen my momma pulled me aside and told me I was the man of the house. I was in middle school. I was the third-oldest brother—one year older than Jeff, and five years older than GMan. Bird (Cherron) is the oldest and Dederrian the second-oldest, but they were living with grandparents. Momma made it real clear she knew I was the one who could handle that responsibility—even at that young age. I promised to take care of her forever, and promised to do whatever it takes. I took that role and that position very, very seriously because I was the one she trusted to step up.

Even with all that, she didn't try to restrict me or restrain me. She just said, "Don't get in trouble."

When you're young and your momma pulls you aside and has a serious conversation with you and tells you you're the man of the house, there's no turning back. It does something for your ego. "I'm going to do whatever it takes to protect our house."

Though I was still a kid, I now had to act like a man.

I took pride in being the man of the house. It fueled me.

Though every kid feels this way, it was now my responsibility to do everything I can to make sure that she doesn't worry. When you see your momma go through so much all by herself to keep our family together, I knew I had to lock in and make sure I do everything that it takes to make sure that lady is good.

I started doing things to get money, to make sure that I was able to provide. Part of being man of the house, you have to be able to bring things to the table. My momma knew I would always come up with some type of funding. She saw my drive, knew she could count on me. When she gave me that title, it felt like a chip on my shoulder. But there came a lot of responsibility too. I didn't follow crowds or anything. I had to make sure I stayed out of trouble, make sure I didn't do anything to lose those privileges. I had to buy my own clothes. If my momma needed something, I had to come up with it. That was my MO. I always came up with it. I took pride in being able to take care of her. I actually took more pride in not having to ask her for anything. That was my drive not to mess around. I had mouths to feed and a momma that needed me to handle my responsibilities.

It was a built-in situation because it wasn't like there was another solution or another option for me. I didn't have anybody to call. I had to come through, or I was going to be somebody that put more stress on my family. Today, when I see kids lean on their parents and ask their mom to stand in line and buy them $200 shoes, I'm like, "That's crazy." I could never ask my momma for those shoes, for nothing like that. My mindset was totally different.

Growing up in a Jehovah's Witness house, I wasn't expecting gifts. I learned how to be independent. That's what being man of the house meant to me.

Even with all that, she didn't try to restrict me or restrain me. She just said, "Don't get in trouble."

When you know, you know. My momma had been around me all my life. Certain things you see in certain people, and my Momma saw it in me. I was only thirteen, but I was a different thirteen. That's what made her give me all the freedom and give me the reins in my younger years. My thing was to live up to it.

* * *

For me, it's always been about football.

When you grow up in a small town—especially one like mine—you had nothing else to do but look forward to it.

My love for football goes way back to when I started playing Pop Warner at age eight.

However, I almost didn't get to play.

Like most parents, my momma was worried about me getting hurt. For me, football is what I wanted to do. I knew this at a young age. So when the chance is almost taken away from you, it made the opportunity to play mean a bit more.

As a kid, you're just happy to be able to play. All the while, you're walking around with doubt.

I'm in Immokalee. There's nothing to do. And football is everything.

At first, I didn't think I would be allowed to play. My family knew I was good. My uncles told my momma, "You gotta let him play." They did that for me, having my family fight for me. That was all I needed—to show them that they were right. That this was for me.

You have to be tough to play running back. You can't be worried or be concerned about getting hurt. You gotta be tough. Then it becomes a mental thing. Worried? Concerned? That's all mental. Your toughness takes all that out the way.

When it came to football, it gave me something to do. Something that kept me out of trouble. Plus, I was actually good at it.

We used to play football in the yard all the time. But now I had a chance to play organized football and play with other kids. Other than that, you're just playing in the projects or playing in the neighborhood. Now you've got a chance to play against people you don't even know. You get a chance to compare yourself to others. There's a difference between street ball and playing on a field, with pads and a helmet. And I wanted that.

Football was my outlet, my chance to do something for myself. It also offered me the chance to experience new things. We can go out of town to play against this team, or that team is coming to town to play us. It was one of those things you sort of gravitated toward. It's like the ultimate game because it brings people together. The camaraderie, being around the guys. It became something I really looked forward to.

When you played Pop Warner, it was a place to hang out. When your game's over, you're able to watch your brother's game, or your cousin's game.

I came from a football family. Everybody in my family played football. All my uncles played. It was a family thing. We all played backyard football. No pads, no nothing. We were really out there trying to mess each other up.

I don't care what city you go to, football is football. In Immokalee, football is life. It's about family. Everybody knows each other and supports each other. One person's success is shared by everyone. Everybody loves football. To be successful there, you've got to put in the work.

Coming from a football family, I was lucky to grow up and play against those older than me. And because my birthday was on August 1, the age cutoff, I actually could have played a level down. But that would have been unfair. I was always the youngest on the team, but I was the youngest and also one of the better guys on the team. There were some other people on the team that were good. I was younger, so I had to take a backseat early on. You had to earn your place on the field, yet I always held my own.

My cousin Dedrin was our quarterback my senior year. After high school, Dedrin played college football at Central Florida. My younger brother Jeff went to Immokalee and played football at Illinois State. My cousin Javarris played football at Immokalee and was a running back at Miami.

If you're killing it in Pop Warner, and you're good, it's usually going to carry over to high school. I was good in Pop Warner. High school, I was good. It wasn't really a surprise to anybody around me because everybody was kind of used to it.

> ## JULIE JAMES DIDN'T WANT EDGERRIN TO PLAY FOOTBALL WHEN HE WAS YOUNG
>
> I was one of those mothers that was afraid for her child to play football.
>
> I grew up with eight brothers. I was the tenth child of thirteen kids. Two of my older brothers, Isaac and Johnny, kept on me until they influenced me to let Edgerrin play.
>
> He was excited because he wanted to play, but he knew how I felt about it: I was afraid of him getting hurt.
>
> I was already into football because I was raised with my brothers, but when it came down to my own child, I was hesitant.
>
> He was excited when my brothers convinced me to let him play, but I was always concerned.
>
> Probably after that first year, I kind of got away from that.

I always give credit to my mom. My mom brought us up under Jehovah's Witness teachings. I'm not a Jehovah's Witness, but we had to learn to accept things. It taught me so much. As a kid, to see everybody get gifts and toys and you just say, "Hey, we don't celebrate." Your birthday comes and it's not a big deal. Your momma tells you: "Every day is a holiday. Every day is a good day. We don't celebrate birthdays." Happy Birthday doesn't mean that much to me. The foundation is set. Things don't matter. None of that material stuff matters. You don't know why. You don't know nothing. But you've got to weather that storm. It gives you a solid foundation of "I can do without." I don't have to have it. I don't have to follow the crowd. I used to hate it (attending Jehovah's Witness services). It was the most boring stuff in the world, but I had to go. I loved watching *The Cosby Show*, but I couldn't watch because we had to go to those services. But you learned to accept things. You learned to accept where you're at. That played such a big part. It came at a time when, dang, everybody's getting something. Kids look forward to things. What made me so happy about my birthday being August 1 was that it was the first day of Pop Warner. I was just born to be a football player.

I found ways to manipulate myself, my mind, to try and trick me. People never knew it was my birthday other than when I had to bring my birth certificate. August 1, the first day of Pop Warner, that's what I looked forward to. Christmas, we don't celebrate, so it don't matter. Everybody else gets all their toys. You watch them. You sit there. You just be happy for people. You can't be happy for yourself because you ain't got shit. You can't feel sorry for yourself. My momma said, "We don't celebrate Christmas," and I ain't going against my momma. Even though I'm not saying I've taken to that religion. That's not my thing. But that was what my momma chose. My momma's birthday was the other day. You say you're going to have a party for her. She's not doing it. You have to really be careful how you word things to her. You learn to respect things like that. You get a great respect for things and people and just life in general. It gave me a nice solid foundation to where things don't matter. I don't have to follow the crowd. The loyalty part? The loyalty goes back to when momma said we ain't doing it. So we're not doing it. I'm not going against her.

* * *

I was always quiet and I watched everything. I paid attention and looked at things from every angle. The more I observed, the more I learned.

When it comes to doing illegal stuff, the hustling and all that, I always say, "God's been had his hands on me." Because you're only one little mistake from not being in the position you're in.

I always think about the hustling part. There are some very interesting stories. I'm like, "Damn. That could have really gone left." But it didn't.

That's why I didn't go into those things because it must not be that important. I don't want to mislead anybody and I don't want to say, "I did this."

What do I mean by hustle?

Hustle is hustle.

The reason I leave it like that because I don't want to paint a picture of what I did.

Say my kids read it and say, "Daddy, you did this?" No, that ain't cool.

When you hustle, you better be smooth. And you better know how to count. You've got to really understand money, and you've got to be smooth in everything you do. If not, you end up making a mistake.

I was in a different space when I was man of the house. If I didn't hustle, I'd become dependent. If I became dependent, I'd have to become a worker. It takes everything out of what I created. I wasn't going to be dependent on anyone or anything, and I wasn't going to break my promise to my momma.

My momma had five boys, and three of them have been in prison for double-digit years. Same bloodline. I don't know why things turned out the way they did. Even so, I do try to take the initiative and hold this thing down and protect my family, no matter what.

The thing about it is, no matter what happens, you learn to keep going. You hope to be an example. You hope to be somebody that says, "Hey, man. You don't have to do all this stuff."

I appreciate my older brothers. They're showing me they're going to take care of themselves.

Hopefully, I get put in a situation where business just kind of falls in place to where it's something that both sides can come to a common ground and actually work together. That's the toughest part to where, dang, I'm doing all this to take us out of this situation. But then, they're doing stuff to put them in that situation.

I have an open-door policy. I make sure every one of my brothers, all of my family members, know they can always stay with me, always have a roof over their head. They've got a place to stay forever.

It's one of those things that tests you as a man, as a family member, and as a brother.

2

MY DREAM CAR

The other kids in the neighborhood respected him. He always hung with older kids. We were riding our bikes and one of my friend's said, 'There's your brother. Let's see if we can ride with him.' Next thing you know, there's thirty kids riding in the park.

—Jeff James, Edgerrin's brother

IN the summer of 1993, I was finally old enough to work with my granddaddy and both of my uncles in Georgia. Most of my friends had three options in the summer. They could work in a program that paid by the hour. They could sleep during the day and play sports in the evening. Or they took their chances selling drugs. None of those options appealed to me. For one, the summer didn't pay enough. Secondly, sitting in the house bored me. Finally, selling drugs was a quick trip to jail.

I wanted to buy my first car, even though I knew I would only be able to drive with a restricted license. My granddaddy and uncles promised me if I saved up all the money I earned, they would take me to buy a car before the end of the summer. I was determined to get a car and worked every day, nonstop, for several weeks. Along the way, I sacrificed a few meals to save more money.

One day after work, we rode past a car dealership where a gorgeous 1975 Chevy Impala sat in the front lot. The green beast immediately caught my eye. Instantly, I wanted it, but had no idea how much it would cost. This car popped, and I knew it would make heads turn back in South Florida. The next day, my Uncle Ike and I drove back to our motel from work and I asked him if we could stop by the dealership to check the price of the car.

He agreed, but only if we had enough time after running errands. Unfortunately, our errands lasted longer than expected. He said we would go there another day.

Days passed and Uncle Ike never took me to see the car. He made every excuse in the book. He dragged out small jobs at work. He would make extra stops that never included the car dealership. Most days he would just say he was too tired. I decided to ask grandaddy if he would take me by the car dealership instead, and he agreed. On this one particular day, I knew we would have time to go because it was a day off from work. Yet, the cycle my Uncle Ike created continued with my granddaddy. He never seemed to have time to take me to look at the car.

As we rode past the car dealership every day after work, I continued to see the green Impala. At some point, I wanted this car so bad that I began to dream about it at night. I envisioned myself driving in it with the newest Krager 15-17-inch rims and Vogue tires. I had even put a coat of fresh candy apple red paint on it, along with a six-pack of 12-inch woofer speakers to beat up the trunk. The more I thought about it, the more the car became a reality.

As the days passed, disappointment began to set in. My frustration fumed toward my uncle and granddaddy for not upholding their word. I thought to myself, "I did everything the right way. I worked, saved the money I earned, and sacrificed all that I could. Yet, they refused to take me to the car dealership." So as time passed and my desire for the car yearned even stronger, I learned a valuable lesson that summer, which would stick with me for the rest of my life: If you want something bad enough, you have to make it happen yourself.

Although I convinced myself I would get to the car dealership on my own, I decided to make one last attempt to ask my uncle and granddaddy for help—even though I knew the outcome. I asked them both again. As usual, they told me, "yes." But, sure enough, they never followed through. I couldn't understand their reasoning for telling me "yes," but never taking me. I thought my grandaddy and uncle were playing a game with me. I mean, yes, we were all busy working, but there was always down time in between. Plus, why would they say "yes" if they really meant "no?"

As much as these thoughts raced through my mind, I decided I was done listening to their excuses. I decided to take matters into my own hands. I had my own money, stood 5-foot-10 with a muscular build of 185 pounds, and tons of confidence. I decided to go to the dealership on my own.

Going to the dealership meant skipping a day of work. Typically, every morning at 7 a.m., we would load a van before heading to work. This particular morning, I stayed in the room while everyone—my granddaddy, my uncles, and the other workers—left moments later. I hoped no one noticed my absence, especially my uncles. The van drove farther and farther away, and was eventually out of sight. I stood alone with only one plan for the day: to get that car.

I began by adjusting my voice to sound older and more sophisticated. Then, I rehearsed my lines for well over an hour, anticipating what the car salesman might ask me. I allowed enough time to pass to make sure the car dealership was open.

Before I left, I counted all the money I had saved. It totaled $650. Unsure about the price of the car, I calculated it would cost $500, which would leave me with $150 to do minor repairs and add some speakers. I had my plan completely mapped out.

Minutes later, I left my room toward the front of the motel hoping I would run into someone who would give me a ride, since the car dealership was a three-mile hike. I stood in the hot Georgia sun for over thirty minutes without any luck. So I decided to walk.

I started walking on the side of the road, not sure how long it would take, but it didn't matter. I watched multiple cars and big semi-trucks pass me by, nonstop. I made sure to maintain a good distance between the road and myself, as I didn't want to get hit by a car on my way to buying my first car.

After walking for a while, fully drenched in sweat from the 100-degree weather, I saw the car dealership a short distance away. At this point, I could only smile. I walked a little faster. I had some pep in my step, as if I were nearing the end of a marathon. Ten feet from the car dealership, I could see the finish line. I could see my future car.

As I approached the lot, I continued to go over in my mind what I was going to say to the salesman.

After what seemed like hours of walking, I finally reached the promised land: the dealership. I walked over to the "Green Dream" and desperately searched for the sticker price to see what the car cost. I spent about fifteen minutes looking at the car when a tall Caucasian man came out and asked, "May I help you?" I instantly added a little bass to my voice as I replied, "Yeah. How much do you want for this car, sir?"

"Nine hundred dollars and it's yours," he responded.

All the air left me at once when I heard that price. I only had $650 saved up, expecting it to cost much less.

Hesitantly, I said to him, "Mister, I've been looking at this car for a few weeks now, and I didn't think it was going to cost that much."

He then went on to talk about the car's terrific condition, including the engine, its one owner, and so on and so forth. I stood there looking at the car in a daze.

"How old are you, boy?" he asked with a strong Georgia accent.

I deepened my voice again. "I'm sixteen years old, sir. My birthday is in August." I mentioned my birthday since I wasn't sure what he meant by asking my age.

As expected, the man asserted, "Boy, you ain't even old enough to buy a car."

But I had rehearsed my lines long enough on my way there to know exactly what to say when the age question came up.

"Sir, my momma is going to put the car in her name. She's in Florida right now and didn't want to drive up until I already had the car. You can leave the title open and she'll take it from there," I said confidently.

The man paused and stared at me for a second. He didn't say yes, but he didn't say no. My confidence started growing.

"Well, the car will cost you $900 if you want to take it." Then he walked back to his office.

At this point, I had only one problem: I didn't have $900.

I could have tried to borrow it from my uncles or granddaddy, but I knew they wouldn't lend me money to buy a car. Plus, I figured I'd probably be in trouble after skipping work. They'd probably even call my momma, and she'd make me come back home.

My spirit had been crushed and I stood in front of the car thinking: "What can I do to get some extra money right now, and fast?"

I got through the hardest parts: saving my money, skipping work, walking to the dealership, and the age limit. Now I faced another obstacle. I started thinking I didn't deserve the car, or that some higher power didn't want me to have the car to prevent a tragic accident.

I did everything the right way, but I still couldn't get my car.

The experience left me disappointed. All year, I talked about the moment when I'd come home after working all summer driving down I-75 in my own car. Now my plan failed, all because I didn't save enough money.

Sweat dripped down my back from the burning heat. My face shined like the chrome rims I imagined on my car. My feet hurt from the three-mile walk. I wanted to cry. I wanted this car so bad.

With both eyes still on the car, I made a promise to myself: From that day forward, I would always have enough money to get whatever I wanted, whenever I wanted.

I never wanted to feel that feeling ever again.

At this point, the day felt like a waste. I spent most of it staring at the car—not even looking at it, per se, but rather gazing in its direction as an unattainable object. Without a doubt, I put hours of thought and energy into getting this car. Now I felt like I had to accept the loss and figure out how to tell the man I couldn't afford the car. I didn't want to beg, that's not my style.

I knocked on his window and signaled for him to come out.

"Sir, I don't have that kind of money, and by the time I earn that much the summer will be over and the car will probably be gone."

The man discreetly looked at me and with his Georgia accent said, "Well, son, how much money do you have?"

I reached down in my basketball shorts, under the top shorts where I kept my stash, and pulled out all of my money. I counted out $650.

"Boy, this must be your lucky day, 'cause we need that space."

He completely caught me off guard with his response, as I didn't expect him to come down on the price.

I smiled from ear to ear.

It became clear that my dream car had become a reality.

I thought to myself, *I walked to the car dealership from the motel, and now I'm about to drive my first car, from the car dealership, back to the motel.* This felt so good—even better than scoring a game-winning touchdown. The salesman gave me the keys and signed off on the title.

After I eagerly hopped into my car, I adjusted the seat, fixed the rearview mirror, and turned on the radio. I shook the man's hands through the car window and pulled off. Pumping the accelerator, I leaned to the side in my seat sitting low like Goldie from the movie *The Mack*. Life couldn't get any better.

As I sank into the green vinyl seat, I even shocked myself. A fourteen-year-old, with no driver's license, no more money, and a half tank of gas, had earned his first car.

I drove the car back to the motel, the same three miles I had walked. I backed my new car in front of our motel room on the first floor so I could make sure nobody broke into it and I could get out faster. All the cool kids did it and I wanted to be cool. You know I had to back that thang in!

As all the excitement and new car blues started to mellow out, reality began to set in. *How am I going to explain this to my uncles and my Granddaddy? How am I going to tell my Momma?* I didn't want to return the car. I especially didn't want to make my momma mad.

Throughout the day, anxiety set in anticipating my grandaddy's and uncles' arrival. I knew they would have something to say in their own unique diction. To ease some of the tension, I decided to go outside to clean the car. I figured I'd play a little music. Minutes later, the work crew rolled in, so I knew it wouldn't be long before I had to face them. I braced myself for what would be a good cursing out when they realized what I had done.

Uncle Ike and I roomed together, so I assumed he would be the first to notice my car. When he approached me, I turned my back to him and continued to clean the car.

"Aye, man, who the heck got you this car?" Uncle Ike asked.

Before I could even get one word out, he yelled for Uncle Johnny.

"Aye, Johnny, this sucker don' went and got that car. Can you believe this mess?"

Uncle Johnny, now alert, looked at me and said, "Man, what the heck is wrong with you? You're only four'teen. You're too young to have a car. Ain't like you can drive that sucker."

It took a second, but I finally spoke up for myself.

"Y'all told me if I saved my money y'all were going to take me down there and get the car. So I saved up my money. Then on the days we're supposed to go to the car dealership, y'all made up excuses. I got tired of y'all lying and faking like y'all were going to take me. So I went by myself." It felt good to speak up.

In the midst of speaking up, Uncle Johnny intervened to tell me the truth and explained why they never took me to the car dealership.

"Listen, Edgerrin, your momma didn't want us to let you get a car. She said you were too young to have one. She figured when you're fifteen next year—about to turn sixteen—it would make more sense for you to have a car. At fifteen, you can't even drive without adult supervision.

Uncle Ike started to laugh to himself in amazement.

"This little sucker crazy," he said.

Both of my uncles looked at each other and began to debate which one was going to be the one that called my momma to tell her the news. Uncle Johnny thought that since he stayed in a different room, Uncle Ike should take responsibility.

Disagreeing with his logic, Uncle Ike said Uncle Johnny should call, and they went back and forth. Listening to them, I started to get scared of my own momma, seeing how much respect and fear they had for her.

Uncle Johnny said, "You call Judy 'cause I ain't!" Then promptly walked to his room.

Still standing outside by the car, Uncle Ike explained the issue in more detail.

"Your momma left you in our hands for the summer, and we weren't supposed to let you get that car," he said. "Since we're responsible for you, we didn't want to let her down by doing something she told us not to let you do. So I'm going to call and let you explain what happened to her on your own."

Obviously, neither one of them wanted to take the blame for my actions, nor should they have had to. Sure enough, resentment kicked in as I wished they wouldn't have strung me along. They could have told me about my momma's wishes when I first mentioned the car, and we wouldn't have been in this predicament.

At that point, I could've lost my car and also would have had to go back home. On a daily basis, I always tried to do what my momma told me to do because I never wanted to let her down. As a result, I had more freedom than all of my friends. On top of that, she treated me like the man of the house. However, she only had one rule: don't get in trouble. Now I felt like I jeopardized her trust and risked losing all my freedom.

I dreaded having to make that phone call. I asked Uncle Ike if he could wait until the next day to make the phone call. That would give me more time to get better acquainted with my car. I wanted to drive around the motel parking lot some more before she made me return the car.

Luckily, Uncle Ike didn't make the call that evening. 'Til this day, I don't think he wanted to deal with the wrath of my momma or her worrying about her son. I psyched myself up to believe that whatever the outcome would be, it wouldn't really matter. If she truly decided to return the car, I already earned bragging rights to say I owned my first car at fourteen.

The next day, I woke up a little earlier than usual. I brushed my teeth, washed my face, and put on my work gear. I peeked outside, through the curtains, to make sure I didn't dream of getting my first car. Sure enough, the "Green Machine" remained backed into the parking spot I left her in. I figured I would use the extra time to sneak out and get more familiar with my car. I got in and started the engine. With the windows rolled up and the A/C on, I listened to Tupac's "I Get Around." I thought to myself, *I'm in love with this car.*

About twenty minutes later, I turned the car off and got ready for work. As we pulled off, I couldn't take my eyes off of my car, because I knew that day could've been the last I officially owned it. I had a flashback of both my uncles' reactions. Then I tried to imagine my momma's reaction.

In a roundabout way, my momma is an easygoing lady, but of course my uncles knew her better than I did. They continued to play hot potato with who would make the call.

All I heard between the two was, "You call Judy"; "Judy is gonna be mad"; "I don't want Judy fussin' at me"; "I ain't about to call Judy." All day they said, "Judy this," "Judy that," "Judy, Judy, Judy!"

I figured my mother had to be a ruthless woman growing up. Then again, maybe she had secrets strong enough to blackmail them or something worse, because they were really stuck on respecting her wishes. On the other hand, I wasn't even sure if they were talking about the same person I knew, because I thought my momma's name was Julie. But, hey, they knew her better than I did. Eventually my anxiety returned; I officially lost all confidence in keeping my car.

As the day went on, I prepared myself to face "Judy, Judy, Judy," as much as I didn't want it to happen. That evening, we got to the motel sooner than normal. I made time to drive around the motel again. My gas tank registered half full when I bought the car, but after all those laps around the parking lot, it quickly crept toward nearly empty in just two days.

I ended up backing into the same parking spot in front of the motel room. I planned on asking Uncle Ike to take me across the street to the gas station. I could use the money I made today so he had no reason to say no. I kept the car running, burst through the door, and said, "Aye, Ike, I need you to put gas in the car."

At the time, I heard Uncle Ike on the phone, and I knew that my momma was on the other end as soon as he reached the phone out and said, "Here, talk to Judy."

I stalled for as long as I could.

I took the longest route to turn my car off. I rolled the windows up one by one, and manually locked each door.

I knew the end had finally arrived. I slowly walked back in the room with a disappointed look on my face and grabbed the phone from Uncle Ike.

"Hello."

"How are you doing, son?"

"Nothing."

I knew she hadn't asked me what I had done, but replied as if she did. Maybe that's what I thought she would ask, I don't know.

She spoke in the calmest, sweetest voice.

"I'll be up there tomorrow, don't you touch that car."

"Okay."

All the air went out of me as I hung up the phone after the shortest conversation ever between us.

Anytime I've left my momma's side for an extended period, we would talk for at least thirty minutes. We always had something to talk about.

For instance, as I got older, she knew I faced challenges and always kept me informed on what my brothers and other relatives had going on back home.

I hadn't had a decent night's rest since I 'd bought the car. So, finally, I got a good night's sleep.

Morning came and so did work. I got up and did my normal routine, except this time I didn't look out the window to check on my car. Even though the car still sat parked outside the motel, it felt like my dream had already driven away. It sucked knowing I couldn't drive it, touch it, and admire it anymore. It became like every other car in the parking lot.

The feeling became more of a reality in my mind when I didn't bother glancing at the car as we hopped in the work van. On this day, rain clouds hovered overhead, making it gloomy and even more depressing. I couldn't stop thinking, *My first car officially became the car that was no longer mine.*

A few hours into the workday, I watched a grey Ford Taurus pull up. At the time, I continued unloading watermelons from the back of a work truck. Then I noticed my momma walking toward me from afar.

I knew that she would be there, but I didn't expect for her to be there that fast. Apparently, she rented the car as soon as she got off the phone with me, and immediately hopped on the road.

Now, don't get me wrong: I'm always happy to see my momma. But knowing I disappointed her and may have let her down for buying a car without her permission pained me.

As she got closer, I watched my uncles and granddaddy each walk up to greet her. Feeling perverse, I continued working, trying to finish unloading the truck before I had to go over there. I heard everyone laughing and talking as I approached them.

Expecting the unexpected, I gave my momma a hug as I would normally do. She took a step back to eyeball me. She looked at me with a certain look—not a look of disappointment, but one of motherly concern.

"Are you okay?" she asked me.

"Yes."

"Are you *okay*, Edgerrin?"

"Yes."

I'm not sure if she asked me twice because she didn't believe me or she thought I was crazy. Until this day, I still don't know what my momma's intent was.

Her eyes then wandered over to the drug users and recovering addicts working alongside me. Then she took notice of my thinner frame and looked back at the addicts again. I could only guess that she thought I got into the wrong crowd and started using. Either way, she didn't buy it and advised my uncles that somebody else needed to take my spot and that we were going to lunch.

Once we got into the rental car, she asked me for a third time: "Are you okay?"

She asked if the other workers had influenced my decisions about drugs. During her childhood, she grew up around people that used drugs regularly. I assume that it taught her not to accept the first answer from anyone, because she asked me over and over again: "Are you okay?"

Maybe my momma, knowing the type of people I worked around—including their behaviors and actions—made her able to better understand how easy it is for someone to get lured into that lifestyle. However, she should have known she didn't raise a fool. I would never do anything to disappoint her.

After perceiving how she looked at me over and over again, along with asking me the same question over and over, I felt the need to man up and speak up for myself. I began by telling her why I appeared to look different and did what I did.

"Momma, after I first laid eyes on that car, I knew I had to have it. I wanted it so bad that I worked harder than everybody this summer. You get paid by the amount of trucks you unload, so I jumped in to do extra work anytime I could. I worked and worked as much as I could to make extra money. I have had to feed myself three times a day, plus pay motel rent, and also wash my clothes.

"So I chose to sacrifice eating. I stopped buying breakfast in the morning and lunch in the middle of the day. I ate watermelons instead. That way I would only have to pay for food once a day unless somebody brought extra food.

"Being away taught me it is every man for himself, and I wanted to prove that I could be a man and provide for myself.

"Overall, Momma, I made many sacrifices to get my car. I only made one mistake: I lied to the man at the car dealership about my age, and that you said I could get the car."

I literally spilled my heart out to her, but I stood by the truth, hoping she believed me. I felt like a weight had been lifted off my shoulders. We discussed the situation a bit more in detail.

After our long talk over lunch and explaining everything that went on, my momma's whole demeanor changed.

She went from a concerned parent to a proud parent. She took pride in knowing her son didn't succumb to a potentially bad environment. Above all, I wanted to show her I grew from her little boy into a man.

After a long ride full of positivity, my dreams turned into reality right before my eyes. The turning point came when she stepped up and bought the insurance for my car. I became flabbergasted with joy. Momma helped me keep the car.

She made it clear that the only way I could ride in my car was if someone with a valid driver's license drove it. I promised her I wouldn't get into any trouble and assured her that I wouldn't drive.

That day, my momma really shocked and amazed me. She showed me how to be a caring parent. She proved I had the coolest momma on earth. For her to rent a car and drive 448 miles to Georgia overnight, knowing we didn't have that kind of money to waste, then offer to put insurance on a car she didn't want me to have in the first place, left me speechless. The universe really has a way of making dreams become reality.

Over the next few weeks at work, I recruited all the workers that had a driver's license, addicts and all. I didn't care. We rode in my car every day after work and on days off. Overall, I explored every inch of Ashburn . . . from the passenger's seat.

* * *

As the summer came to an end, work began to slow down. By this time, getting home, back to Immokalee, became my top priority. I didn't call my momma or let anyone know my plans.

I approached an older man named K. C., the only person I trusted behind the wheel, and asked if he would drive me home.

Overhearing him talk earlier in the week, I could sense he wanted to leave, too. A couple of beers and he said he was ready.

I didn't have much money left after joy riding in the car every day, but I did have enough to buy him some beers and twenty-five dollars (ninety cents a gallon at the time) to fill up my gas tank one time. I packed my belongings quietly and did my normal routine after work. I didn't go to my room, leaving behind my work clothes, but I didn't care to get them. So with my driving partner by my side, I headed home to Immokalee.

As everyone slept, we jumped on I-75 that night. I co-piloted in my own car. Despite being broke as a joke—just as I'd been when I first arrived to Ashburn—I had never been happier.

I wanted to be one of the youngest people that got his own car. No handouts. Nobody giving me nothing. I wanted to come back to Immokalee and show all my peers, show everybody, that I got a car. Getting a car on your own, that says a lot about a person. You've got grown-ups that don't have cars. Grown-ups would come to me and say, "I'll give you some gas if you take me over here." That's how neat it is to have a car. That right there gives me an advantage to separate myself from the pack and say, "This is a man right here. I'm doing man things."

This kid is fourteen got his own car. It shouldn't surprise anyone to see where I am right now, years later, and how I'm handling things. When you start looking at those little things right there, if I want something, I'm gonna do what it takes to get it. I'm gonna take a shot at some stuff, I'm gonna take some risks. If I want something, I'm gonna do what it takes. That's how driven I've always been—from the time I was young until now. I'm gonna be super successful. I'm gonna make a lot of money, and I'm always gonna be a boss and I'm always going to keep my freedom. You'll never see me lay down, throw in the towel, go begging for a job, just so I can be comfortable. You'll see me starve first.

> ### JULIE JAMES SAID EDGERRIN GREW UP THE SUMMER HE BOUGHT HIS FIRST CAR
>
> My brothers took him with them to Georgia one summer to harvest watermelons. I allowed him to go with the thought in mind that my brothers are going to look after him.
>
> They called me on the phone frantic one day.
>
> Edgerrin had bought a car. He was fourteen years old.
>
> They said, 'Julie, we tried to stop him. We told him not to go down there. He played like he was sixteen to the man that had this car. He went back there and bought this car, you hear me?'
>
> Once Edgerrin called me and told me about the car, I thought about it. I said, 'For him to go after this car like this, I have to rent a car.' And I did not have money like that. But I rented a car, I took off from work, and I went up there, got insurance on the car, and calculated somebody to drive him that had a license for him to bring his car back.
>
> When I saw him, trust me, I said, 'Oh my God. My brothers have allowed my son to get on drugs.' Because the way he looked, he was so skinny. I was like, 'What did I do? Maybe I shouldn't have let him go.' My brothers explained to me, 'No, Julie. He wanted that car so bad he would only spend five dollars a day on himself.'
>
> I kept asking him, 'Are you okay? Are you all right?'
>
> I was looking at my son. I left him plump and he got up here and he's skinny.
>
> Honestly, I didn't know how to go about that. But I said he had to really want that car pretty bad.

PART II:
HIGH SCHOOL (1993–1996)

3

SCHOOLBOOKS AND PLAYBOOKS

Edgerrin had unbelievable vision. He would see things on the back side. He never made those crazy, dance-in-the-hole cuts. It was always one foot and go. He was a physical, physical kid.

—Gary Meadows, Edgerrin's high
school coach at Immokalee

HIGH school was a means to an end.

I was in school mentally. If you memorize stuff the way I did, you're going to test well.

In my mind, and even at a young age, school was just so I could stay eligible for sports. That's all I was worried about. You did enough so you could stay on the field. I didn't set out to make straight A's—nor did I need to. I set out to make sure I could play football. I knew I'd be fine if I just kept my GPA over a 2.0.

For me to be able to go to college on a scholarship, I had to repeat some classes. I had a guidance counselor, Audrey Moss, who put in a lot of time with me. She told me that if I was willing to commit, she was willing to commit as well. We worked out a schedule, and I ended up using my lunch period to retake some classes.

You used to have to score a 17 on the ACT to get into college. The NCAA changed that rule my senior year. If your GPA was low, you had to get your test score higher. My grade point average was 2.0 something.

The first time I took the ACT, I scored a 16. I did better the second time and scored a 17. But it wasn't good enough. It was one of those things where, if they went off the previous year, I would have made it on my second try. But because they switched to a sliding scale, along with the other college requirements, I needed a 19 to get into college.

My senior year in high school was twofold. Football was easy for me. That's why so many colleges were recruiting me in the first place.

But I had to do better on the ACT, as well as retake classes that I blew off.

I knew I could do the work, but I wasn't applying myself like I should in the classroom. When I saw that football could go out the window and that I might have to go to a junior college, that motivated me to work harder and do better. I started showing up when I was supposed to show up, and I did what I needed to do to improve my grades and get my test scores up. I wasn't worried about the testing part because once you study and become familiar with something, you realize, "Okay, this is how you do it." What you're strong in, you need to do a little bit better in so your overall score is better. Give a person direction and they'll know exactly where to go. I was given direction: "This is what you need to get on your test." Anytime somebody put a number or a goal in front of me, I usually attained it because I locked in to get it.

Nobody was going to keep me from playing college football, and so I put in the work and got the 19 that I needed.

IMMOKALEE HIGH SCHOOL GUIDANCE COUNSELOR AUDREY MOSS DESCRIBED EDGERRIN AS A DRIVEN YOUNG MAN DETERMINED TO ATTEND COLLEGE

I ran a competency-based computer lab after school where kids could work at their own pace to earn class credits. Edgerrin needed a higher score on the ACT. He also needed to get his grade up in Algebra. If his GPA was higher and his test score was higher, he would be eligible for college. That's how we connected, him working in my computer lab and me working with him one-on-one.

We had an unusual connection.

I was never really his classroom teacher and I was never really his counselor even though a lot of people gave me credit for what was done. I was sort of a mentor-tutor. More of a tutor than anything. I only worked with him directly his senior year. I showed him how to do math problems because I was a math teacher.

He was this big name as far as being a popular athlete on campus, but he never brought attention to himself. He was quiet and unassuming and didn't talk a lot.

We ran an after-school study hall for athletes. They were basically required to come to after-school study hall. He would come after school and do his work. The first time I met him, I mispronounced his name. I'm from Tennessee originally and I have a Southern accent. The longer I talk, the faster I talk. And the faster I talk, the more the accent comes out. Me saying Edgerrin's name wasn't always the way it needed to be said. I

(Continued on next page)

didn't call him by name a lot because I was afraid I'd mispronounce it. Instead of him getting upset, he joked about it.

I worked with him and helped him and did what I could. He did all the work. He saw this as a way to get out of Immokalee and make a name for himself and help his family. He was like, 'What do I need to do? Whatever it is, I'll get it done.' When he did need help, I tutored him.

The NCAA eligibility rule for college-bound high school seniors had changed. The previous year he was eligible, but that first semester his senior year he had to do some things to get eligible so he could sign with Miami.

Other schools didn't have faith in him. They didn't think he could do it. But Miami believed in him all along. They didn't have a lot of scholarships because they were coming off probation, but they saved one for him.

That was all he needed to know.

He needed to improve one letter grade in Algebra. It wasn't a traditional classroom setting where he had to take the class. It was you did it, and when you got it right, you moved on. He had to improve his SAT score at least two points.

Back then, Immokalee High students all took the ACT. We didn't even offer the SAT.

The reason was because minority students typically did better on the ACT. Partly because the way the teachers taught was more geared toward the ACT-type standard or what the ACT consisted of because our state test was similar. The only time a kid would take the SAT, they would first have to go to another high school. The closest school was twenty-five, thirty miles away and they would have to travel on a Saturday morning to get there.

They would only do that if they were going to a northern college that required the SAT. Miami and all the schools that were looking at Edgerrin were accepting the ACT. It was just

(Continued on next page)

something in the South, you took the ACT. Now kids will take both tests and do as well on the ACT as they do on the SAT. The state testing is different and the teaching is different.

For Edgerrin to get accepted to Miami was a major accomplishment.

Edgerrin set the bar at Immokalee High. When I became a counselor several years later, I helped a kid get into Miami based on his academic record. He had a full-ride academic scholarship to Miami, which was unheard of. In my thirty-five years, we had two students attend Harvard. We had one student go to Columbia. Two or three is all we had go to Miami on academics. Our kids go to either Florida, Florida State, South Florida. They go to the state universities. They don't go generally outside Florida. First of all, they can't afford it. Secondly, they don't get accepted with full-ride scholarships.

The atmosphere when Edgerrin was there, especially his junior and senior year when he was big in football, was electric.

Because it is a small, agriculture community that's not near a big city, you have to drive to get to Naples or Fort Myers. There's no movie theaters, there's no skating rinks, there's no shopping malls, there's no nothing in town.

Football is huge. To have someone of Edgerrin's ability and the way he played and the fact that he got to Miami, was just huge.

More so than he probably even realized. Because he was this low-keyed person that did not make a scene.

I grew up not too far from the high school; the football field was about two minutes from my house. That's where I would do all my early morning work. I would get out there before everybody else, before school, and put in work just so I can have an advantage. I always wanted to have an advantage on everybody else.

When you're so driven and committed and you want to be the best, you want to be better than everyone else on the field.

I always wanted to be one of the big boys—but I wanted to be better than the big boys. The guys I hung out with were two grades ahead of me. To catch up, to be on the same level, I knew I had to do something more.

It was just me wanting to stay ahead of the curve; my little secret. I wanted to do more because I wanted to be good.

I never had a problem putting in work. That was always easy. When you see that you're getting results, it drives you. Even if it doesn't work, it can become a placebo effect. If your mind thinks it and it works, you're going to be doing it.

In high school, I just wanted my coach to coach me. Coach Gary Meadows was legit. He watched me grow. He saw my potential.

I wanted Coach to be honest with me. I want to be one of the best, and I wanted to learn how I could be. I needed him to be honest with me. That's all I ever looked for.

One thing I did every offseason, beginning in high school all the way to the pros, was go to my coach and ask what I needed to work on and what things I need to improve on. I wanted constructive criticism—be honest and not hold back. I just need to know what you want from me and I'll do the rest.

One way I knew would help me improve was working out. I know some people see it as tedious, but that wasn't my case. I just wanted to see myself improving, and this was the perfect way to see those results. I love to measure everything. When you measure things, that's what gives you a gauge or a goal to shoot for. I would run and I would lift. And then I would run and lift some more. Then I would set goals for certain goals and weights

I wanted to reach. Okay, I need to be running this time. I need to be jumping this high. I need to be able to lift this much.

If these things improve, I improve. If I improve, I'm a better player. If I'm a better player, I've got a chance.

At the end of the day, there's two keys to such success: work ethic and purpose. Working out is nothing. There are twenty-four hours in a day. You mean to tell me you can't give two hours out of the day to what you love? I don't understand why. It doesn't make sense. What's more important than what you came for?

As a freshman, I played a lot on our undefeated junior varsity team. I moved up to varsity as a sophomore. In Immokalee, there's a lot of good players. I wasn't the only good player on the team. I had people ahead of me that were good too. I didn't get to play a lot, but I learned a lot. I learned how much I liked to play football and how I would do anything to get on the field. I was a running back, but I also played linebacker. Offense or defense, I liked to hit.

In tenth grade, now you get a chance to be one of the boys. I was playing with juniors and seniors. No matter how good you thought you were, I still had to wait my turn. That's just the way it was. There was always somebody good in front of you.

But even though I wasn't playing as much as I wanted, I was learning how to play the game, learning how to play running back.

It starts with the mindset. Football is a warrior sport. You have to be a warrior. I always had a warrior mentality, man vs. man. If it's one-on-one, I plan on winning. It was going to take two or three of them to stop me. They're gonna need some help. I wanted to be one of those guys you wanted to take to the foxhole with you.

In football, sometimes people get hit and they'll show weakness or they'll use it as an excuse. Who's going to take a hit and jump right back up? The guy that's always going to show up on every play, that shows real toughness. You can say my ankle's hurting, you can make an excuse. I took that as there's no excuse for me to be laying out here.

Growing up, I only saw so many football games on TV. I had this one VHS tape. It was called *Sweetness*, and was about Walter Payton.

In the video, as part of his training, he ran up a hill. It was a steep hill, but it made him stronger and tougher. I learned so much just watching how hard he trained, how he played. He was super smooth. But he was also super tough. There was one scene in the video where he was hurt, but he jumped right back up. I incorporated that into my game.

When my junior year finally came, it was the first time I was able to say, "I am the man." Before that, I wasn't the man. I was one of the guys, because everybody had to share the ball.

It was more of a coming-out party. Everyone knew I could play, but you have to share the ball. You've got to make sure everybody gets the ball—especially when you've got a loaded backfield like we did. We had a very talented backfield, and most of those guys were two years ahead of me. So when I got the opportunity to showcase my talent, I didn't hesitate.

It's kind of how it happened for me at Miami with the UCLA game. I finally got the opportunity.

My junior year in high school, that's all it was. Opportunity.

It was the same game. Same players. Nothing really changed. It's just now I'm out there dominating.

Being from such a small and poverty-stricken town, most people didn't know much about me. But when I rushed for 2,000 yards in a season, that's when people started taking notice. But those numbers were the same ones I put up in Pop Warner football, against a lot of the same players I played against back then. It wasn't a surprise. It was more you're finally getting to see who Edgerrin really is. I'm still little Edgerrin doing the same stuff in high school that I did in Pop Warner. Just now it was on a larger stage.

I knew that a lot of college coaches came to our practices because I was there. I knew that (former Florida Gators head coach) Steve Spurrier showed up and that other coaches from the SEC and other big conferences were watching.

Those things aren't something that you need to rely on. I never relied on "I'll practice harder because this coach showed up to watch me practice." I practiced hard because I wanted to be better, and I liked to show the person next to me that "there's a difference between me and you, and the only way I can show you is every day in practice, day in and day out."

We didn't always have the best offensive line, but it didn't matter. You just had to learn tricks. You just had to find a way.

I had to make a hole. I had to figure it out. That was the only way. Because on the other end of breaking a tackle is a big run.

When the defense has eight men in the box, that means there's three in the secondary. When you play running back, you just do the math.

If they have five up front, there's six in the secondary. If its seven in the box, there's four back there. When there's eight in the box, your receivers are on those three in the secondary.

If you bust through the line, you're pretty much gone or you've got one man to beat. If you break that tackle, you're gone. I broke the game down to its simplest form.

When I say football was easy for me, that's what I mean.

Don't make it complicated.

I decided I was going to use football to get a college scholarship. My Plan B was that, if I didn't play football, I was going to Florida A&M and would study business. I already knew how to hustle. I was going to make some money either way.

Growing up in south Florida, the University of Miami was everybody's team in the '80s and early '90s. It was an easy decision for me to play with a team that was my favorite growing up, as I never had an NFL team that I really followed. Plus I was able to stay close to home, which was important. I always wanted to be close to home because I'm big on family, big on friends. I always wanted to see people in the stands that I grew up with. That motivated me, helped me, pushed me to play at my best. Whenever they got a chance to see me play, however, I took it to another level.

Miami was always my No. 1 school, but they were going through probation when they recruited me. I really didn't know how things were going to shape up, so I looked at other schools. I visited Ohio State. The University of Florida was on the radar because it was also close to home. But, at the end of the day, Miami was always my first choice; I only wanted to go there.

When you looked at the direction Miami's program was headed, they were coming off probation but they were headed in the right direction. During the time I was being recruited, I found out that the right pieces were being put in place and that the program was being built up.

I weighed all the pros and cons, and even knowing everything with Miami being on probation, it was still an easy decision. I felt comfortable about going to The U.

For me, I know that if I did what I was supposed to do, that I would end up in the pros. Miami was in my backyard. It's not something they had to sell me on. At the end of the day, and even with the school on probation it was never close, because my heart was always home.

There was this drive in me to bring Miami back to the top, and also position myself to get to the next level.

Miami only had thirteen scholarships that year, but they held one for me. That's how I ended up at The U. They knew about me, they came to my school, and Butch Davis, the head coach, held that scholarship for me.

They knew what time it was.

IMMOKALEE HIGH SCHOOL HEAD FOOTBALL COACH GARY MEADOWS COACHED EDGERRIN FROM 1993 TO 1995

I'd never been to Immokalee before I took the job. When I drove through there I was like, 'Wow. This is interesting.' in the 1990s when Edgerrin was growing up, there were a few traffic lights. Burger King was just coming in. There was a Winn-Dixie.

It was the best decision I ever made. I was an assistant coach when Edgerrin was a freshman. I became head coach in Edgerrin's sophomore year.

The kids there just grab at you because they're such hard-working, humble individuals. Very prideful community when it comes to Immokalee playing Naples High, or Immokalee playing Bishop Verot, or one of the big-city schools in Fort Myers.

(Continued on next page)

FROM GOLD TEETH TO GOLD JACKET

It was a humbling experience for me watching these kids grow, and how hard they worked. Kids in Naples and other cities didn't have to work at a packing house at 4 a.m., then turn around and come to school at 7:30 in the morning. If you started practice at three in the afternoon and got done at six, these kids are going home real quick to grab a sandwich and go to work at a packing house until twelve or one in the morning.

Edgerrin was one of them. His family was one of them. No one ever complained about their work. And they always worked.

Edgerrin's personality comes from his family. They were very private people. They weren't like the families of today: 'Hey, Coach, my son just rushed for 250 yards.' That didn't really affect them like that because they knew when the sun rises on Saturday morning following the game from the night before, they all had to go to work. They all had to take care of business.

I'm not sure today's kids could do what that group of kids did. They all went to work in the spring because that was watermelon and tomato season. One year we only carried thirty-five kids on the roster. Most of them worked. I've never really seen a community get along with each other with the different nationalities like they did. Blacks. Hispanics. Guatemalans. Haitians. They all went to school together. Their parents worked together. Where else are you going to see that? It's like the melting pot of the country.

It's everything you think about America. Hardworking people. Opportunities. My Dad always taught me you make every opportunity with what you have. That's what I believe those people were like too. No matter what size the opportunity, you make it the best you can.

You have to understand where these kids were coming from. They were grinders. As a coach, you had to under-

(Continued on next page)

stand that. You had to try to work your schedule around them. They're supporting their families. They're supporting their households.

Hauling watermelons isn't easy. The players took me out one weekend to do it. I couldn't move for two days. I was still in pretty good shape. I worked out with the kids. I played linebacker in college at 215-220 pounds. You're bending. You're always doing something physical. You're throwing watermelons up in the truck. It's almost like a power clean (weightlifting maneuver). You have to keep up with the truck. Those kids did it all day on Saturdays and Sundays. And they did it all summer. After seeing that, you never doubted that they would come back in shape for football.

I knew who Edgerrin was through some of the guys on the coaching staff, and Pop Warner. I wasn't the kind of coach to go out and recruit kids. I was just watching and observing. I was always the coach trying to figure out is that talent going to translate to high school; is that really going to translate to college. He was very impressive as a young man in Pop Warner, I'll say that.

When Edgerrin was a freshman, he hit the field running. He was solid rock muscle like he was his whole career. He was a very talented running back that I wanted to play defense because he was a heck of a linebacker too. He could have played linebacker in college, or in the pros. He averaged over 100 tackles a season when he played defense for us. He also kicked off and handled extra points.

Edgerrin's junior year was his breakout year. He rushed for over 2,100 yards and 29 touchdowns.

No one ran a lot of zone back then. Now everybody's running zone stuff. We were a Wing-T, multiple, motion offense.

Edgerrin had unbelievable vision. He would see things on the back side. He never made those crazy, dance-in-the-hole

(Continued on next page)

cuts. It was always one foot and go. He was a physical, physical kid.

Just the way our kids blocked for him. He was a 205-pound tailback-halfback-linebacker. We had guards that were 160 pounds. But those 160-pound guards would fight like hell for Edgerrin because they knew he was going to fight like hell for them and never complained to that O-line if he did get hit in the backfield.

On his first carry against Fort Myers Riverdale in our first game in his junior year, Edgerrin ripped off a 60-yard-plus run. He ran over an inside linebacker, hit that hard cut like he always did to the outside and there he goes down the sideline. Me and a couple coaches looked at each other like: 'We got ourselves one.'

He went over 2,000 yards that year in a game against Clewiston.

Recruiting back then wasn't as it is today. Edgerrin would have been a five-star recruit after his junior year. Going into that year, we hosted a jamboree. The quarterback and offensive lineman on one of the teams was going to the University of Florida. We had Steve Spurrier and all the SEC coaches there. Next thing you know, everybody was in our fieldhouse after the game wanting to know about Edgerrin.

What's he like? What's his character?

Who didn't show up to our practices?

SEC schools. Big Ten schools. Ohio State and Michigan hardly ever recruited Florida back then.

They could talk until they were blue in the face. There was only one school that he wanted to go to, and that was The U.

Coach [Art] Kehoe was Miami's recruiter for our area. When he watched our spring practice and brought back Coach Don Soldinger, that just made Edgerrin's day.

(Continued on next page)

When Miami offered him that piece of paper, it was a done deal in his mind. That's where he wanted to go. That's what he wanted to do. No doubt about it.

Edgerrin loved The U. When he was young, that's when The U was the bomb. They were demolishing everybody.

What Edgerrin needed was what Coach Soldinger gave him. Stability. Structure. Discipline. Work ethic. Love. Everything he got in Immokalee, he got from coach Soldinger at Miami. Coach Soldinger was the head coach at Miami Southridge High School where he coached the same type of hardworking kids who wanted to get out.

Edgerrin had some extra work that he had to do in the classroom. He just had to finish it up academically and it was a done deal.

4

DREADS AND GOLD TEETH

I remember having that conversation with him where they said you have to cut your dreads off. Why do you have to cut your dreads off? Go out there and be you and do what you do on the football field. Carry yourself off the football field the way you were taught. If thy want to profile you, they got the wrong profile of a young man with dreads.

Know who you are. You can't please everybody. Don't let anybody define who you are because you've got dreads. Don't let anybody define who you are because they don't know you. If you ever get caught up in what other people think about you, that's when you're gonna be put on pause and you're gonna stop moving forward. If they want to say you're a thug because you've got dreads and you know you're not a thug, just laugh that off. Keep on going, but know who you are. He's always been about that.

—Luther Campbell, rapper and record executive

THE grill is a South Florida thing.

It's super popular. Everybody had gold in their mouth.

You can always tell when somebody's from Florida, or from the South. The way they look, the way they talk.

Growing up in South Florida, that's one of the things that's the norm, that's one of the things a lot of people do. That's one of the things I ended up doing at an early age.

I was fifteen.

That's our culture. That's South Florida. It's your flex as an individual. In South Florida at that time, when you had gold teeth, it's a statement. Gold teeth. Gold chains. All that stuff goes together. That's one of those things from a cultural standpoint that I've arrived. Especially when you're younger. The cool dudes were doing it. The younger that you're doing it, it's like, "yeah, look at me."

My momma said you can get one, maybe two. I came back with five. Three up top, two on the bottom. It just felt better to have five. That was a big issue for her, a typical mom response. It wasn't so much me sweet talking her about getting five gold teeth. What's done is done.

I was like any other kid that was getting something he wanted.

I spent my own money; I was thirteen the last time I'd asked my momma for money. It cost me one hundred dollars for each gold tooth. That was a lot of money back then. I got them done in Miami. I had different family members who had already gotten their teeth done, so I knew where to go.

When I had gold teeth, I had to take the crowns out and put veneers on it. Everybody gets fake veneers. I went to a Black dentist, a brother out of Jacksonville. He went to Florida A&M pharmacy school with my brother Ed. I said, "My teeth have to look how they always looked." He said he never had nobody go back and forth, back and forth, until they were perfect, like me. I said, "Man, but that's how I am."

"

PRO FOOTBALL HALL OF FAME QUARTERBACK KURT WARNER MISJUDGED EDGERRIN AT FIRST GLANCE

We're at a time in our country where perception has become reality between the races.

You could easily look at Edge and you see the persona, you see the gold teeth, and develop some sort of perception about who he is.

One of the biggest problems in our country is that too many of us have those biases and you make an assumption about somebody based on how they look.

I think he's a perfect example of why it's so important never to make those presumptions.

Yet you get to know him and you go, my gosh, there are so many things about the two of us that were so similar, that really brought us together, that I never would have thought of beforehand.

I didn't know anything about Edgerrin.

But when I got to know him, we were able to easily connect because of the person that he was and the father that he was.

I had no idea what I was getting into when he came to the Cardinals other than he was a really good football player. I found out I got to play with a great man and a guy that I respect greatly both on and off the football field.

That to me is what I love about the locker room. It brings people together of all different shapes and sizes and different races and backgrounds.

I just can't speak more highly of how I see Edge and the kind of person that he was and the things that he taught me when we were together. **"**

FROM GOLD TEETH TO GOLD JACKET

I got rid of them when I was older when I played for Arizona. I knew I would get rid of them at a certain point in time, but I wanted to do it on my own free will. I didn't want to do it because somebody told me to do it.

I'm satisfied with the way that it turned out because that's where I was in that space. I wouldn't change that for anything. You can always look back in hindsight. But you are where your are. In the midst of it all, I was comfortable. I didn't have guidance. I didn't have somebody to tell me what to do and what not to do. Everything I did was off natural instinct, and I'm satisfied with the outcome. But I'm mature enough to grow and say, "That was cool back then. But this is what's cool now."

Cool never stays the same. It was cool at one time to wear big, baggy clothes. It's not cool anymore. It's cool to rock gold teeth when you're young. It's not cool anymore. Cool moves. You have to be able to move with cool.

> ### DR. BENNIE CLARK PERFORMED EDGERRIN'S DENTAL WORK
>
> Edgerrin's brother Ed and I were roommates at Florida A&M. We graduated from pharmacy school together. Ed told me his brother was going to play in the NFL. Edgerrin was in high school. I was like, 'Dude, for real? Let's go to medical school and make this money.' He was like, 'I'm serious. I've got to go home and help him with his ACT because he's going to the NFL.'
>
> We put a lot of peer pressure on each other to succeed. We were two over-the-top dudes trying to conquer the world. But Ed went back home and worked for a year, helped Edgerrin,
>
> *(Continued on next page)*

and then he went back to medical school. You don't see that very often.

The first time I met Edgerrin, he was in high school. I couldn't believe that a person of that caliber had gold teeth. I used to make comments to Ed because I knew him. I didn't know Edgerrin well enough to say that to him.

That look was not what the NFL was looking for. Ed, Pierre Rutledge, and all of Edgerrin's other handlers were like, "He's not going to take them out."

I had been to Indy a couple of times when Edgerrin played for the Colts. When I went to his house, I was floored. I walked in the door, and he was on a laptop. I expected to see people hanging from the ceiling.

Ed, who Edgerrin put through medical school, was one of the smartest dudes I ever met. He was my classmate and roommate, so I don't know why I didn't expect that from Edgerrin.

After that, I always defended Edgerrin. This dude has never gotten into trouble. Never blew his money. The only thing people know about him is being in those Trick Daddy videos. They don't understand the way he evolved to be that stand-up guy.

Coming from where they come from, people don't come out of there. It's a migrant town. Ed got out because he was smart. Edgerrin got out because of his athletic ability.

One day Edgerrin gave me a call.

'Whatcha doing?'

'Working.'

'I'm on the plane. I'm coming to see you right now.'

Edgerrin had just signed with Arizona. He said, 'I'll be there at . . .' I think it was twelve or one o'clock.

He walked in the door. His mother was with him.

He said, 'Take 'em out right now.'

(Continued on next page)

'Really?'

'Yeah. Right now.'

My wife is a dentist too. Both of us, which we never do, we did his case together

Edgerrin was detailed, as detailed as I was.

Most people are not. Most people can't see the stuff I'm looking for.

He had veneers on his teeth. His mouth was immaculate.

That was the other thing that surprised me. Most football players, I hate to say this, their mouths are like train wrecks. I was like, 'Why'd you put this gold in your mouth?'

Usually a procedure like that is actually not as involved because those things come out pretty easy. It took me longer to put it back together than it did for me to actually do what I needed to do. Probably two, two and a half hours from start to finish.

I was able to make him have a really good experience and do exactly what he wanted. It's hard for people to pull that off because they don't have the experience, nor do they listen to what the patient is saying. I was very keen on doing exactly what he was telling me. It's almost like he had done some real, in-depth research. It surprised me.

I also had long dreads. We're known for being creative with our hair in South Florida. We're not pretty boys. We're rough, rugged. We just kind of let our hair do whatever it do. Dreads were a part of my makeup. I looked at myself like a lion. A lion has a mane. You look at his mane, that shows his strength.

But dreads also made me a target on the football field. Defensive players were pulling my hair. Really—intentionally pulling my hair. Being a football player, you understand it's within the rules. After one particular game, after they pulled my hair twice, I went home and cut my hair. I know I'm difficult to tackle, but you don't have to do that. So I did what I had to do: removed one easy way to bring me down. Now they had to work for it even more.

MUSICIAN LUTHER CAMPBELL OFFERED SOME WORDS OF ADVICE ON NOT CHANGING HIMSELF TO APPEASE OTHERS.

I remember having that conversation with him where they said you have to cut your dreads off. Why do you have to cut your dreads off? Go out there and be you and do what you do on the football field. Carry yourself off the football field the way you were taught. If thy want to profile you, they got the wrong profile of a young man with dreads.

Know who you are. You can't please everybody. Don't let anybody define who you are because you've got dreads. Don't let anybody define who you are because they don't know you. If you ever get caught up in what other people think about you, that's when you're gonna be put on pause and you're gonna stop moving forward. If they want to say you're a thug because you've got dreads and you know you're not a thug, just laugh that off. Keep on going, but know who you are. He's always been about that.

PART III:
THE U (1996–1998)

5

A CANE AT LAST

From that point on, I was like, okay. I respect Buddy. Now let me find out who Buddy is.

I went to my room, looked at the media guide and realized that Buddy was Edgerrin James.

That's how we started. As my college career went on and on, my relationship with EJ got bigger and bigger. He was one of those dudes everybody on the team respected.

—Reggie Wayne, Edgerrin's teammate at The U and
with the Indianapolis Colts

I DIDN'T go to Miami to get a degree. I went there with the mindset of: "I'm going there so I can get to the NFL, make a lot of money, and take my family out of poverty."

That was always the plan.

I totally committed to football, even adjusted my school schedule. Everything was based around football.

Once you get there, they ask what you want to major in. I wanted to major in business. But I looked at the classes and was like, "Hold up. That's a lot of work."

My plans changed. I needed to know the easiest degree I could get. They told me a Bachelor of Liberal Arts. Okay, put me in there, because I came to play football, I'm going to make this football thing work. If football doesn't work, I'll deal with the consequences.

My goal was to go to Miami so I could play football, work hard, and prepare myself for the NFL so I could take care of my family.

I did everything in my power to make that happen.

In college, they gave me way more than I was used to having. When I was growing up, I always had to figure out ways to get money. When I got to Miami, they gave me a Cane Card and I had so much money on that card. I could go to Burger King and all these places. Then they gave me a Pell Grant (need-based federal financial aid that doesn't have to be repaid) and there was so much money on that. Then we'd get to go to the cafeteria; we were so creative that our meals looked like they came from a restaurant. So now I had more than I'd ever had before.

The U is a special place. College is a special time in one's life, but this felt different. We're in a city unlike anywhere else. With some colleges, it's the school and nothing else. But this was Miami. You're seventeen, eighteen years old, just outta high school, and are now a college freshman in Miami, Florida!

One special thing is that Florida colleges spend a lot of time scouting local high schools, which means you end up playing ball with kids you grew up with. The South Florida connection is strong; it's a close-knit group. Everybody kind of knew each other, or knew of each other when they were in high school, or played in an all-star game together. We actually became dependent on each other. You grow together. The bond was there from the beginning.

Being a Miami Hurricane is something you can't really explain. From the outside, you can see it but you can't really feel it. It's bigger than just going to school. It's your lifestyle, it's everything.

When you get to the University of Miami, like with most schools, you form a certain brotherhood that lasts forever. The things you go through, the life lessons that you learn, it's something that you cherish forever. We take pride in taking care of each other. But being born and raised in Florida, and then going to The U with those you grew up with and played with. Well, it gave us a sense of pride in having "Miami" follow our name.

As I said, playing college ball builds a bond with your teammates—as well as those who played before and will play after—that lasts a lifetime. We hang at the same spots that we hung at coming out of college and then into the pros.

It's easier for us. If you played at Nebraska, people don't go to Nebraska to hang out in the offseason.

SANTANA MOSS ON RESTORING THE U'S TRADITION OF EXCELLENCE

It's hard to say what started it, or who started it, or what made it what it is. It's like something you can't shake when you get on campus. The older guys who paved the way, they came back. That's something that when I watch UM games now, it makes it hard to believe that these guys don't feel what we felt

(Continued on next page)

> when we played there. Because if they felt what we felt, they would want to be better. They would have made a pact to be better.
>
> When I got there in '97, EJ was in the class right before me. Instantly, you could feel that his class wanted to bring the tradition of old back. They had EJ, Al Blades, Nate Webster, James Sutton. That core group of guys set the tone that the groups behind them had to set the bar to restore what we had. Being the class behind them, we had no choice but to look up to them. EJ was one of those guys; he was the leader of that group. When I came in the door, he liked what he saw. In football, and in sports, you get recognition from the other guys, from the upperclassmen and veterans, by your play. So, before you say anything, it showed them on the field between those white lines that you're for real and can make a difference to that one common goal. That's how I became close to a lot of those guys, especially EJ, knowing what he did there. And now to be in that same locker room with him, he's going to lean on those guys that were similar to him. We did the same thing when we became leaders on the team.

Everybody comes to Florida. Everybody comes to Miami. Miami is college football. It brings another level of excitement. College football needs the University of Miami doing well.

Miami lets you be you. You can have dreads, you can have gold teeth, you can wear gold chains. It doesn't matter.

We had our own artists, like Trick Daddy and Uncle Luke, prominent Miami figures that were successful entertainers. We've got the Rock, who also played at The U.

In college, after a game was over, I'd jump in the car with Trick Daddy and we would hang out. That's my buddy. Same thing when I got to the pros. Uncle Luke, same thing. Me and Uncle Luke are tight friends. We're still bouncing ideas off each other, still lean on each other when it comes to business and advice.

We take pride in The U because everybody's always against us. Miami is the school that made a name for itself taking a risk on a certain type of athlete. Once they got away from that, the football program went down.

But that's what Miami is built on. It's about that rebellious type: being you, doing you, having fun. We're outworking everybody in the hot sun. If you ever went to the Orange Bowl for a big game when we were doing well, you saw some serious fans. And you saw all the former players come back. You looked on the sideline and you saw everybody. The University of Miami is the meeting spot for all former players. As I said, while many colleges have successful guys that went to the pros, it felt like our school was the one where they always came back to visit. They had moved on to bigger and better things, but it was still home.

I was lucky to be put in a situation where I touched on multiple eras. When I was coming in, Ed Reed was there. When I was leaving, Clinton Portis, who's one of my closest friends, was coming in. I kind of bridged the gap between everybody.

All of a sudden, I went to the pros and hit the ground running. Michael Irvin. Warren Sapp. You have a bond with all those guys. But I also have a bond with the young guys.

In the locker room, there were a bunch of couches. There was a rule that freshmen were not allowed to sit on those couches. There was a TV on the wall, with a couch on each side, plus one in the back. Guys would watch TV and hang out. Some guys would tussle with each other, and we'd have actual bouts between us. I personally wouldn't be the one that would actually tussle with the guys, unless I had my own personal one-on-one match. I was actually stronger than everybody thought or realized. It was just one of those things when you get in the center of that ring, it's man-on-man. Everybody thinks they're tougher than the other guy. But then you're isolated and you're in that ring, and you've got to do your thing.

It was tradition. We all went through it. I went through it as a freshman.

That part was easy for me. I had been living like a man way before I got to college. Mentally, I was ahead of the guys when it came to that. I always fended for myself. It's part of my DNA. Nobody's going to handle me. Plus, I was stronger than I looked.

> ### REGGIE WAYNE WAS AT THE CENTER OF THE LOCKER ROOM INCIDENT
>
> The University of Miami had rules that freshmen didn't really know about. The rules were that freshmen weren't allowed to sit on the couches in the locker room. The only time anybody was allowed to step on the 'U' on the carpet was when guys wrestled.
>
> If somebody got called out, you had to go out there and wrestle. If you didn't wrestle, then you've got to wrestle everybody.
>
> It was all freshman in the locker room one day. We sat on the couches, kind of taking it all in. Then the rest of the team walked into the locker room. They saw freshmen sitting on the couches.
>
> They had this code at Miami. They would say: 'WHAAAAAAT . . . WHAAAAAAT.' Whenever they made that call, it was like the Batman signal. Everybody comes running.
>
> *(Continued on next page)*

There's a couple of us sitting on the couches. We didn't know what was going on. We just know we was getting surrounded.

All of a sudden, somebody said, 'Y'all not allowed to sit on the couch.' But they were more aggressive with it.

I'm like, all right. I'm going to have to be rebellious. I have to bring my New Orleans out.

I didn't move. I stayed on the couch.

They started surrounding me.

My thing is, they might whip my ass but somebody is going to feel me.

Nothing happened.

And the reason nothing happened is because of one guy out of all the upperclassmen kept it 100 with me.

Only thing EJ did was he said, 'Yo, freshman not allowed to sit on the couch.'

That's all I needed. Tell me the rules, and I'll listen to the rules. Don't try to muscle me.

From that point on, I was like, okay. I respect Buddy. Now let me find out who Buddy is.

I went to my room, looked at the media guide and realized that Buddy was Edgerrin James.

That's how we started. As my college career went on and on, my relationship with EJ got bigger and bigger. He was one of those dudes everybody on the team respected.

Me and EJ took trips together. Like the time we drove to Dadeland Mall in his hooptie, an old box Chevy. We're driving through South Miami and the police get behind us.

We're cool. We ain't did nothing. We wasn't speeding. I look over at EJ and he's sitting up straight like he's in the military.

'What's wrong, bro?'

He looked at me.

'We ain't got no papers on this car.'

(Continued on next page)

"Why didn't you tell me that before we got in the car?"

The police came up to the car. Asked EJ for his license and registration. EJ gave him his license and told him there ain't no registration.

I just knew we were going to jail.

The police went back to his car.

I guess he ran EJ's license. He came back and told us, 'Y'all better be glad that my computer is down. Have a nice day.'

I'm like, Computer down? Have a nice day? Whatever.

As we pull off, I'm thinking we dodged a bullet, we're going back to the dorm. But he's driving in the same direction.

'Bro, where we going?'

'We're going to the mall.'

I'm saying to myself, 'I'm with the right guy. This is who I need to hang around with.'

Looking back, the one thing that stands out in my mind was my first practice. It's my first day I go out there, and I'm not really understanding the drill. All I know is that I'm standing across from a linebacker, and we've gotta go at each other. Well the drill starts and this linebacker pushes me into the ground. You only get one shot, and I got taken down. And so everybody looked at me like, "Hey, I thought you were legit?" I knew I had to wear that until I got another chance to prove myself. From that day on, I said never again will I step on a practice field and take it lightly or let somebody get the ups on me.

Leaving Immokalee and going to the University of Miami, I didn't really have a measuring stick.

When you're coming from high school, you really don't know. You're only as good as the people in your hometown, or your area. In Immokalee, you hear about all these guys that were No. 1 in the nation. In your youth, you value rankings. But once you get to a school like Miami, you start seeing, "This guy right here, I used to play against him, or I used to practice with him, and now he's in the NFL."

Once you start measuring up, that's when things change. It pushes your confidence to another level.

They would call out your bio in front of everybody. My bio's short. Their bios are long as hell. I remember thinking, *Damn. They did all that?*

Everyone thinks they're good, but you really don't know until you get to college. Once I got there, I was expecting it to be tougher than this. Our coach, Butch Davis, came from the pros. He had been with the Dallas Cowboys. So, being a guy fresh from the pros, he made sure we practiced like the pros. The way he ran offense, it was a pro-style you see on Sundays. It was a pro atmosphere. Guys were being groomed to play at the next level. Our practices were intense. It was fun, but you had to really compete. We worked so hard in practice that games seemed easy for us. That was the mindset in place. When I got to the pros, it was the same type of practices I'd had at the collegiate level. I thought that my first practice in the NFL would be *much* different than my first one here.

But then you suit up and play.

It usually starts in practice. You start practicing against the best of the best. You see guys who are All-Americans and have all this publicity, who are juniors and seniors. They're five-star recruits, and you measure up, you dominate these guys and realize you're as good or better than them. That's when you know it's a bunch of BS, it's not what it's made out to be.

"Hold up. Nah, this dude can't touch me. He's a senior, and I'm doing this to him."

That's when I said, "Bump all this. I'm going pro. I'm going to make it to the NFL."

For the first time, I can see it. I can really feel it.

I think the hardest thing for me to accept when I got to Miami was playing on the scout team.

I'd been busting my ass since Pop Warner. I knew I was good enough. I'm thinking, *You told me if I'm good enough, I can play. What's up?*

My running backs coach, Don Soldinger, pulled me to the side and explained how things worked at Miami. Coach Soldinger taught me that it wasn't about me and what I wanted. It was more about what was best for the team. He told me my time would come, to just be patient and wait my turn.

"Edgerrin, imagine you're a senior and you've got a chance to go make millions of dollars. And this hotshot freshman comes in and he takes carries and he takes opportunities from you. If he does great, he still has to stay in school. But if you do great, you can go to the pros. Now imagine that."

That's when it all began to make sense. I'd been worrying about myself, my family. But these guys *were* my family. I accepted that my time is going to come, but for now my job was to help my brother. And when my time came, I wouldn't want somebody coming in and taking part of the opportunity that can take me to the NFL and change my family for the better.

It finally clicked. Now I knew how to practice. My mindset changed. I went from *I'm better than all these fools, get me on the field* to *Let me go out here and do what I'm supposed to do and not trip on not getting on the field.*

Playing running back at The U raises your level of play because you know that, if you don't make something happen when you get on the field, you're going to be on the bench. It makes you pay attention to the little things. I better make the most of my opportunity because there might not be another one.

It's two things you can get from competition. You can get put on the bench. Or you can get better.

So you compete. Then it comes down to who's available, who can do more, who takes better care of their body, who knows their assignment, who can the team count on. Little stuff like that starts to add up.

To get to the next level is the norm at Miami. You see people dealing with things more there than you would at other schools. That's one thing about going to Miami. You see it all the time.

You learn what to do, what not to do, firsthand.

I knew exactly what I was doing. I knew where I was going. I knew this was my chance, my way out. You never do anything on your own. You find people that fill that void or fit the description. People who can say, "I tried it this way." Or they give you information. Information is key. When you, as a young Black man, face a situation similar to mine, we lack information. Who gives you this information? How do you receive this information?

Thankfully, at Miami, there were so many people you could actually ask those questions to, and get an honest answer.

I sat with every guy at Miami that was going to the pros. I went to Miami's pro day. I would watch them and tell myself, *One day, this is going to be me.*

I hung around school all day. If guys were preparing for the NFL, I was there. As a freshman, I was there. As a sophomore, I was there. Anytime the NFL guys would come around and train, I was there. I kind of invited myself. I wanted to see what's up. If this is where I'm going, this is what I need to be doing.

I always trained hard and pushed myself. No one had to tell me what to do to make myself a better football player. I was self-motivated. But Michael Irvin was someone who motivated me at The U. I would see him running his 110s in the hot sun with nobody pushing him and telling him what to do.

Not only was he running 110 yards in the hot sun with nobody pushing him, he was doing it wearing his shoulder pads and equipment. And he's in the NFL! Seeing that would motivate any player that was able to witness it.

It opened my eyes.

The NFL is a dream. That's where you're trying to go. If you ever thought about cutting back and not working as hard, all you needed to see was Michael Irvin working out in the offseason to understand, "This is what it takes to get to the NFL." You add it to your workout if you really want to make it to the pros. I've got to do what these NFL players are doing so you mimic them.

When I ran my 110s in the hot sun, I could have done it early in the morning, but I took pride in working out during the hottest part of the day. Michael Irvin did it, so there must be something to it. Seeing him do it gave me even more confidence that I was doing the right thing.

When I would see opponents' wills being broken and their bodies shutting down in games, I would look back at all the work I put in and tell myself this is why I do what I do. When we saw UCLA's players cramping up and complaining how hot it was, we were laughing at them. It was because of all the work we put in in the summer, running those 110s in the hottest part of the day and pushing each other no matter how hot it was or how tired we were or how sick we felt. Those conversations came up in the middle of our workouts. We would talk about the teams on our schedule and how when a team came to play us in the Orange Bowl, they were going to feel the heat. We wanted to play in the afternoon when it was the hottest part of the day. That's what motivates you to work harder than you ever worked before.

It was one thing to see Michael Irvin train on his own in the hot sun wearing shoulder pads. That was one kind of motivation. But he was already in the pros. The veterans who were on the team were another kind of motivation. They meant so much to the younger players. Veterans like Duane Starks and Kenard Lang. Kenard and Duane were first-round draft picks, but they weren't too busy to give us some of their time. Kenny Holmes was someone else who went in the first round who reached out to younger players. You could talk to them. You watched them and listened to them and learned from their examples. It was the Miami way. It meant something because they didn't waste their time with just anybody. They saw something in you.

That mindset was passed down from the veterans. When I was a sophomore, I met a freshman named Reggie Wayne. It's me and Reggie to this day. He was one of my first encounters. He was a younger player but he had that 'it' factor. He stood up for himself. You've got an incoming freshman class of fifteen to twenty people. And then you've got sixty other people on the team. If you've got somebody willing to stand up like Reggie, that stands out.

I would always hang with the linebackers. There was a natural connect between running back and linebacker. To be a tough running back, you've got to understand what it takes to play linebacker too. Linebackers were super tough. I was super tough. Running backs and linebackers have to deal with each other on the field. So I always worked out with the linebackers. Rod Mack. Nate Webster. Dan Morgan. That was the ultimate push for me.

We would be in our dorms the night before practice. We'd play video games and get into it about who's better. As soon as the sun came up the next day, we would go to the facility and compete. It all stemmed from the night before in our dorms.

You couldn't stop guys from hitting in practice. We were competing. You always had to have your guard up because somebody would knock your head off.

To us, practice was more than just practice. To others, it may have looked like practice. It was more personal for us. Some people dreaded practice. We loved practice. We turned practice into a game within a practice. It came from our coach, Butch Davis. He was our coach, but he was also a leader of men. He understood every aspect of the game. He could be a player's coach where you thought he was out there playing and seemed like one of the guys. His pedigree was tight. He came from the University of Miami under Jimmy Johnson, then went to the Dallas Cowboys under Jimmy Johnson again. When a coach has that type of background, he's going to have every ear on the team. When he talks, people believe. He got everybody on the team to believe and buy into what he was saying. With his words. With facts. He'd come up to me and pull out film of Emmitt Smith at the Cowboys' practice and show you things. He'd say, "This is Emmitt. This is how Emmitt does it. Look at how he runs. Look at how he plays."

I'm going to do everything my coach tells me to do, and I'm going to do it hard, and I'm going to do it right. I never had a problem being coached hard, or taking criticism from coaches. I respect you as a coach, but I'm no whipping boy. I respect you. Treat me like a man. I would ask my coaches what can I do to get better. Write it down. Let me know. Don't hold back. As a running back, running is running. My running backs coach at Miami was not into all the BS. He taught the fundamentals and the details. I could make a fantastic run, break tackles, reverse the field, but he would feel like it was a bunch of wasted movement. The good coaches already know what you can do because they see it in practice. They know when they've got somebody special on the team. Every running back on our roster pushed each other. They were your measuring stick. You pushed and pushed and pushed.

Our coaches emphasized blocking. I hated blocking drills but they made me a complete running back. One of the reasons the Colts drafted me as high as they did was because of my blocking skills. You've got to sit there and wait on somebody that's bigger than you coming at you at full speed and you've got to stop him. That wasn't easy. It was hard. Real hard. But it helped me. Running is a natural thing. You develop that skill as a child. You didn't have to learn how to block as a kid. I learned how to block at the University of Miami, and that carried over to the pros. That's what made you tough. We had a blitz period at practice. It was the craziest thing, but you had to do it. Blitz period might last fifteen or twenty minutes. It was a pass pro drill. You've got to stand there and stop linebackers like Dan Morgan and Nate Webster in their tracks. And then do it all over again.

In the summer, you could stay on campus or off campus. We would choose to stay off campus because you got the money from the school to live off campus. They had empty dorms. So we would set up shop in the empty dorms. Why not? The power and water was on. We ate on campus. That was a hustle that we had. We kept the money and set up shop in the empty dorms. The school was empty, so it worked out. You were supposed to spend that money on your apartment. But we kept that money for ourselves. That was one of our easy hustles. Sign up for off-campus housing, but stay on campus. If they shut down one dorm, we would just find another dorm to stay because the power and the water was still working on campus. We had some good summers. But we were never in our rooms that much because we spent so much time at the facility.

At Miami, the players held each other accountable. Guys had goals. They didn't want to be on the side that loses. Guys didn't want to not put in the work. We would get into it with our teammates for not completing a drill. The coaches didn't have to say much to us. Once you understood the culture and the expectations, the coaches didn't have to say nothing.

It's cut and dry why you're there. The University of Miami isn't an easy school to get into. It's a private school. It's very expensive. When you're a football player there, you understand, "I didn't meet the [academic] qualifications. I didn't score crazy high on my test to get in. We did the things that they allowed for athletes. We're in a different bracket." You have to understand your position. You had people who were straight A students who had to fight to get into The U. Some of them came from wealthy families. It's a very expensive school. We were the balance to the school. Football was a big deal at the University of Miami.

* * *

I was preparing for my pro day, and decided to work with our school track coach, Amy Deem, so that I could improve my 40 time. I didn't really know how fast I was since I was never officially timed in the 40. Andreu Swasey, our strength and conditioning coach, put me together with coach Deem. He felt that she could help me run faster.

Coach Deem helped me with my start of the race, but I trained for my pro day with coach Swasey. He was the go-to for every single thing I did. He wasn't too much older than us. He'd go out there and bust your ass in a drill. He was able to not only tell you what to do, but actually show you by being actively involved. That meant a lot to me. You gravitate to someone like him.

It's easy to say, "Go run these 110s." But when he goes out there and does them with you? Well, you take what he says a little more to heart. That was major. When he told me about Coach Deem, coming from him, I knew she could help me run faster.

Coach Deem was a really good coach. She worked with male and female runners. I learned a lot from her in a short period of time.

I ran a bit of track, mostly the 4x100 and at times the 100. Back then, all I did was just line up on the field and go. I was fast, but I didn't use any special technique.

I was a north-south runner on the football field, but I could cut it up or break it outside. I was comfortable running inside with power. But this was different.

Everyone knows that a fast 40 time at pro day could improve your position in the draft. I didn't want to leave anything to chance.

I told coach Deem I needed to work on my speed because if my strength numbers went up and my technique improved, I'm automatically going to run faster. My weight room game was strong. I was already explosive. I did everything else I needed to do . . . it was just a matter of learning how to run.

She got me to concentrate on my takeoff. She taught me not to pop my head up real fast at the start. How to stay low and how to come out of the blocks at the right time. But she also helped with the things I didn't initially take into account. Like understanding when the coaches in charge of the 40 started timing you. Coach Deem showed me that when you move your hand, that's when the clock started. I didn't know any of those things, and if it wasn't for coach Deem I probably wouldn't have.

Everybody was trying to tell me what to do to get me to run faster. I didn't want to make any mistakes, so, thanks to coach Swasey, I decided to go with the best of the best. That was coach Deem. I worked with her for several weeks leading up to pro day, which took place at UM's soccer field. I ran the 40 twice and felt good both times. After I ran the second time, they told me I was good. Nobody showed me their hand, but I knew that it felt good; that I did what I needed to do with NFL teams watching and timing me on their stopwatches and clocks. Anything 4.5 or faster was good.

I was timed at 4.4. Some people had me at 4.38. Some people had me at 4.41. Some people had me in the high 4.4s. It didn't matter because it exceeded everybody's expectations—except those who already knew. My coaches and teammates weren't surprised by my numbers. Also, having home-court advantage was definitely an added bonus. I was doing it in front of my people. When I ran, all my friends and the same people I trained with were there.

* * *

As someone that trained morning 'til night, day after day, one thing that stood out for me was how some guys only started working when football season ended and were trying to get to the pros. It made no sense. I was with you during the season. I was with you in the gym. I saw you skip weight training. Not doing the things you're supposed to do. Now you're going to all of a sudden get serious? You can't wait until the end of the season to get serious about playing pro ball.

I'd see these guys eating better and working out, and be like, "Not you. You're the king of ducking out on workouts." You need to give it 100 percent day after day. Nobody can just start getting ready and, in a few weeks, be at the top of their game.

They get with these agents. They get with these trainers. And they don't get drafted. You realize that they took the wrong approach. You can tell who's going to get drafted and who's not going to get drafted.

Miami always had first rounders, guys getting drafted. So with the amount of former players coming by and those getting ready to hear their name called, I didn't sit back and wait. You could go to your dorm or go hang out or you could watch pro day from the sidelines—that's where I was.

Micheal Barrow was one of those guys. He was in the NFL, taken in the second round in 1993. He would come back in the offseason to train, spend time with us kids, offer advice. In fact, he gave me some of the best advice I could get from a guy who already made it. It was the summer after my sophomore year, and I was training before my junior season. I put in so much work every day out there on the field, I was probably in the best shape of my life.

After a day of practice, Micheal sat me down and went right into it, telling me all the things I needed to know. "Make sure you position yourself to go pro as a junior," he said. "Now, I'm not telling you to leave school. But have that option. Do whatever you have to do to have that option."

That stood out to me. A lot of times you could wait until your senior year, but he told me to give myself that option—to turn pro as a junior—because you never know what could happen as a senior.

At Miami, you always heard stories about Melvin Bratton, guys that played their senior year and ended up getting hurt.

I had major respect for Barrow. He was a big dog at UM. Everybody knows him. Student of the game. Sharp. He's that player. Before it was me, it was that group. The linebackers. Micheal Barrow. Jessie Armstead. They were the dudes who were actually in the pros. You listened to what they had to say.

It was never brought to me that way before.

It was always, "If you do well, you do well. If you play well, you might get a chance to go pro, you might not." But nobody ever said you don't want to depend on your senior season. Nobody ever said that before.

6

FOOTBALL AND FAMILY

Growing up the way we grew up, there's a responsibility you have. You dive in headfirst. You tell yourself, This has got to work. *There's no way around it.*

YOU have to be honest with yourself. You've got to believe in yourself.

But you've also got to be realistic.

I could catch. I could run. I was tough. And I'm 6 feet tall. I'm not 5-8, 5-9. I weigh 208 pounds. I've got everything that it takes. Plus, I was considered a smart football player. I was a thinker out there. Understood the offense, understood what was going on. I learned all the tricks of being a running back.

I didn't drink. I didn't smoke.

And then, in my sophomore year, my daughter QuiQui was born. Up to that point it was still a game. Yeah, I wanted to make the NFL, get money, and help my family. But now it was personal. Now I had a child to think about, to take care of.

I was seventeen when I got to Miami. A year later, as an eighteen-year-old sophomore, I'm a father.

My momma had all boys. We didn't have a girl in the house. My daddy had girls, but I didn't have a sister in the house that I grew up with. So this was all new territory for me. Plus, it's not just a girl, it's my daughter. It makes you really dig deep and tell yourself, *I've got to tighten up. I've got to make sure that every move I make is serious.*

Having a child doesn't scare our family. Everybody has a bunch of kids. In our family, it's scary if you don't have a child.

Before she was born, things seemed easier. It was me against the world. All I had to do was play football and everything else would work out.

But then things changed. Now I had a daughter that relied on me. It changed my mindset and helped me grow up a lot faster. You have to get more strategic, be more calculated in the moves that you make.

Growing up the way we grew up, there's a responsibility you have. You dive in headfirst. You tell yourself, *This has got to work. There's no way around it.*

You start taking your training a little more serious—not that I didn't take it serious before, but now it'd gotten real, real fast.

Thankfully, I had a support system behind me. Plus, I always made a way. I knew how to hustle and get me some money, so I never worried about that part. I mean, I was the man of the house as a kid. This was just another responsibility I needed to take on.

I've got to figure out a way to make all this stuff count.

Make every rep count because every move matters. You become more focused and locked in. Then you start looking at the calendar and mapping out your life. *If I do this and this, I can get to the pros.*

As I said, I already had the mindset of *I'm going to take my family out of poverty, I'm going to do this for my momma.* But once you add another level of having a child when you're still in college, knowing that you're going to be a father, you add more fuel to the fire.

When you have a child, you look at the world totally different. You look at your workouts totally different.

And when you grow up without having that person, your father, in your life, and it's your turn to be a father, you say, "I'm going to be there every step of the way."

You always want to be given what you didn't have.

It was one of those things that drove you.

I put in the work. I know I'm really good. And I just can't wait to show these motherfuckers.

When you get drafted, you become rich instantly. You're still that same person. The day before you sign your contract, you're the same person. But then you sign that contract, and it's official. Now you have money. But you're the same person. That stuff's still in you, it doesn't go away. I had to get it out of me. That's when I started removing myself from being on the corner.

I know people that had potential who didn't make it. When you go through certain things, that's what makes you value certain things a lot more.

That's been me, all the way up to the University of Miami. I didn't go home any more in the summer. I stayed at school. I took preventative measures to be around certain situations. That was my mindset. Even to this day.

I made it. I really, really made it, and I take that seriously.

7

JUNIOR YEAR AND THE UCLA GAME

Everybody asks who was the best running back I coached at Miami. I had so many great athletes, great guys. Clinton Portis. Frank Gore. Willis McGahee. James Jackson. Najeh Davenport. Jarrett Payton. Everyone could play. There were so many guys, one after the other. The competition is what made them special. They competed like crazy. They all had something a little different.

EJ was, by far, probably the best athlete of all of them. He could have been a receiver. He could catch the ball. He could run. He could block. He was smart. He didn't make any mistakes. He could be anything he wanted to be.

— Don Soldinger, Miami assistant coach

GOING into my junior year, I put in more work that offseason than I had ever before. That's definitely why I was frustrated with how the season started.

Things just wasn't happening for me. I started out kind of slow.

It was more of a thing where you were just pressing because you expect to get good results. And I wasn't getting the good results I was expecting.

I would have a turnover, or I wouldn't have a big game. I was grinding real hard but I wasn't having the kind of year that I wanted. I think the coaches were about to put me on the bench.

The UCLA game was my big opportunity.

We had just lost big the previous week at Syracuse. That kind of kills your momentum, so now we've got to do something big. It started with Butch Davis. He told us, "We ain't got nothing to lose."

Everybody is totally against us, but our coach sold everybody on everything about this game and our program and we bought into it. We knew our program was on the way back. Let's end this the right way. Let's go out with a bang.

Me, personally, it was one of those things where the running backs had to share the ball all year. And then James Jackson, my backfield mate, got hurt and couldn't play. Here is my opportunity. No sharing the ball. I appreciated that they did it that way during the season because it preserved my body. But in the midst of all that, I wasn't too happy about it.

I'm supposed to be playing. Players play.

You know what time it is. This is my opportunity.

And the Orange Bowl is going to be packed.

There were movie stars at the game. They were filming *Any Given Sunday* in Miami. You came to the sideline and there was LL Cool J.

UCLA didn't know anything about this Florida heat. They were a finesse team. We pounded them.

I would have turned pro even if I didn't have the game that I had against UCLA. I was at a point where I didn't feel like I had anything more to prove. The only thing that could have happened the next year was that I would have split more carries. You don't want to be a senior playing running back. Your junior year is the year.

I was used to making all my decisions. I can't go ask my momma. She doesn't know anything about that. She was like, "I got a son in college. That's all that matters."

Black moms back in the day, if you've got a son in college, you've got the whole world. Not only is he on scholarship. I don't have to pay for anything. That's a big deal for a parent.

> ### ASSISTANT COACH DON SOLDINGER KNEW EDGERRIN BETTER THAN ANY MIAMI COACH
>
> When I first saw him, I went to Immokalee to watch him play. It was like an adult playing with little kids when little kids are trying to tag you and can't get ahold of you. You couldn't touch him.
>
> He came to Miami on a visit. He was very quiet and laid-back. Never talked. Matter of fact, his first year at Miami he hardly talked at all. He never said two words to me. He'd sit in the back of the room and watch me. He evaluated you before he made a decision. He'd check you out pretty good because he wanted to find out where you're coming from.
>
> He shied away from me because I got on guys pretty hard. He was taken back a little bit.
>
> *(Continued on next page)*

FROM GOLD TEETH TO GOLD JACKET

Once he sees you know what you're talking about, and that you care about your players, he changed his whole demeanor.

There were two guys you didn't mess with. There was Nate Webster and EJ. When NFL teams wanted to talk about EJ, I told them that our guys were so competitive and the culture was so different at Miami than it is now. Guys wanted to check you out and make sure you fit in, see how tough you were. EJ was undefeated in those unofficial wrestling matches the players had. For two years in a row. That included offensive linemen. D-linemen. Nobody could touch him, so they quit messing with him. He would just slam everybody.

EJ was splitting time with James Jackson. James was pretty damn good. They were splitting time, and EJ hated that. I said, hey, don't make any mistakes. The guy that's got the hot hand is the one who plays.

EJ came back to me afterwards when he was in the pros. He said the best thing that ever happened to him was splitting time with James. 'When I went in, I was fresh,' he said. 'I had no injuries. I felt great.'

Everybody asks who was the best running back I coached at Miami. I had so many great athletes, great guys. Clinton Portis. Frank Gore. Willis McGahee. James Jackson. Najeh Davenport. Jarrett Payton. Everyone could play. There were so many guys, one after the other. The competition is what made them special. They competed like crazy. They all had something a little different.

EJ was, by far, probably the best athlete of all of them. He could have been a receiver. He could catch the ball. He could run. He could block. He was smart. He didn't make any mistakes. He could be anything he wanted to be.

Me and Coach Davis had a great relationship, one of the best. As time came for me to make the decision if I was going to the NFL, that tells you a lot about your relationship with your head coach when he can use you or need you to stay another year, but gives you his blessing to leave.

I sat down with all my partners, my teammates, and people I was close to before I went to see coach Davis. Rod Mack, one of my close friends, and everyone else was in the locker room, was talking it out. Rod said, "Coach Davis is going to try to convince you to stay. He's not going to be supportive." We go through our whole prep talk. I'm like, "My mind's made up. I don't care what he says."

I'm twenty years old, and I've got to talk to coach. I hope this comes off right because he can say good things or say bad things about you.

We talked in his office.

"Everybody's talking about you going to the NFL," he said. "What do you want to do?"

"Coach, I'm leaving. I think I'm ready."

As soon as I said that, I was expecting a different response. We had already prepared for the worst. To my surprise, coach Davis pulled out a sheet a paper.

"I want you to look at this," he said. "I've spoken with a number of scouts and a number of people in the NFL. Worst case, second round. This is the type of money you can make in the second round.

"But I'm hearing that you will be drafted in the first round."

That was shocking.

Me and my peers were thinking he's going to try to keep me in school. It was a big sigh of relief.

"Edgerrin, I want to support you," he said. "I want to make sure the University of Miami supports you. I want you to be an example for everybody else that comes here. When you go through the agent process, utilize our facilities, utilize everything we have. You don't have to train anywhere else."

Coach laid it all out for me. It was such a relief to know that you've got the support of somebody who it will probably be in their best interest if I stay another year. I'm leaving after my junior year. I really haven't played much college ball. But Miami was good with how they went about things.

We held our meetings on campus. I stayed and worked out with the strength and conditioning coach. I didn't have to spend no money. I could stay right there at school. We've got facilities, I've got everything I needed right there. It was one of those things that worked out even better than I anticipated. At first I thought there would be a little resistance. Sometimes when players say they are going to leave school early, the coach doesn't really get behind them. That wasn't the case with me, which was great.

Coaches really understand the business side now. I think they're being honest and realistic. Their reputation's on the line also. You can't tell a player that's going to be drafted in the first round that he's going in the third, fourth, or fifth round. That says a lot about you and your judgment and your thought process and your insight.

I didn't have an agent yet. I just had a bunch of hard work behind me and knowing that I'm going to the NFL, and it didn't matter where I get picked. Most likely, I'm going first round. But it really wasn't that big a deal for me. My thing was, just get to the NFL. It's what you do where you go. I just have to put in the work and everything else will take care of itself. I'm just here to take my family to a whole new level. From the time I entered college until the time I left, it was strictly business.

PART IV:
NFL BOUND (1999)

8

TEAM EDGERRIN AND THE NFL DRAFT

Steinberg and Moorad did the contract, but everything else, they worked for us. They ran it back to us. Our sole goal was protecting the future assets and finances of Edgerrin James. When we look back twenty years later to now, we made the right choice.

—Pierre Rutledge, a member of "Team Edgerrin"

IF you're looking at the time and the era I played in compared to how things are today, you'll see that the salary cap is way up. But for football players of my era, none got more bang for their buck than me. You get what you negotiate. The NFL is all about leverage; it's business at its finest at the highest level.

Football comes easy to some, but business is the hard part for most. Sometimes your feelings or the fact that you want to play so badly will get in the way of you making the best business decision.

If I was drafted five picks later, I probably would have made $30 million less on my contract. If I had been picked No. 10 (instead of No. 4), I would have been able to live with that because that's where I was picked. But because of where I was drafted, and what I deserved, I understood what the numbers should be.

Those of us picked in the first round, some of us got picked in the money spots. Thankfully, I happened to be one of those players.

Let's do this thing accordingly. Unlike most players, I made sure to be part of the whole decision-making process—and that began with picking my representation. Anybody that does business—or is in business—would respect my position. When you're sitting across from a business person, they're going to respect your position too because they know we know what we're talking about. Sometimes people check your temperature, see if you're really firm or if you'll go for anything. That's fine because we had time.

Selecting an agent is a little deeper than what people think. First of all, I had balls going into the league. I didn't do none of that traditional stuff. Most players get their representation before the draft. I, on the other hand, was fine with waiting until after the draft to make that decision.

I made the decision to form a group of professionals that would help me select an agent, so I wouldn't have to talk to those agents by myself. There were a lot of agents that wanted to talk to me.

We put together a group that had all the qualifications. It was my half-brother Ed German, who was in medical school; his buddy, Pierre Rutledge (a lobbyist), and Tyrone Williams (an attorney). The group was designed for more structure and to put a fortress around myself and those who might have been looking to take advantage of me.

We called them Team Edgerrin.

I can't say everybody on Team Edgerrin agreed with every decision I made, but they always got behind my final decision.

Most agents prey on athletes. I made sure that wasn't going to happen to me.

When I showed up on the practice field, they showed up. They were everywhere. Like the movie *Blue Chips*, for real. And if it wasn't an agent, it was a runner for the agent.

I would meet with agents that were trying to recruit me. Then I would introduce them to the group. The group would catch people off guard. It was a buffer system for me. I made sure we did things the right way and so I put them in front of my people. Professional people. It was good to have people in my corner to get a certain level of respect because they're not nineteen, twenty, and twenty-one-year-old kids. Agents are going to talk to them differently. It wasn't like a cakewalk where agents could just tell them anything, make empty promises. You're talking about three brothers that had their stuff together.

> **PIERRE RUTLEDGE, ON "TEAM EDGERRIN"**
>
> Initially when we started, it wasn't something that was planned. But what we soon figured out was the nuances of boiler-plate contracts. Edgerrin had enough trust in myself, who had an MBA; Tyrone, who had a law degree; and Edgerrin's brother, Ed, who was in med school. We were all in college together at Florida A&M. It wasn't rocket science. The best thing was he wasn't motivated by the money. His motiva-
>
> *(Continued on next page)*

tion was if you negotiate a contract where you have attainable benchmarks, your play will speak for itself.

You've got to understand the psychology behind this.

You struggle all your life. Then somebody tells you, because of a God-given talent, you're getting ready to run into about $5 million. As long as you stay alive, it's coming.

There's so many external pressures. If you're not strong, if you don't have a detailed plan, you don't know what to do.

You're trying to appease everybody.

You've got your crew. You've got your homeboys.

We looked at the track records. We looked at the total presentation. The propensity for negotiating big contracts. We knew that we might be in a protracted holdout. It was a very deliberate process. At the end of the day, it was close. Leigh Steinberg had the name. He represented a run of quarterbacks that had done well in the NFL. With that comes some level of notoriety. Jeff Moorad was more of a guy who really crunched the numbers. Leigh was the face. Both of them were very bright, but they were two different personalities. Steinberg and Moorad did the contract, but everything else, they worked for us. They ran it back to us. Our sole goal was protecting the future assets and finances of Edgerrin James. When we look back twenty years later to now, we made the right choice.

I don't think anybody will do it the way I did it because I took a real strong stance. In my personal opinion, it all came down to common sense. Why pick one agent when I can have all of them?

I was recruited by all the big agents so, in my mind, there was no need to make a decision before the draft. I didn't have a credit line; I didn't need one. I didn't owe nobody nothing. Anything an agent did for me, they did it from the kindness of their heart, or their business heart. I didn't have these tabs that the other kids get. Once you sign with an agent, you get a tab. I knew that. So I realized that I could either get a tab or wait to sign and get stuff like meals and travel for Team Edgerrin to meet with agents for free.

When you sign with an agent, they get you a credit line. They keep a tab of their expenses and things that they've given you. Once you sign your contract, you start paying these things back. I'm still being recruited. I had the longest recruitment of them all. I don't have a credit line. Which one makes the most sense?

I took a different approach. Usually, as soon as you declare that you're going with an agent, a guy usually has an agent that's been courting him. A lot of guys start getting frustrated. They can't take it. They feel like, "I'm tired of all these people calling me," so they just want to commit to somebody. That's when the agent does the smothering tactic and won't let anybody else get next to you. Some players become dependent on that agent because that agent starts showing them a different lifestyle or being that person in their corner, or that person they feel they need in their corner. The player doesn't even realize they hold the power. By the time you realize you hold the power, sometimes it's too late. I witnessed that, and you still witness that to this day. It's one of those things where if the player is not on his "A" game, he can become the victim very quickly.

I got the same benefits or better than the players that were being recruited by agents. They were all trying to sign me and for the longest time I didn't tell any of them no. I got courted longer than most others in my position. I probably got courted longer than anybody in NFL history. From the day that I declared for the draft, I went all the way through the draft without signing with an agent. Players never wait that long. I'm talking about getting heavily recruited and courted. Anything you want. Anything you want to do. Remember, you're about to become a millionaire. They're going to shower you with whatever you want. They're going to be right there by your side. Their whole thing is, "What do I have to do to seal this deal?" Now it comes down to a pride issue for them where they have to make this happen.

You know how hard it is for a player to be struggling and walking around campus, and now you have a chance to get a brand-new Cadillac Escalade? The hardest thing I had to do during that process was turning down ringside seats to a Mike Tyson fight. Tyson was fighting for the first time since he was suspended after the Evander Holyfield fight. I was a big-time Mike Tyson fan. Growing up, he was the man. Damn, I wanted to go to that fight. But I had to sit back and keep my distance. That's when my discipline was really tested because I really wanted to go. But I said I'm not leaving Miami. I'm not taking on none of that stuff until I become an NFL player. I stuck by it. But that was the one time I really wanted to go. I don't know what would have happened if I went to the fight, but I felt like it would have softened me. Like going on the banquet circuit. Start going places because I had access. I might have started cutting my workouts.

You've got to remember, I grew up without having things. I learned how to do without at a young age. I always knew how to make a few dollars. In college, if you've got a couple hundred dollars, you're good. If you've got a thousand, you're really good. As long as there are opportunities out there, I'm going to find them.

I didn't need things because Miami provided me with everything I needed to make it to the pros. The weight room. The facility. I still had my apartment on campus. I was good. This was a new process for me, so I made sure to get all the information I needed to make a good decision. It wasn't so much that I wanted to use them, as much as it was that I don't believe in making a decision until you absolutely have to. When I see people rush and make a decision, I believe they're not doing their due diligence. That was part of the process. But along the way, I never got a tab. I never got a credit line. I never got to where I owed anybody money. So when I signed my contract, I didn't have to pay an advance. My money came from when I signed my contract.

I mean, there's no way an agent is going to give you a $50,000 advance and not recoup that expense. They're only making so much money off you. They're also in this business to make money. They only know you because you play football. They only know you because you're good. Nobody's going to just give you money. It's the reason why people give you things. I don't take offense to that, but let's do business. I've always treated everything like business. I had my team, and we went over everything, we observed everything. We took a true professional approach. That's what it really came down to. A lot of people have trouble separating the personal and professional side. I went in being professional, and made sure to handle everything that way moving forward.

Even so, I was honest with everyone from the beginning. I made it real clear exactly what I was aiming for, what I was trying to accomplish. Everybody understood what I was doing—they just didn't think I would take as long as I did to sign with an agent. I just don't think you have enough time to make a good decision within the time frame they give you. This is a very important decision, so why the rush? I never understood that part. What is everybody rushing for? You don't know these people. I understood the process. I understood the game. I just wanted to make a good decision. I'm going to make every decision based on what's best for me, not what everybody else is doing.

From my first days at Miami, I made sure to watch, to observe the entire process. Because of that, I became a student to the situation. I watched every single thing that everybody else did. Every decision I made was based off what I'd seen others do. The way some players went about getting agents. The days from their first conversations all the way to draft day.

I would hang out with guys going to the pros. I would work out with them. For me, I was always watching real close to gain a little insight. Once I gained the necessary insight, I know that when I got my turn, I'd already know how to handle things. Some guys left school to train. Some guys stayed at school to train.

When my time came, I did it the way I planned. As I said, there was no reason to go anywhere else to train, when I had everything I needed at Miami.

When it was only a few months until the draft, I started breaking things down to ninety days—January, February, March. You have the combine, and the draft is in April. I went eighteen, nineteen, twenty years with no money. A couple more months really didn't move me. I didn't need a new car right away. I didn't need a new house right away. My mentality was, why not wait a few months living as I have since Immokalee and then make a deal? I saw no reason to owe someone for all my hard work when it wasn't necessary.

To me, agents don't deserve to be on a pedestal. I knew from the beginning that they work for me. Some agents do a great job, don't get me wrong. I just wanted to make sure they did a great job for me, for what I needed.

The recruiting process can go in many different ways. A lot of times it's heavy recruiting and a lot of uninformed athletes. It's the first time a lot of families go through that stuff. It's competitive to where you kind of get smothered. There were so many games being played. People were saying, "If you don't sign with an agent you're not going to get drafted." All right, cool. But the agent isn't running the combine. They ain't running the pro day. If I get drafted, it'll be because of what I did on the field. Not who my agent is.

Then, next thing you know, I'm the fourth pick in the draft and I don't have an agent. They say I gotta give the name of somebody for the team to call. Hey, they can call this little phone I got, here's the number right here. I sat back and witnessed all the games being played. I was going to be fine regardless.

When you're unsure or don't know, that's when people can persuade you into doing things against your better judgment. My mindset, my vision, was already intact. I already had a purpose. When you have people who are wandering, a wanderer can be pushed either way. But when a person's head is in the right place, you have to go through a lot to convince them. There has to be a trust factor. I was walking around not trusting people. When you start looking at things from that perspective, I knew what I was trying to accomplish and others didn't.

At first, they can't help but do what they're known to do. Your MO is your MO. The process is the process. It's all part of the game. I was always my own person. I was comfortable with my circle. The whole wine and dine process? Nah. My mom didn't take part in none of this stuff. She could care less. She just wanted to make sure I was doing the right thing. Some parents were more involved, but as I'd been doing since becoming the man of the house, I took care of myself.

After all my watching and studying, I started to learn and understand about leverage with agents.

Agents can charge some players three percent with no pushback from the player. But if you're a superstar, you can negotiate. I had already gotten myself drafted—fourth overall, for that matter—and knew I wasn't going to be paying three percent. Why should I pay an agent three percent when I have leverage? Why should I have to do this when I already got myself drafted, without their help?

People overvalue things. As I've said, football is a business, and the real question is: can you play ball? Once you accept those things, everything falls into place. You can't mix business with personal. When a team has to make a decision about you, you have to accept the fact they have to make a decision. Now more than ever, players are understanding that and are starting to make decisions that are in their best interests. If you don't take care of yourself, and you're hoping somebody else does it for you, then you need a lot of luck, and hopefully people do right by you. But them doing right by you has to also be doing right by them. And then it comes down to business. Anybody that's not of that mindset . . . well, you could find yourself in trouble.

The key is that you can't let people leverage you. Once you let a person leverage you, it's over. It's a saying: "He who cares the least has the leverage." I'm not going to let somebody put me in a position where I have to accept something that I know I'm due. I'm due those things. If they tell me I'm supposed to get two dollars to sign and that's the going rate, guess what? Give me them two dollars. Because that's the way it goes. But if this is the way things go, don't try to shortchange me, or try to play me. All my life I've always been aware of that.

People look at me and they look at the history of guys who come from where I come from. The African American or the ballplayer that comes from a single-parent home. A kid that has a grill and dreadlocks. They look at you a little bit different. I'm used to people misjudging me. Get to know me first. You're going to see this dude's different.

Some agents told me, "I can only do it for this percentage." I told them, "This is what I'm paying. Who wants to work?" That's kind of what it came down to. Anybody that gave me anything leading up to the draft, that was on them. It wasn't because I was signing with them. That was all part of their recruiting budget. It's part of their investment. A lot of agents have a budget where they can take you out to eat, hang out, whatever. But they do it with the intention of signing you. If they don't sign you, it's a tax write-off for them. When Pierre and the rest of the group would meet with agents, the agents would have to pay for their expenses, fly them if they had to travel somewhere, etc.

At the end of the day, when you start breaking it down, you realize: "I'm about to get millions of dollars in a little bit. I can get my own credit line." That took that weapon away from agents. Once you take that weapon away, they don't really have much to fight with.

Once you get through all the BS, you start looking at how agents treat their clients. You can't work with somebody you can't get along with. You can't work with somebody who's not going to be there for you. Won't have your back.

Now it comes down to who is this person going to be? Now you start getting down to what this is really about: negotiating a contract.

We did our homework, and decided that Leigh Steinberg and Jeff Moorad were the best team. They had a person in Miami, Gene Mato, who became a lifelong friend and was always real with me, even to this day. They had a history of doing big things, and had two people that were strong in Steinberg and Moorad. Steinberg had the name, but Moorad? That dude was on point, a serious businessman. There was something extra about him. He ended up leaving as an agent and became a part-owner of baseball's San Diego Padres. The two of them, Steinberg and Moorad, they were a team. They had a nice pedigree.

The best thing about Steinberg-Moorad was me and Moorad had a great relationship, and me and Steinberg was always cool.

Even so, I had all the leverage. You didn't have to wine and dine me. You didn't have to recruit me. All the money you spent on those other guys, you didn't have to spend it on me. This is what I'm paying you for. I'm not budging. And the biggest law firm at the time accepted exactly what we said, and we had a great relationship. There was a mutual respect. They knew what they were doing. Plus, if they get me, that gives them the opportunity to get other players. That also carries weight. It worked for everybody involved all the way around.

We did a confidentiality agreement. If I feel like it, I can give you a bonus at my discretion. They respected it wholeheartedly. Anybody that knows me understands I'm never going to take advantage of anybody, but I'm definitely not there to let somebody take advantage of me. You didn't get me drafted, so let's do things the right way.

I never went to their office. I don't have to see your office, I just need to meet you. Talk to you. Learn who you are and how you handle things for me to know if I want to do business. They couldn't sell me on *come in here and look at this*. It was straight business. We met with a lot of agents, but when it came down to what we were looking for, they were our choice. History shows we made the right decision. After all these years and salary cap movement, my first contract still stands tall.

I did all the legwork and I ended up signing with the top firm in the country for the least amount of money possible. It was a historic deal.

We were in a situation where the contract behind us was unusual, because there was already another running back more popular than me. And we had a contract in front of us that was similar to that of a quarterback. We said we were going to hug the quarterback contract. You can pick where you want to go. You can let people put you in a box, or you can stick with the normal pattern.

Nobody had to twist anybody's arm. They're doing their job, we're doing ours. If both parties keep doing their job, we'll get there. What's right is right.

" LEIGH STEINBERG SAID EDGERRIN WAS A TOUGH NEGOTIATOR

Agents across the country were soliciting him. I'm sure he was interacting with all those agents because he couldn't avoid them. They'd just physically be present on Miami's campus.

I want you to understand the atmosphere at Miami at the time. Miami had the best football players in the country. And they had players who not only were great college players and high draft picks, but instant successes in the NFL. The atmosphere there was really wild and raucous. Some agents would go right to the edge of practice. Edgerrin was offered tons of money to sign. How he dealt with that, I don't know. He had the good fortune of having a brother and a family who interceded. He had exceptionally sharp people asking exceptionally probing questions.

It was an unusual circumstance because he was picked by the Indianapolis Colts. The general manager of the Colts was Bill Polian who notoriously did not like agents. He was an explosive figure. He would get angry and throw things. Since I had the largest practice, I was sort of representative to him of ultimate evil. Bill Polian may not like agents and may be explosive and has a really big temper. But he is really talented when it comes to judging talent. He put three franchises in playoff contention.

Edgerrin put absolutely no pressure on me. As smart as he was and as concerned as he was, he trusted me to understand the market. I had a little bit of leverage because I also had Akili Smith, who was the No. 3 pick in the draft that year by the Cincinnati Bengals. Edgerrin went next. We were sitting back-to-back with a contract that had been done for Ricky Williams by Master P at No. 5. It had a signing bonus and it had base salaries and all the rest of it was stacked up into incentives

(Continued on next page)

he would make if Ricky exceeded the first four-year yardage that Terrell Davis had amassed. There was no way to make that incentive. We were exceptionally resolved not to accept something like that.

Now with an ordinary player, they probably would have been anxiety-ridden, right? Normally a player in Edgerrin's situation goes between telling somebody I want to hold out until the number's right and then two hours later, are they going to pay me, I've got to get into camp. You could already tell Edgerrin was impervious to that. He had trust in the process. He believed in his own value. Even when the results were not encouraging in the first couple months of discussions, he never put any pressure on me. He was totally behind me. Which gave me more strength in the negotiation process. What we did was more incentives than I had ever put in a contract. You're trying to put as much money into his guaranteed signing bonus as possible. But he was fine with it because he believed he would make an instant impact. We needed that belief in him in order to construct.

What happened was he had two sets of incentives. One of them was crushing figures and the baseline was 740 in terms of yards. He bet on himself. Well, that gave him hundreds of thousands of dollars of revenue right there. And then it had a rollover effect because all the money he earned rolled into the base salary the next year. He ended up making the most money any rookie had ever made, even though he wasn't picked first. He was Rookie of the Year. He made the Pro Bowl. He gained a ton of yards. He caught a bunch of passes. He blew out every single incentive and rollover.

Under today's salary cap, the picks are essentially slotted. Nobody holds out because teams make the maximum offer they can make. They come right out and offer the top amount they

(Continued on next page)

can offer. There's nothing really to argue about. But in Edgerrin's day, half the first rounders were out of training camp. I had done a contract back in 1993 that was under the first salary cap. It was written to take money away like the current salary cap from rookies and proven starters. That was the intent, but it wasn't written tightly enough. So we ran rings around it. I had the first pick in the draft in '93, '94, '95. By this unique contract construction, Edgerrin got every bit of the signing bonus he should have gotten, but he got millions of dollars more. He made the most money to that point that any rookie had made in the first four years of his contract.

We wanted an $11 million signing bonus. We ended up signing for $9.5 million, but we got the roster bonus to get us back to $11 million, so it was just word play. We ended up getting what we wanted, and they got what they wanted.

During negotiations they said, "We can give you $8.5 million." I'm looking at everybody like, "That's a lot of money." You're looking at a piece of paper and all I could think was, "Damn, $8.5 million. We're tripping over $1 million more." That's when I said I'm staying in the house for real. I'm scared to leave the house now. It would be just my luck that something happens to me. You start thinking about your momma. Man, I got a daughter. I got everything mapped out. I did it. I made it. And we're tripping over $1 million.

At the end of the day, when you have a number that you're trying to reach, sometimes you realize in this business it's more perception as to who won and who lost. We wanted $11 million. It was the number we had and we ended up getting $9.5 million, but we still got $11 million regardless. It's one of those things where you get exactly what you wanted but it may not look like that to whoever's watching. It was win-win all the way around.

We put in reachable incentives to where it was realistic to myself and what I could accomplish on the field. We knew that if I got to these certain numbers, I'm going to hit it. If I didn't hit all my incentives, I still would have a good contract. But by me hitting the incentives, it would go from good to great. That was the difference. I expected to hit it because it was based off a couple things. It was based off yards, touchdowns, and receptions. Aside from the UCLA game and the Micron PC Bowl, most people didn't get to see me play. Yeah, I was taken fourth, but to many I was still an unknown—and I used that to my advantage.

Ricky Williams signed his deal first, which made things a bit more challenging. He was looked at as the more popular pick, but he was still taken after me. We never lost sight of that. We never looked at it any other way than: "I'm the fourth pick. I'm right behind quarterback Akili Smith. I want my deal to be closer to the quarterback with the third pick than the running back taken fifth. You can't be the fourth pick and make less than the fifth pick."

Once we started working with those numbers to separate ourselves, we came up with the incentives. To get 1,000 yards, all I needed was 60-something yards a game. It was a calculated decision. And not just me saying "I can get a thousand yards," but I put together a chart with expectations for myself.

I knew exactly where I wanted to be, and where I was at after every game. I took it very seriously. Every game, I had to get this number. I knew that if I stay on the field . . . every team averages a certain number, running versus passing. In training camp and all the minicamps, I'd tell all the backup running backs you better get all your work in right now because when the season comes, I got you. All you have to do is make the team. If you make the team, I'll carry the load during the regular season. The Colts had also just traded their starting running back, Marshall Faulk, so I knew I was the top RB on the depth chart, and by playing the way I knew I could play those numbers were well within reach.

If you ask me, I think the incentives in Ricky Williams's contract, if you go through the history of the game, people didn't do those things. It wasn't realistic from my understanding. It wasn't something that had been done before.

You get drafted, you think you're Superman. But the reality of it is history is the real Superman. If you look at history, you can see that Walter Payton only did this; Emmitt Smith only did that. Look at Marcus Allen, he played a long time. Yet he only had one season with more than 1,500 yards. You start breaking people down, you see this is not realistic. These are some of the greatest backs ever and they weren't able to reach those feats that were in Ricky's contract. Why would they even put you in a situation where you sign something like that, or they even agree to something like that? All you can do is end up being disgruntled. Everything we did we tried to make it realistic and have it make sense.

As a player, the locker room, your teammates respect it, they love it. They understand what you're doing. I shouldn't have had to hit incentives. I shouldn't have had to do all these things. When a quarterback is drafted as the second, third, or fourth pick, they get a certain amount of money. When it came to myself, when it came to other running backs, we had to hit incentives to get that money.

> ### SANTANA MOSS ON HOW NFL PLAYERS WERE IN AWE OF EDGERRIN'S ROOKIE CONTRACT
>
> The Colts thought giving EJ that deal with the incentives that he put on it, there's no way he's going to reach all of that. He wanted it for that reason. EJ was a guy that always wanted something that he could go after.
>
> I remember that story of him telling me about getting that contract. It may have seemed like it was impossible, but they didn't know who they were dealing with.
>
> Just use myself as an example. I didn't know enough about what I was getting into when I got drafted (16th overall in 2001). All I knew was I made it: 'This is what they say I'm worth for this particular round and spot in the draft. Everybody in my spot gets this much.'
>
> EJ was ten steps ahead. He's like, 'I ended up jumping in front of the guy y'all said was better than me. Now I'm going to leverage this contract and show that you made the right decision.'
>
> All of us don't have the sense to go out and do something like that. Imagine a twenty-one-year-old having that much sense and that much knowledge about money and putting a deal together to benefit him down the road with incentives like he did.

Even though we get that money, to get that *extra* money, the things that quarterbacks didn't have to fight for, we have to as a running back. Different ballgame.

When it's a consensus and this is what running backs are doing, it makes you believe who you are and who you become, and people are not going to go against it.

I'm supposed to be compensated the right way. If I didn't hold out, if I didn't stand up, you know what I'd get? I'd get the bare minimum right within what they're giving versus pushing the envelope. I fought for what I fought for and after doing what I did, it's somewhat justified. It's a thing where it was earned, and I shouldn't have been put in that situation.

Running back is a tough position, so you have to know what you sign up for.

It's one of those undervalued positions, which I really don't understand. The running back position reflects the fact that this is strictly business.

You're talking about a position that has to do it all.

The ballcarrier has to be able to catch. He has to be able to run. He has to be able to block. He has to be able to do all those things—and do them well.

The toll on a running back's body, the value of a running back, is so much more than people actually give us credit for. When it comes down to the toughest position, hands down, it's the running back.

Quarterback is the toughest position mentally. But, overall, running back is the toughest and most dynamic position. When you see somebody who's a running back and he's able to play

Wearing No. 3 in my Pop Warner days.

Big man on campus!

On the sideline during a game at Immokalee High with my "family," Walter James II (25), Dedrin Smith (8), and my younger brother Jeff (14). *(Images courtesy of Julie James)*

No. 5 making moves for The U. *(Getty Images)*

My breakout game against UCLA during my junior season. Racked up 299 yards and the game-winning touchdown. *(Getty Images)*

With Colts GM Bill Polian after being drafted.

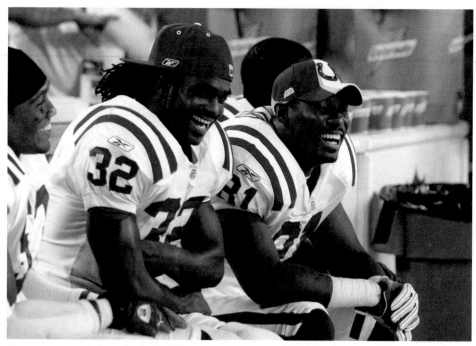

Having as much fun on the sideline as in the game, having a laugh with tight end Marcus Pollard (right). *(Images courtesy of the Indianapolis Colts)*

Using speed and agility to my advantage against the Pittsburgh Steelers in 2002. *(Indianapolis Colts)*

It was always a big game when we went against the New England Patriots. No matter the weather, you always have to bring your best. *(Indianapolis Colts)*

Always good to compete against your personal friends, here going against Samari Rolle in 2003. *(Indianapolis Colts)*

Racking up 204 yards and a TD on the ground as we pummeled the Chicago Bears in 2004, 41–10. *(Indianapolis Colts)*

Standing with my brothers, plain and simple. *(Indianapolis Colts)*

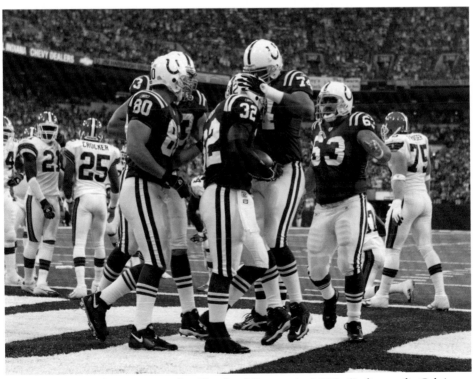
Getting in the endzone against the Cleveland Browns in 2005. *(Indianapolis Colts)*

Posing with the great Marshall Faulk and our running backs coach Gene Huey. *(Indianapolis Colts)*

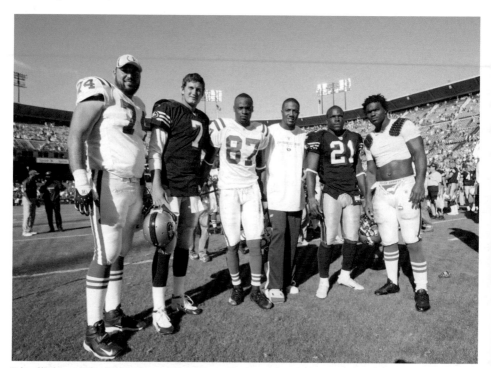

It's all about The U. Left to right: Joaquin Gonzalez, Ken Dorsey, Reggie Wayne, Mike Rumph, Frank Gore, me. *(Getty Images)*

The Colts Big Three: Peyton Manning, me, and Marvin Harrison. *(Indianapolis Colts)*

It's always an honor to make the Pro Bowl, but it's even sweeter when you can enjoy it with your teammates by your side. Left to right: Cato June, me, Dwight Freeney, Marvin Harrison, Peyton Manning, Tarik Glenn, Jeff Saturday, Bob Sanders. *(Getty Images)*

Two men I greatly admire: My head coach with the Colts, Tony Dungy, and my head coach with the Cardinals, Dennis Green. *(Getty Images)*

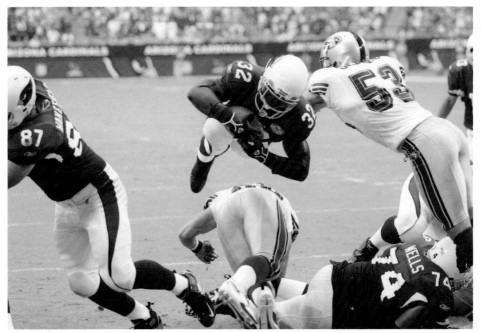

First game as a Cardinal, doing what I do best: getting into the endzone. *(Getty Images)*

NFC Champs! Celebrating going to the Super Bowl after ten years in the league. Tampa, here we come! *(Getty Images)*

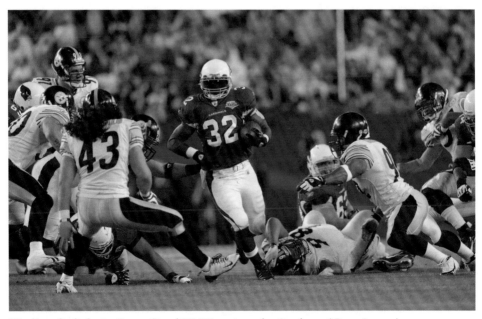

Finding daylight in Super Bowl XLIII against the Steelers. *(Getty Images)*

On September 23, 2012, I had the pleasure of being inducted into the Colts Ring of Honor. *(Indianapolis Colts)*

South Florida Car Culture was represented well at HOF weekend.

First time seeing my bust at the Pro Football Hall of Fame induction ceremony. Unveiling with my presenter, Colts owner Jim Irsay, with Hall of Famer and fellow Hurricane Ed Reed as the photographer. *(Pro Football Hall of Fame)*

Inmate #336. *(Pro Football Hall of Fame)*

Posing with fellow inductees Steve Atwater (left) and Jimmy Johnson (right). *(Pro Football Hall of Fame)*

Immortal. *(Pro Football Hall of Fame)*

The James GANG (from left to right): my daughters Emani, Qui, and Eyahna, and sons Eden, Euro, and Edgerrin Jr.

five, six, seven, eight, ten years, that says a lot about that person to be able to withstand that, because it's not easy.*

I knew what I was getting into. I know I'm not going to come out of here physically normal. I know I'm going to come out of here with some broken bones.

If you look at my running style, it was always a protect-me-first style. I didn't take a lot of hits. I would always end my runs falling in a certain way. I would always fall forward.

I had a defensive mentality. I would attack the defender.

I was put in an unusual spot. My draft year went quarterback, quarterback, quarterback, running back. And the running back—me—turned out to not be the popular running back. The popular running back was Ricky Williams, who was taken right after me.

I was put in a spot where you had to be somewhat creative with your contract. But I made it work. I got what I wanted. But if I don't hit those incentives, things changed.

My contract was earned, but I shouldn't have been in that situation. I shouldn't have had to do all those things.

---

* Editor's note: In a study published in 2018, it stated that the average career length for NFL players was approximately 3.3 years. However, for running backs, it was 2.57.

> ### ED GERMAN, EDGE'S HALF-BROTHER, ON "TEAM EDGERRIN"
>
> When EJ first came up with the idea, he said, "I don't want an agent. Those guys are no smarter than you are." He said agents made players think they could position them to get drafted. I told him I would talk to Pierre and Tyrone about helping him select an agent.
>
> It was big news that he didn't sign with an agent right away, that he was doing it with guys that had no agent experience although Tyrone knew how to read a contract.
>
> When we met with agents, Tyrone would always present first. I said very little and usually wouldn't talk until the end. Tyrone and Pierre loved to chop it up, so I let them do what they were good at doing. I would listen and come up with questions at the end that no one asked, or I didn't think they answered to my satisfaction. Tyrone and Pierre would take turns bringing it home. Ultimately, the decision was EJ's to make based on our due diligence.
>
> Some agents didn't do their homework. They could be very condescending. Some of them were taken aback by how well we spoke and our knowledge of football outside of EJ running up and down the field.
>
> In case we weren't sure exactly what the three of us had gotten ourselves into, they would get straight to the point.
>
> 'Let's cut to the chase,' said one prominent agent. 'We're prepared to give you guys a check right now for this amount if you get EJ to sign.'
>
> The money wasn't for EJ. It was for the three of us.
>
> I looked at Pierre to my right, and Tyrone to my left. We got up and walked out. The money was an insult.
>
> Imagine the offers that EJ encountered that I knew nothing about. There were just so many. I started getting calls all of a
>
> *(Continued on next page)*

sudden. I said, 'EJ, who are all these people calling me?' He would answer, 'Yeah, bro, I gave them your number because I don't want to talk to them.'

After EJ was drafted fourth overall by the Colts, we actually had a copy of Peyton Manning's contact from the year before. We wanted to know how much the Colts valued their first-round quarterback. We had Peyton's contract along with contracts of running backs from the year before and the contract of the fourth pick that year [Charles Woodson] and the year before that [Peter Boulware].

9

EDGE AND RICKY—THEN AND NOW

It didn't feel like there was competition between me and Edgerrin. More like appreciation. Game appreciating game. Every time I saw Edge in person or watched him play, that's always how it felt to me.

—Ricky Williams

THE thing that went down with me and Ricky and the draft. Well . . . that's just a matter of popularity.

Half the people didn't know what they were talking about. It's easy to go with what's popular instead of doing your homework. But when you actually do your due diligence, it made sense how I fit into the Colts' system.

Plus, keep in mind that Miami didn't have much TV exposure, I wasn't a household name. We played on national television only once during my three years there, but it was the UCLA game, which obviously brought me a lot of attention. But the scouts knew who I was. Those who mattered knew who I was.

I always understood why people would say "I like this person over that person." But for me, I never played the politically correct game. I never once did an interview saying I'm the best running back or this team should have picked me. All I said was I'm going to train and I can't wait until I get drafted and get to the NFL and show everybody what I got.

For me, it was never an issue or concern; I never wasted energy thinking about it. People tried to force a competition between us—especially in my early years. Things were working out for me, and people would try to get me to talk about the situation. They wanted drama, and I wasn't interested in any of that. I'm still not.

For me, it never had anything to do with other peoples' view of me, or trying to prove myself to others. I wanted to be the best for myself, for my family. That was always my focus.

If it wasn't my focus, after things didn't work out for Ricky, or when things weren't going well for him, I could have said something about it, but that's just not me. I always respected Ricky. I loved his game. But we didn't know each other personally, and I'm not one to be competing with nobody. I'm competing with myself. I'm trying to improve myself. If you get caught up in trying to compete with this person, that person, you're going to lose yourself.

But that's what the media wants. They want negative reactions, headline quotes, scandal, etc. Too bad they weren't getting that from me. I understood what they were trying to do. If the Colts would have picked Ricky instead of me and they had the camera on me at the draft, you never would have gotten

that reaction from me because it didn't matter. I wasn't competing to be the first back picked. I wanted to play in the NFL. I
wanted to be a first-round pick.

Everybody tried to say there was a competition between us.
I'm coming from the University of Miami. All we care about
is us. That's what people don't really understand. We focus on
ourselves and try to better ourselves at Miami. People tried to
make it like it was me versus Ricky.

Plus, aside from me, it was really unfair to him. He's his own
person. I don't know him; he don't know me. It was like a forced
relationship, a forced beef, a forced competition.

Even when it came to our contracts, it would keep coming
up. I didn't have to get a contract like his. I utilized the leverage
I had because he was more popular.

I was the fourth pick in the draft. He was the fifth pick.

He won the Heisman. He had the most yards in college.

But I know business. And I got balls. That's a deadly combination. Business and balls.

Even though neither of us planned it this way, we've always
been connected.

After being drafted by the Saints, where does Ricky end up
playing ball?

The Miami Dolphins.

We go through the whole thing with the draft in 1999, and
Ricky ends up in Miami with the Dolphins. My backyard.

For one reason or another, our careers have always been
entwined.

Ricky was a great running back. I have so much respect for
him as a ball player and the way he carried himself on the field.

But people had an agenda. So many times they tried to pull me in to say something about him.

That was the weirdest shit that I still can't get my head around. That's a brother doing his thing. I know it's good for ratings, but I never thought it was good for me because I didn't have any value in any of that stuff. And I'm sure he felt the same.

It was always, "Oh, you have this many yards." I'm with the Colts. We're winning ballgames. I'm trying to get to the Hall of Fame. I'm trying to be one of the best of all time. I never understood why, as a player, you would entertain the fact that you're competing with somebody that's right there in your era when I'm chasing the football gods.

I'm chasing the Jim Browns. I'm chasing the Tony Dorsetts. I'm chasing the Emmitt Smiths. Why would I waste my time entertaining something about one of my peers?

I remember when me and Ricky were in the same room for the first time at the NFL combine. That's when I saw how popular Ricky was.

There were coaches and scouts in the room. You stood up and told them your name.

I got up and said, "I'm Edgerrin James from the University of Miami. I'm not working out today."

They weren't happy. They wanted to know why I wasn't running. I'm getting all these questions, you know?

They kept pushing, but I stuck to my guns. I told them I would run at my school's pro day.

I'm still in the room. Ricky stands up and says, "Ricky Williams, University of Texas. I'm not running today."

Silence.

Nobody said nothing.

They lashed out at me when I said it, but didn't bat an eye when he did. When he said it, it was like a god said it. He was the big thing, and apparently I wasn't.

I'm like, "Damn, he got juice."

> ### *RICKY WILLIAMS ON THOSE FIRST FEW PICKS*
>
> We went four and five in the draft. There's that connection and parallels in our careers. I think it's something I thought about earlier in my career. But after going through all that stuff, it shifted everything for me. I didn't really think about it much after that. Or at least I thought about it in a very different way after that.
>
> It wouldn't have been such a big story if Mike Ditka didn't make that trade.*
>
> If Washington keeps the pick and drafts me at No. 5, it's a completely different scenario.
>
> I think people would still say Edgerrin James and Ricky Williams being drafted at four and five, that's a good story. But I don't think it would be anything that people would still be talking about.
>
> It was a surprise the way things turned out. But, for me, it was a layered kind of thing.
>
> First of all, I didn't want to go to the draft. I really wanted to stay in Austin and hang out with my friends. But my manager convinced me to go and said it would be good.
>
> There was talk about the Browns taking Tim Couch with the first pick. I thought I would have done really well playing in a
>
> *(Continued on next page)*

---

* Editor's note: The Saints traded all their picks in 1999 (first, third, fourth, fifth, sixth, and seventh), and their first- and third-round picks in 2000 to Washington for their fifth pick in 1999, which they used to draft Williams.

> town like Cleveland where there's a history of Jim Brown and a history of running backs. I thought that would have been a great fit. And being the No. 1 overall pick would have felt good, too. But I wasn't the first pick.
>
> I met with Andy Reid, who was head coach of the Eagles. They had the second pick. You can kind of feel when you meet with the teams if there's a connection. I didn't feel a connection, although I thought I would have been a great pick for Philly. Again, a big football town and, by nature, I'm a West Coast offense running back. They took [Syracuse quarterback] Donovan [McNabb].
>
> I knew the Bengals were taking Akili [Smith]. They had Corey Dillon, so they weren't taking a running back.
>
> And, so, for me, it was just whoever was next.
>
> I was already reeling. I was like, 'Damn,' you know?
>
> It got to the Colts, and I just assumed that I would be the next pick.
>
> And then when I wasn't, I'm like, 'Wow!'
>
> I was shocked. And then everything started to move really fast with the Saints trade.
>
> At the time, I thought I would go to Washington because I felt like I had a pretty good meeting with Norv Turner. But then, Mike Ditka made the trade.

Another thing that didn't sit well with me . . . well, this was where my business instincts kicked in. We get through the draft. Now you deal with the people who handle player trading cards, and they reached out to me.

"Edgerrin, who do we call about your player cards?"

"Me."

"Who's your marketing person?"

"Me."

"Oh."

They tried to lowball me. They wanted to pay me $20 a card.

I was the fourth pick in the draft, so I asked, "What did everybody else get?"

Obviously, the three quarterbacks at the top of the draft got their money. When you get drafted, the first pick gets more than the second pick. The second pick gets more than the third pick. The third pick gets more than the fourth pick. And so on.

Right behind me is Ricky. They knew it and I knew it.

"What did Ricky get?"

"Well . . . " They told me this and that.

"Okay, cool. I ain't doing it."

I knew that they needed this collection.

What they didn't know was that I didn't need the money. I didn't care about those cards, but they did.

I called around and found out how much Ricky was getting for a card. I told them I've got to get more than that.

"Well, you're not popular," they said. "Ricky won the Heisman."

"Okay, that's cool. I don't have to do it."

That's when the negotiations started.

Guess what? They doubled back because they needed me in the collection. They gave me what I'm supposed to get.

Always know your leverage.

I knew I didn't have to be popular, but I got picked where I got picked, and therefore I'm supposed to get what I'm supposed to get.

All I had to do is wait a couple months and I've got millions of dollars coming to me. I don't have any bills. I'm still staying in my college apartment. I didn't do like other players where I created bills. Nobody had leverage on me.

The toughest person in business negotiations understands how leverage works and knows their value.

That was me.

An article came out that, when I met Mike Ditka (who was coaching the Saints), my handshake wasn't strong.

I'm a player on the field, but a person off it. I'm physical when I gotta be physical. When the game is on, you ain't gonna find too many motherfuckers tougher than me.

So you judge me by my handshake?

So if you read the article, they wanted you to believe that I wasn't that tough. But for those who thought that? Well, put them across from me and see what happens.

RICKY WILLIAMS SPEAKS TO COMPARISONS WITH EDGERRIN WHO WAS SELECTED ONE PICK AHEAD OF HIM IN THE DRAFT

It didn't feel like there was competition between me and Edgerrin. More like appreciation. Game appreciating game. Every time I saw Edge in person or watched him play, that's always how it felt to me.

We hadn't even met. We were at a distance.

I was starting to figure it out, but it was so early in the process that I didn't understand what was really going on.

And I think that my behavior from the end of my college season to the beginning of the draft was unconventional and created some concerns that I was a different kind of person.

(Continued on next page)

I was embraced at Texas. I think I did a good job of choosing a college where I would fit, where I was embraced for being myself. People loved it, and it was something that felt good to me. So I just assumed, you know, doing it this way got me to break all these records and win the Heisman Trophy.

I just assumed I'll keep on being myself and these things will keep happening for me. But I started to realize that when you get to the NFL . . . these NFL owners . . . and I get it, they're making a big investment. They want to know that their investment feels safe. I think, especially, people that look like me, don't seem to care what they think. That doesn't feel like a safe investment.

I had this idea in my mind that my personality was an asset. But, more importantly, that it didn't matter as long as I could play football.

And, so, at that moment, I think it was that kind of wake-up call. I didn't realize it then, but, looking back, I realize it was a message that you might not be accepted here the way that you think.

Looking back, knowing what I know now, slipping to No. 5 in the draft, I just should have said, 'No thank you. Bye.' Not forever, but if this doesn't feel good to me, maybe I ought to take a trip and get to know myself better and come back next year.

When you look at me and Edgerrin, in the media's defense, being part of the media is looking for the lead. What's the headline? What's the story?

Me, the draft choice that Mike Ditka made, and Edgerrin, the draft choice the Colts made, it got peoples' attention to watch how it played out. It's interesting. Because Edgerrin's kind of a reserved, quiet guy, and so am I, we never did anything to take the bull by the horns and create our own narrative.

(Continued on next page)

From my perspective, he was drafted by the Colts and it was a surprise. There's pressure around that. But also going to play with Peyton Manning. It's not fair to say his success was surprising. It definitely wasn't surprising to the Colts and anyone that played at Miami that really knew him.

Just the quality of the experience, it's interesting to think of the differences.

The situation I landed in going to the Saints was almost the opposite.

We had two quarterbacks named Billy Joe [Tolliver and Hobert], and there were tons of expectations. I think it would have been a different situation where it would have been more under the radar for me playing with a good quarterback.

I'm more than happy with my career. I'm thinking about the quality of the experience. Aside from numbers, playing with a quarterback the caliber of Peyton Manning, just the way my mind thinks about the game, that would have been fun.

My motivation to structure my contract the way I did had very little to do with money.

It had more to do with me making a statement that I wasn't playing for the money.

I was twenty-one and a little bit naïve. My signing bonus was almost $9 million. That's great, that's paying me for what I did in college.

To me, it was already a win.

What I make at this level should be based on performance. That's the way I was thinking.

The reason I got a new agent is because the first agency, No Limit Sports, collapsed. I needed to find a new agent.

In my mind, it was this great opportunity to show the world what I can do and I'm going to get paid to do it. It didn't make sense to me to think about what's the most money I can get. I saw it as an opportunity to make a statement.

PART V:
AN INDIANAPOLIS COLT (1999–2005)

10

INDIANA, HERE I COME!

I've always said the greatest part about football is you've got guys coming from all different backgrounds. Edgerrin James is from Immokalee, Florida. I'm from New Orleans, Louisiana. Marvin Harrison is from Philadelphia, Pennsylvania. Three different backgrounds, but you're all on the same team. You're all accomplishing the same goal. At one o'clock on a Sunday afternoon, it doesn't matter where you're from. We're all together. I loved that.
—Peyton Manning, Hall of Fame quarterback and teammate of Edgerrin with the Indianapolis Colts

I **NEVER** knew the Colts were going to draft me.

I didn't visit them. Our meeting at the combine was brief. They did the barely-talking-to-me thing and the keep-it-under-your-vest thing. I was clueless to the entire situation.

But then the day before the draft, the Colts traded Marshall Faulk, their starting running back and future Hall of Famer. That's when things got weird for me.

When I saw the Colts trade, I knew I was going to be one of the top backs taken in the draft. What you do is you look for teams that need running backs. That was four or five teams.

Everybody said the Colts were going to take a running back. I figured if the Colts drafted a running back, that makes it even better for me because I'll get picked pretty early. The higher you go in the draft, the more money you make.

I knew the Dolphins and Saints needed a running back, too. So did Washington. Now the Colts threw their hat in the ring. That's all I looked at: teams that needed a running back.

If the Colts drafted a running back, it was going to be either me or Ricky. There was a coach with the Miami Dolphins who used to coach at the University of Miami and said the Dolphins were trying to trade up to get me. I didn't care where I went as long as I was drafted in the first round.

The Philadelphia Eagles had me come in before the draft. I know people in Philly wanted them to draft Ricky. I didn't even work out for them. I just sat on the curb. They didn't even really talk to me, but brought me in to say, "We had Edgerrin James here." It was part of their little game for the draft.

The team that drafted me didn't bring me in, but the team that didn't draft me, did.

Then you realize that you're just draft bait. It's smoke and mirrors. They bring you up there to take part in that. It's weird. It's crazy. I didn't know what team was going to draft me until the Colts called my name.

From that moment on, everything took off.

Life was going at its own pace. But from that one phone call, everything picked up and went to going full speed. It's just amazing how you can be sitting there on one side and then after just one phone call, you're in a whole other world.

The Colts did what was best for them—I was best for them. It had nothing to do with, "Oh, they did me this favor. They did me this solid."

They did their homework. They made an assessment that was right for them.

Ricky could have gone to the Colts and been successful. But they wanted somebody with my skill set that fit what they were building.

At Miami, you weren't getting on the field if you couldn't block. We had great running backs at Miami. It made you raise your level of play. It forced you to sit back, look at the situation, and say, "If I don't make it happen this time, I'm going to be on the bench." So you just compete. Then it comes down to who's available, who can do more, who takes better care of their body, who knows their assignment, who can the team count on. Little stuff like that starts to show up. It makes you pay attention and puts you in a situation where I better do something. Lots of people can carry the ball and get a chance to do it again next time. With us, there might not be a next time.

The coach we had and the things we had to do made us professional ready.

That was the difference.

FROM GOLD TEETH TO GOLD JACKET

REGGIE WAYNE RECALLS THE DAY EDGERRIN WAS DRAFTED

At his draft party, we're in Immokalee. We called it the Little I. When EJ throws a party, it's a party. Everybody's there. The whole team's there. His family was there. Everybody in Immokalee was there. Everybody in Fort Myers was there. Everybody in Naples was there.

It was a celebration.

We knew EJ was going to get drafted high. We knew he was going to get drafted in the first round. But where? He killed the individual drills at his pro day. But he surprised everybody when he ran a 4.38 40. We didn't know he was that fast.

When I tell you time stopped when the Indianapolis Colts drafted EJ . . . he shook up the world.

Everybody thought it was going to be Ricky Williams. We thought it was going to be Ricky, too. Ricky won the Heisman. EJ had the stigma that we felt like nobody wanted. Dreads. Gold teeth. South Florida. Coming up from the mud. Coming up the hard way. We figured that wasn't the look people wanted. They're going to give it to the clean-cut dreaded dude, Ricky Williams.

Back then, it was Miami against everybody. Nobody really wanted to give Miami no juice. It's going to be Ricky Williams first, and EJ is going to fall in somewhere after that.

They picked EJ.

The town shook.

I really believe there was an earthquake in Immokalee that day. The town went crazy.

This is how crazy it was. EJ still had his Chevy convertible that he had since he was fourteen. It was orange. Miami orange. He treasured this car, right? When I say treasured, it was his baby. Tell you how much he didn't give a shit. When he got drafted, people were dancing on top of that car.

(Continued on next page)

144

> We're like, 'Get down. You know that's his baby.'
> EJ said, 'Man, you know what? Let 'em dance on it.
> I can get a new one now.'

I didn't go to New York City for the draft like a lot of the other top picks did. I never left my comfort zone. All my life, I've always been in my comfort zone. Me not going to the draft was just another example. I've always been around my people. If I went to New York, I could only go with a limited amount of people. If I went, I wanted to bring the whole city with me. I wanted to bring everybody with me, and that wasn't allowed.

I understand why people were concerned and shocked when the Colts picked me over Ricky. That made it even easier for me to stand out because when I do something big, it's really going to stand out because it wasn't expected.

Maybe because of Ricky's Heisman award-winning season, he was very popular and had a lot of pressure to become the first pick. That may have been the thing that made it kind of disappointing for him. We had different approaches.

That day once the holdout was over and we agreed to terms with the Colts, when I got to training camp, they handed me a check.

I glanced at the check and went to practice.

I was so gung-ho about getting to practice, I didn't really get a chance to just sit there and look at the check. One of my agents was with me. I handed him the check. I wanted to get to practice. That was my main thing, getting to practice.

It was more like, "I'm glad it's over." My holdout lasted twenty days. I wanted to get to practice to show what I could do. That was more important to me than anything.

When you're missing training camp, everybody feels like you're not going to be ready. I wanted to make sure I showed that I was actually more than ready.

I didn't do anything with the check. I glanced at it, handed it to my agent, and then went to work.

I wanted to practice. I wanted to play.

The deal was done. Now it was time to show that there's a reason why I'm here.

I knew I was behind, so I wanted to do everything I could to catch up.

> **"**
>
> ### AGENT GENE MATO DESCRIBED WHAT EDGERRIN DID WITH HIS FIRST NFL PAYCHECK
>
> When Edgerrin got his signing bonus, I told him put your money in a bank. I said, 'Pick the biggest bank. Pick any bank you want. Let's walk into a bank, blind, and we'll put your money there.'
>
> We're walking around the streets of Indianapolis. He sees a bank and says, 'Okay. This bank right here.'
>
> It was called Key Bank.
>
> We walked into Key Bank and I walked up to the people working in the bank.
>
> "Do you have anybody that does investments?"
>
> They said, yes, of course.
>
> 'I'm here with Edgerrin James. He's a rookie who just signed with your team, the Indianapolis Colts. And he's got I don't know how many millions of dollars. And he'd like to put them in your bank.'
>
> So, of course, they were very, very happy that we walked in. Very surprised.
>
> We met a fellow there that worked in the bank, and that's who EJ gave his money to. It was just to open an account, so
>
> *(Continued on next page)*

he wasn't interested in stock—none of that. It was just literally opening up a savings account.

That's kind of how our relationship went through the years. I always felt I needed to show him that he was making the decisions, that I wasn't trying to steer him in the wrong direction.

He literally put his money in that bank for years and years.

He was always very street smart, so that wasn't a problem. He didn't trust at all, which was really the best thing you could have as a player, to not trust. You're better off not trusting than trusting.

The fact that he didn't trust I think helped him in making decisions. I think he needed somebody to trust that came from a completely different circle of life than he did. But I wanted to be very careful with how he trusted me. I wanted to earn the trust, but I also didn't want him to completely trust me.

I wanted him to understand that there can be people in your life that you become friendly with and you're close to and you think you can trust, and then eventually something happens. That was my way of showing him that when it comes to business, you have to be very, very careful.

It was an exciting time because everybody was young. Nobody knew what the Colts could do. Nobody had these expectations of us. You had guys getting together who wanted to work hard.

When I arrived in Indy, I didn't know Peyton Manning. I didn't know Marvin Harrison. I didn't know my new teammates. But I knew how to work hard. And I knew if I did my part, and everybody works hard and everybody outworks everybody, after you do it, people will say, "I see why we won. I see why we were so good. I see why their offense was so fast." You had hungry people who wanted it.

You didn't have to tell these guys to dedicate their lives to the sport. We did it on our own. We were a bunch of hungry people that nobody was really talking about. You can't judge a person's heart or their work ethic or the things that matter to them.

Remember, this was a 3–13 team when I got there. It ain't like I was going to the defending world champs. I'm going to a team that's been getting their ass kicked. You didn't know what to expect. But the thing about it was they put together a group of people that were committed to working hard. Everybody was going above and beyond.

We got the right people, but I didn't go into it thinking we're about to run up and down the field.

They traded Marshall Faulk. I just got here. Everybody's wondering. They don't even know if I'm any good. So you just work, work, work, and the next thing you know we're 13–3. Aside from Marshall, it's the same exact team from the previous year. That running game fit my style, which was why I was able to fit in so well.

When you go from college to the NFL, the difference is that in college you may have a couple guys that are good. In the pros, you find out quickly that everybody's good. So it becomes more detailed.

Physically, you may be faster than the person trying to tackle you. But playing in the NFL shows you the power of the mental. You can run a 4.3, 4.4. Another person runs a 4.5, 4.6. But he has years on you, he has experience on you. He'll be able to cover you, he'll be able to stop you, he'll be able to outsmart you.

You learn quickly that the difference is the speed of the game and everybody being good, everybody knowing exactly what you're going to do.

They know your tendencies. So it comes down to: How good are you?

If you're good, it's going to show. If you're not that good, it's going to show. At some point in time, the truth reveals itself. So you've got to be good because they're studying your movements, they're studying everything you're doing.

For me to line up across from you and you know exactly what I'm going to do, and for me to beat you, that says a lot about me.

You always have to be on your "A" game and understand that they know you, know what you're going to do. It's man-on-man.

That's why I love football because it's one of those sports where you know what I'm gonna do, I know what you're gonna do, now let's see who's the baddest out there.

I was way better than what was advertised in college. Everybody goes off perceptions. At Miami, they were about to move me to receiver as a freshman. You don't just move somebody to receiver unless he's got hands. The wide receiver position took some injury hits to the point where they were considering a position change. I'm really a running back, but I can catch the ball with the best of the receivers. I was a freshman and just wanted to get on the field. As far as running the ball, I could do that all day. I'm tough as all outdoors. And I can catch the ball. They didn't realize I was this good. It caught people off guard.

That was part of my thing. Doing things that not everybody else is going to do. What people ain't willing to do.

So I created my own workouts. My workouts would always be more than what the team was doing. I kept the University of Miami workouts and I stuck with that my entire career. I just trained, and trained, and trained. I had the weight limit

I wanted to be at. I had certain weights I wanted to hit, so it became the norm for me.

Not only were we all young and bought into what the team was trying to accomplish, but everybody got along, everybody worked hard. You had hungry people who wanted it. You didn't have to tell these guys to stay after practice. We stayed after practice on our own. You didn't have to tell these guys to dedicate their lives to the sport. We did it on our own. You can't judge a person's heart or their work ethic or the things that matter to them.

I knew my role. I was the missing piece, so to speak, to that offense. The things that I did complemented my partners, and what they did. It just clicked. We never had that top-ranked defense, but we had a high-powered offense.

Throughout all my preparations, and I trained and worked hard to make sure that, if there was a mistake, I wasn't going to be the reason why something went wrong. I've never been one to get caught up in the popularity thing, where you say, "If it wasn't for me . . . " I know what the team did. I know it takes a lot to make a change or make a difference. I just made sure that there was never a concern of my ability or being prepared.

Football is the ultimate game of life. It tests you. I don't care how talented a person is. I don't care how tough a person is. Football pushes you to the brink of who you are at times because you have somebody on the other side—they want it, too. It makes you dig deep. It's like in life, you have to dig deep. You have to separate yourself. Trying to get that one yard is not easy. You're on the goal line. You're right there. You can see the end zone. But I can't get there. You have to will your way to those things. That's how it is in life. I look at football like if you really want something you've got to take it. Or you can take what they give you. I look at life the same way.

From football, I was able to take control of my life. I was able to position myself to be able to do all the things that I wanted and not be dependent on anybody or anything. That's what football was able to do for me. It tells you how important people are. You can't execute a play if everybody doesn't do their job. I don't care how good you are. If a guy jumps offside or a guy doesn't make his block, then it's all for nothing. For me, everybody has value. And with that, you have to find that value and you have to put it together. Put it together so we can execute what we're trying to accomplish, and that's trying to be successful in life. Football is the same exact thing.

> ## LINEBACKER CATO JUNE SAID EDGERRIN WAS THE GLUE THAT SOLIDIFIED THE COLTS LOCKER ROOM
>
> Edgerrin was calculated and very well read and detailed. Everything he did had a purpose. Whether you understood him or not, this was the purpose and this is why he did it. And him believing in that purpose. And believing in that ability to not really care what people think or believe and sticking to his guns.
>
> That part of it is unique because most people can't do that in that environment, especially in the locker room. Especially in that locker room. Our locker room was very conservative compared to a lot of NFL locker rooms. Which was not necessarily a bad thing. But it was conservative in approach. You didn't see a bunch of people driving big cars, talking about how much money they had. It wasn't that environment at all, which was awesome because now you have an opportunity to truly know who people are. Because sometimes that can mask everything in that environment.
>
> *(Continued on next page)*

FROM GOLD TEETH TO GOLD JACKET

When your best players practice every day, when your best players work harder than everyone else, the impact is obvious, you don't have to say anything. You just understand this is the way it is. The impact is priceless because anytime you have your best players that can be so-called cool, it can be somebody that you can actually have a conversation with.

He challenged me to be consistent in my thinking, in my actions, and be deliberate in everything I do. As a young player, I think that's very much needed. When you come out of college, everything is structured. And then you go into the league, and everything is on you. You have to figure out what structure is for you. That veteran in the locker room is very important to the success of the team. I think that's getting lost with everybody having to have the new this, the new that, in the NFL. It's kind of destroyed the veteran, and the importance of the veteran, and the importance of the real team captain—the captains that control the operation. I think that is what separates some of the really good teams.

When Edgerrin lived with me the year he played under the franchise tag, he was planning on being a free agent, seeing where he was going to end up, and selling his house. First call, he told me, 'I'm going to park my car over here.' Next call was, 'I'm gonna live with you.' I was like, 'All right, cool.' It was that simple.

We had a routine, and we stuck to that routine.

Everybody thought we were always just kicking it and partying. We had a good time, we were social. We didn't really drink during the season. People would always think the opposite. Basically he was showing me, 'This is the way you can do things, play at a high level, be consistent, create your study habits for football, protect and maintain your body, all those things a young player really needs.'

Going from South Florida to Indianapolis, you think it's going to be a big-time change, it's going to be different. But once you get there, you realize you're playing in a dome (the Colts played their home games at the RCA Dome). The temperature is the same no matter what. In South Florida, we played in rain and all different weather conditions. In essence, it's actually better, because it's always a beautiful day in the dome.

This wasn't about me just getting to the NFL. It was about me making my mark and doing what it takes to be one of the best all time.

In my first NFL game, I rushed for more than 100 yards and scored a touchdown. We beat the Buffalo Bills, 31–14, at the dome.

My first NFL game wasn't this, oh, wow, wild moment. I felt like I was supposed to be here.

I've played this game thousands of times in my head. I dreamed it. So when I was there, I was comfortable. You have to see it before you can be it. I saw myself as a ballplayer, I saw myself playing. I was never nervous before a game because I was always prepared. There were many nights as a kid, I was already there.

Jim Mora was my first NFL coach. I was young, twenty-one years old, when I got there. I just played football. I didn't know him on a level other than him being my coach. I didn't have a problem with the way he coached. He held people accountable. I know a lot of people looked at coach Mora like he was very vocal, but he never bothered me, he never said anything to me. If you didn't do your job, he got on you. If you weren't prepared, he got on you.

But I did my job. I was prepared. As such, I didn't give him a reason to bother me or say anything because I was going to outwork everybody at practice. I love football to death. There was nothing he could really say to me when it came to football.

We never clashed, we never had an issue or anything like that. I went out and did my job, and he coached.

Though I never got to know him on a personal level, he was always super cool with everything.

In my seven years at Indy, I only had two coaches. And while it was all business with coach Mora, the only coach I felt like when you got around him, "This is a cool dude," like a father-type coach, was Tony Dungy.

Coach Dungy was totally different. He had your best interest at heart. You just respected him to a whole different level.

It was always "If you had an emergency, go take care of your family." A lot of coaches aren't going to say that.

He was the only coach I ever looked at like, "That's how a dad's supposed to be. That's how a father's supposed to be. That's how a coach's supposed to be." Because you respected him so much by the way he carried himself; by the way he treated others.

Not from him yelling at you. But from him treating you like a man, respecting you like a man.

But also by not putting the game first.

Not that the game didn't come first. But coach Dungy made it real clear: family is first. That always left an impression on me—and I'm sure anyone else that played under him.

There are so many parallels in football and life. We had this thing in the Colts meeting room with Gene Huey, our running backs coach. We would always talk about, "Coach, we don't play for the big run." The way I live my life is one yard, two yards, zero yards, seven yards. It doesn't matter, I'm going to keep grinding, keep pushing, keep getting after it. At the end of the day, I'm going to end up with that same 100 yards. The other guy might get a 60-yard run. I never banked on that. I banked on staying the course, steady pounding, steady chugging away. Eventually, I'm going to end up where I want to be anyway. Not taking losses. It might take me more carries. But at the end of the day, when ESPN rolls at the bottom of the screen, they're going to say in Week 13, Edgerrin James had 100 yards rushing. It doesn't say Edgerrin James had one big run for 78 yards and 19 other carries for 22 yards. Me and my coaches, we embraced that.[*]

What I am going to do is go after the little things, the RBIs, getting on base, to where I'm not losing yards. It may be seven yards. It may be 12 yards. But at the end of the day, I'm going to end up just like everybody else, or better, because I'm going to be more consistent and earn those things in the toughest situations. I know how to squeeze out a yard when there's nothing there, when the team really needs it.

I worked with coach Huey and then I went from position coach in meetings to working with Peyton to understand the offense. We played in a loud stadium. You couldn't hear things. So I tried to get a beat on what is the quarterback thinking if he changes the play. It kind of built from there, little by little. I would ask everybody a thousand questions.

The game slowed down when you know what the quarterback knows, when you know he's going to change from a pass to a run, or a run to a pass. Other than that, you just react because in reality you don't know why he would go to this play or that

---

[*] In Edgerrin's seven years in Indianapolis, his longest run was 72 yards—in his rookie season. His second longest, in 2003, was 43 yards.

play. It was more about me understanding what he sees when he does it.

When the defense was in a certain front and the linemen in the middle would move, I would know exactly what play Peyton was switching to. The game slowed down for me.

It was years and years of film study. Everything was a progression. You're always looking for ways to get better and continue to improve. Otherwise, the game's going to pass you by. There's always somebody gunning for your job. Everybody's improving. If you're not improving, you're doing yourself a disservice.

> ### COLTS OWNER JIM IRSAY ON EDGERRIN'S IMPACT
>
> We really arrived when Edgerrin arrived. Obviously, Peyton is the quarterback and you understand the man and the legend and the teammate he is of Edgerrin. But, still, you know it started when Edgerrin came in. We were 3–13 with Peyton as a rookie. Marshall [Faulk] did some great things. Eric Dickerson was here, and Eric was such a great running back. But the way Edge catches the ball out of the backfield and was able to block a linebacker, he's a complete guy. We knew we were looking for a back that could be there for a long time. Bill Polian is a master of looking at a draft and really seeing the best player. He saw Ricky Williams and he saw Edgerrin, and he knew it was Edgerrin all the way.
>
> Mike Ditka with the Saints offered us the whole draft for the fourth pick. We said we wouldn't take his whole draft, plus the one next year. It was going to be Edgerrin. We knew we had zeroed in on someone special.
>
> Dwight Freeney is only six feet tall, and Bill he knows it's Freeney. He's tremendous at that. Edgerrin came in, and we had such expectations because we knew how special he was. In his first preseason game he takes it to the house.
>
> *(Continued on next page)*

156

We really knew about what type of man he was. We knew about his mom. We knew about his grandmother. We knew about his upbringing. It was something I could totally relate to only because my grandparents came across Ellis Island with just the shirt on their backs. My mother raised five kids in the inner-city of Chicago. My grandfather died in 1927 and he was a poor tailor. My grandmother raised my mom.

Just like in Chicago, you don't put out any airs. It's no bullshit. With Edgerrin, it's real. You realize every time Edgerrin's in the room with you and there's other people there, he's probably the smartest guy in the room. Most guys coming out at twenty, twenty-one years old don't have that kind of wisdom or maturity.

Edgerrin was out of the mode that I was taught when I came into the league fifty years ago with Johnny Unitas and those guys way back when. That no one can outwork you, that's in your hands. Given all the God-given talent that he had, God's gift to us is the talent he gives us. How we use those gifts is our ability to pay back God and show appreciation.

I would always watch Marvin, Edgerrin, and Peyton come out of the locker room before games. I'd be in the tunnel and I'd see the fans. I'd get behind them and see No. 18, No. 32, and No. 88 and I always told myself to just lock this image in your mind, man, because you're not going to see this again. You don't see Montana and Rice and Ronnie Lott walk out of the 49ers locker room. It just doesn't happen. It was such a special team because they love each other, they fought for each other, the fans just loved them.

When you looked at the horseshoe, when you look at what it stands for, when you look at why people love it and respect it, it's because of people like Edgerrin. Only a handful of guys you can point to and say he created this legacy.

(Continued on next page)

Peyton was there. Marvin was there. But this was a different team in '99 when Edge came in. He changed everything. He was the glue that finally made things happen.

At that time, the conference was a lot like it was back in the '70s when we had Bert Jones and couldn't get past the Steelers and the Raiders. In later years, the Patriots-Colts rivalry was as good as its ever gotten.

It was a special time in my life. When Edgerrin came to the Colts, I was thirty-nine years old. Those guys from that era, you have to understand, that Colts team in that decade won 115 games. That's averaging 11.5 wins a season, which is incredible. Seven seasons with 12 or more wins.

Edgerrin was special from the beginning. You can talk about his siblings seeing him working when he was eight and nine years old, doing things that sixteen-year-olds couldn't do, he was so strong. To overcome adversity. To be given that talent but not fall prey to the dark side, which can so easily happen with great young talent in sports and entertainment. If you really want to be the best of the best, it's going to take everything including an immense commitment to hard work.

His grandmother was very strong in his life.

We played the Detroit Lions and we dominated the game and we took him out late in the third quarter. After the game he came out of the locker room and I met with him. I had a chance to meet his grandmother.

I walked up to her and said, 'Hello, ma'am, such an honor to meet you.' She grabbed my hand. Her grip was like Mike Tyson; it was unbelievable. She's like eighty-something.

'Now, listen. That's my favorite boy out there and when you take him out when I'm at the game, I don't appreciate that!'

'Yes, ma'am. I'm so sorry.'

Edgerrin was laughing. He's like, 'C'mon, Grandma.'

She said, 'I don't care who he is.'

We were the first team to perfect the stretch play. It was actually the best thing for me. It was more my style. It was a match made in heaven. You've got to have patience. If you don't have patience, it's not going to work. You've got to pick your hole. There's no direct hole. Once you feel that this is the right way to run, you plant your feet and go.

The beauty of the stretch play is based on personal decisions. Whatever I felt was best were things that I saw. It wasn't like you were running like a robot. You run, you get to an area, and when you see it, you go. It's not like other plays. You get to make a decision.

I love that, and I always compare it to business. I'm going to make the best business decision. I'm not here to lose yards. I was an incentive-based runner. I had to make the right decision to get paid.

The stretch play holds everybody accountable. You have a dominant running back, a dominant quarterback, and a dominant receiver. It holds the defense accountable because you never know if Peyton is actually going to hand me the ball or pull it back and pass. If the safety sits up there and tries to cheat, most likely they're going to get burnt by the receiver. Would you rather give up the big pass, or the run?

So you punish them with the run.

It's hard because the quarterback is detailed and takes it all the way to the last minute. He sells it, whether he has the ball or not. That's what makes it so powerful. Everything looked the same at all times. From down and distance, you couldn't tell if it was a run or pass.

As a running back, the thing that made that play so beautiful was that it was less about hitting the hole—you just had to stretch it as long as it needed to take.

Sometimes it comes short and you don't have to go as far; you just hit it and get yards. You get to make a decision on the go. They're outside, so I'm going to turn it up right now. Or it's nothing on the inside, so you go all the way as far as you can go, right before the sideline—I'm going to get these two, three, four yards.

That was the beauty of running the stretch play. Everybody did their job and everybody held the defense accountable. That's the one thing that made it so special.

11

GOOD TIMES

In the early years, the entire passing game was built around the stretch play and his ability to run the stretch play and play action. The ability to make safeties adjust to Edgerrin James is what drove the offense and set up the big plays for Marvin Harrison, Reggie Wayne, and Dallas Clark. They had to honor the stretch play, the outside zone play, which he was so adept at running. And if they didn't, we simply dumped the ball off to him and he took off and ran with it after the catch. There was really no antidote for him.

—Bill Polian, Hall of Fame executive and former
Colts president

WHEN it comes to winning championships, I understood that it takes a team. No matter what you do, if you don't have all the pieces in place, it's just not going to happen.

I'm just glad that I was part of helping one team get to a Super Bowl, and helping another team become a Super Bowl–winning franchise.

It was one of those things with the Colts where everybody got along, everybody worked hard. I knew my role. I was the missing piece, so to speak, to that offense. The things that I did complemented my partners, and what they did. It just clicked. Everybody knew their role; everybody worked extremely hard.

It was the best time ever for a Colts fan because every week you knew you were going to see some points going up on the scoreboard. You were going to see some excitement. And it was done over a long period of time.

And then, the way it happened. You've got the face of the franchise, Peyton Manning. You have somebody like me, the unexpected. I surprised a lot of people.

We made the playoffs my rookie season after going 3–13 the year before. When that happens, sometimes it's the missing pieces falling into place. And those pieces getting better. I brought an element to the game. The quarterback stepped his game up. Everything just came together. And then a lot of people didn't expect such a quick turnaround. They expected 8–8 or 9–7 or 7–9. That would have been more like the natural progression after coming off a three-win season. But when you have it all together like we did, it *really* comes together.

The organization moved in a direction together, no matter what they did. You had a gang of people putting in a lot of work that were dedicated to their craft. Expectations were raised and we lifted each other up. There were no prima donnas. There wasn't anybody that didn't have to practice. Everybody practiced, everybody worked, from top to bottom. Everything was earned. Coach Dungy treated us like men. You treated football like a business. It wasn't where you were just happy to be in the NFL. You wanted more. We all wanted more.

When the heads of the team are always working, always putting in extra time, it sets a standard. If guys at the head of the team didn't go hard or didn't take practice seriously, it would have trickled down to the rest of the team. You felt uncomfortable not going hard. You felt uncomfortable missing practice.

> ## PEYTON MANNING SAID EDGERRIN KNOCKED THE COLTS SOCKS OFF FROM DAY ONE
>
> I wasn't surprised because I had been there one year, but Bill Polian talked to me early on, kind of told me he was interested in this guy. Bill kept his cards pretty tight and pretty protected, so he wasn't telling me who he was going to pick. I remember him telling me he really liked this guy.
>
> I certainly knew that Bill wanted to get a running back. Champ Bailey was there too, we certainly had a lot of needs. When you're 3–13, you're going to have a lot of needs. It was my first year, so I was kind of still feeling my way out and maybe got a little more involved as I got older and maybe knew who we might take and share input. I certainly didn't know him at that point, but I'd seen him play and was putting my full trust in Polian that we were getting a good player.
>
> I think the biggest thing was there was a lot of pressure on this player because we had just traded Marshall Faulk. He had a great individual season in '98. Our team wasn't very good; he was traded. Whoever this player is has got to be a great player. I think that's why Edgerrin's great accomplishment is that he came in and silenced people trying to make comparisons to Faulk and Ricky Williams. He didn't talk about it.
>
> *(Continued on next page)*

FROM GOLD TEETH TO GOLD JACKET

I've always said the greatest part about football is you've got guys coming from all different backgrounds. Edgerrin James is from Immokalee, Florida. I'm from New Orleans, Louisiana. Marvin Harrison is from Philadelphia, Pennsylvania. Three different backgrounds, but you're all on the same team. You're all accomplishing the same goal. At one o'clock on a Sunday afternoon, it doesn't matter where you're from. We're all together. I loved that.

That first year in '99 was awesome. I still remember a one-handed catch he made with his left hand down the sideline against Washington. That play always jumped out to me. He set the rookie rushing record and led the league in rushing.

Our coaches, one of their things was if a play was working, they were going to keep calling it. They would keep calling the same pass plays and keep calling the same run plays. We'd get in the second half of games, third quarter, fourth quarter—These are close games, right? Those linebackers and especially the safeties, they just got tired of tackling him. The first quarter you come out, everybody's fired up. The safety comes down and he's going to pound you. Well, for the twelfth time that safety comes up to make that tackle, I would just see it. These guys were saying, 'Know what? No. This was okay in the first quarter but I'm done with it. It's too much.'

He was so strong and so physical. When I saw him in the weight room, I knew how strong he was. I know he lifted weights but he didn't have to. He was a naturally strong guy. And he ran so hard, those guys got tired of it. We kept running the same play and I used to always be concerned. We'd run him three times in a row. I'd look at him and go: 'Dude, are you alright? Are you okay? If they call the run play again and you need a rest, I'll change the play.' Every time I would ask him if he was okay, he'd just give me this look like how dare you ask me if I'm okay? I'm okay. Stop asking me. It was almost like I had insulted him because he had great endurance, he could run all day, he was tough.

Peyton and I couldn't have come from places that were more different. It's impossible to find two people as totally opposite all the way around. We didn't speak the same language. We didn't talk the same talk. We didn't go to the same venues. I'm coming from South Florida. I'm rough, rugged. We had none of that in common. We developed that over the years. The thing we did have in common was our work ethic. Nobody had to tell us to work harder. When it came to football, Peyton and I spoke the same language.

The way I got along with my offensive line, it was easier for them when we ran the ball. It was harder when they had to pass protect. When it came to pass pro, they knew I always had their backs. If there was a missed assignment or mistake, I would deviate from my pass route and stay in to block. You develop a relationship and they'd be like, "That's my boy." Or you'd have a conversation with them and ask them what they were looking at, how could I make it easier for them. They appreciated that.

I was one of the boys. It was bigger than football for me. We might crack a joke. I'm with y'all. We've got to be out here working, but we can joke, we can laugh. If we don't, that makes practice even longer and tougher. That's kind of the relationship we had. It was real all the way from the top of the roster to the bottom.

It was natural for me. I wouldn't say it was strategic. It was more like a combination of it being good for the team and me enjoying it. I always hung out and kicked it with everybody. In college, you had friends and family. But when you get in the league, everybody forms their own cliques. So it was rare to do what we did.

People thought we were a finesse team on offense. We were not a finesse team. The way we did things, it may have appeared that way. But our team was tough. We had to be tough. When you're in a one-back system like I was, you have to break tackles. We didn't have a fullback. We didn't have big linemen.

When people said we were a finesse team, all they were saying was we were smooth with what we did and how we did it. I guess because of the play-action fakes we ran and the art of the whole thing, it made it seem like we weren't grimy. But we were hard-nosed and more than happy to hit you in the mouth.

> **COLTS PRO BOWL CENTER JEFF SATURDAY SAID EDGERRIN WAS THE PERSONIFICATION OF TOUGHNESS**
>
> Probably one of the toughest teammates I ever played with. I don't use that term lightly.
>
> He played with a ferocity that was very quiet. It wasn't spoken. It was performed.
>
> It was just the way that he went about it. You could give him the smallest windows, and he would make the most out of them.
>
> If a guy didn't quite get his block done, he didn't come back complaining and bitching and being upset. Instead, he would say, 'Hey, man. Get your head on this side and I'll make it happen.'
>
> We would talk about the screen game and he would tell me, 'Just go make up your mind and do it. I'll make you right. Whichever way you decide to do.' He was always that guy that was trying to tell you, 'If you go do this, I'm going to make the most of it for both of us.'
>
> There would be dudes that had him dead to rights, linebackers bearing down about to blast him. He would buck one and then go and get four or five more yards. No one ever talked about that part of his game, but I'm telling you, it was so essential
>
> *(Continued on next page)*

> for our offense because he got us so many first downs where you could get the defense fatigued. He was like a freight train. Whether he was making a catch out of the backfield or running it, he was going to punish somebody. It was a beautiful thing.

That was the perception people had for the Colts because they really hadn't seen an offense like that before.

We made people think.

Not only did we make people think, we were tough about it.

If I'm doing my job—and my job requires me to pass block—it takes a tough person to do that. You're also talking about a job requiring me to run between the tackles and deal with the biggest and toughest interior linemen.

We would do it all—run and pass. But the way we did it was different.

I remember we played the Thanksgiving game against the Detroit Lions in 2004. Peyton threw for six touchdowns. I did all the blocking and play-action fakes. We were up by a lot, and so Coach Dungy started pulling us starters toward the end of the third quarter. However, I realized that I only had 91 yards—not 100—and so refused to come out of the game. I stayed in there with the backups until I got my 100, finishing with 105.

Jim Sorgi was the quarterback. He looked at me in the huddle like, "Edge, WTF are you doing in here?" I gave him "STFU and hand me the ball, kid."

They would signal for me to come out of the game, but I stayed in anyway. I wasn't coming out until I hit that number. I wouldn't even look at the sideline . . . I sent the backup running back to the sideline and ignored them.

FROM GOLD TEETH TO GOLD JACKET

With my incentive-based contract, I knew the numbers I
needed to reach every game. Against sorry teams I better get 100
or I'm mad.

We never had that top-ranked defense, but we had that high-
powered offense. If we had any defense at all, we would have
breezed to the Super Bowl.

That tells you about the game, and how important people are.
How important it is for all of it to come together, and how hard
it is to get there.

> ## COLTS PRESIDENT BILL POLIAN PINPOINTS EDGERRIN'S "GREATNESS"
>
> Edgerrin had only been on national TV once because
> Miami had been on probation. The talking heads on television
> and the prognosticators in the press didn't know who he was.
>
> We'd already seen him. I saw him live twice prior to the
> UCLA game. The UCLA game just convinced us it was further
> proof that he was the outstanding back in the draft and the guy
> for us. It was icing on the cake.
>
> We had traded Marshall Faulk because of a contract situa-
> tion that was nobody's fault. He was no longer under contract,
> which made renegotiating impossible. Marshall deserved a
> renegotiation. So we traded him. And then we were obviously
> going to take a back, and the world decided it was going to
> be Ricky Williams. The only problem was [personnel director]
> Dom Anile hadn't decided that.
>
> We went through the scouting process and Edgerrin had
> every trait we were looking for in a running back. A person
> taken that high in the draft, the hope would be for a bell cow
> for you for a long time. He had size. He had speed. He had vi-
> sion. He had acceleration in the hole. He had balance. He had
>
> *(Continued on next page)*

168

innate ability to run routes. He could catch the ball. He could run after the catch. He had tremendous ability to make people miss at the second and third levels. And he was a tough guy and a really good blocker. He was a complete back, so much better than Ricky Williams. In our minds, it wasn't even close.

We never did publicize our thinking or our choice prior to the draft. So when we took Edgerrin, it came as a shock to everyone. Not the last of which was our fans in Indianapolis. They lit up our switchboard complaining. I was Public Enemy No. 1.

Edgerrin's talent, toughness, professionalism, and his ability to play sixty minutes every week was what drove the offense.

There was really no antidote for him.

It used to drive me wacky when I'd hear people say, 'You know he played with Peyton Manning and Marvin Harrison.' What are you talking about? You're crazy. Can't you see greatness?

At the end of the day, it's about the bottom line. We didn't get it done.

Indianapolis is a small market. We made a small market bigger than it was. If we had this same team in a big market, you would have talked about us non-stop. We took a small market and turned it into a big market, a big name, that was well-respected around the league. That's saying a lot.

You have a great organization, and a great organization can go far. But if you have an organization that's missing things, they're not going to get there.

When we played the Steelers in the 2005 playoffs, whoever won that game was going to the Super Bowl. That was the real Super Bowl. The league's two best teams played in that game.

The thing you take away from that game is the good teams know how to win and the bad teams find a way to lose. That's where experience came in.

That's where the Steelers, with their experience, came in.

They'd been in that situation over and over again.

We didn't answer the bell at that moment. It's not that we played bad. We just didn't capitalize on opportunities.

New England is used to it. We had some tough battles with the Patriots. They played all the way to the last second. Those games showed us that stats were irrelevant. We would march up and down the field, but sometimes we didn't get it done. We would have a gang of stats, we would have all the numbers that said you're supposed to win this game, but we'd have a turnover or a mistake and lose.

When the Colts played the Patriots, they were real strategic chess matches. You loved those games. You loved the environment. They had older players. They weren't the fastest, but they were always in place. They were always where they needed to be. They would have little to no representation at the Pro Bowl, but they were always represented at the Super Bowl. They made you bring it every play. They're not going to give up big plays. That was the mental part of the game that always stood out to me.

As far as the era we played in, there were some good teams. We were one of those teams. But we were just being put together.

Heavy on the offense, but your defense is flat. The year I got hurt, 2001, I will never say it was all because of me, but when you have a big part of your offense out, it just really exposed the defense. Our offense was able to cover for our defense a lot. We would give up a lot of points, but we would also score a lot of points.

That was probably one of the best things to happen to the Colts organization because now we have to fix the defense. We know we had the offense. The offense can cover for the defense all you want. When you score all those points, the defense gets to pin their ears back. But when you're going score for score, that means the defense is really going to be put on display.

We bring Tony Dungy in after the 2001 season. He made the defense go. We already have the offense, and now we had the defense. Everything is finally rock solid.

When you're in those situations, you just keep plugging away.

That's what we did. We kept plugging away and eventually figured it out. The Colts finally became a complete football team.

> ### REGGIE WAYNE AND EDGERRIN WERE VIRTUALLY INSEPARABLE
>
> EJ led the NFL in rushing his first two years in the league. Some of the stuff he did in those years are still records. As college players, EJ was the closest thing to us that he was in the league. Miami would play on Saturday, NFL games would play on Sunday. If we could get EJ's game on Sunday, everybody watched in the locker room. We piled up in the locker room watching EJ. We're cheering in front of a big ole flat TV, a big screen on wheels. Whenever he played the Miami Dolphins in Miami, we all had tickets. It was nosebleeds, but we appreciated the tickets. We were happy just to be in the building. As college players, we were like, 'Why he got everybody up here?' But then when you play in the NFL and see the price of those tickets, okay, now I get it. We were kind of living our NFL dreams through him.
>
> *(Continued on next page)*

Time goes on and 2001 comes. I'm up for the draft. My teammate Santana Moss, who also plays receiver, he's in the draft. I'm at my draft party. The teams tell you to keep your phones available in case they need to call you.

My phone rings. It's EJ.

'Bro, you know that it's draft day. Why are you calling me? I'm thinking you a team, and it's you.'

'I know. I know. I just want to tell you I think the Colts are going to draft you or Santana.'

'Get the hell out of here. They must gonna draft Santana. I talked to every team at the combine except the Colts. I know they ain't drafting me.'

'Nah, Weez. I think they're coming after you.'

'It don't make no sense. How are they going to come after somebody they didn't even talk to?'

'If they draft you, I told you. Just remember that.'

And then with the 30th pick in the first round, that 317 area code pops up on my phone, which is the Indianapolis Colts saying they're drafting me.

After I get drafted, probably about twenty minutes later, EJ calls. He was laughing.

'I told you,' he said. 'We're right back in the box Chevy all over again.'

12

WOUNDED KNEE

Seeing him like that was surprising because we thought he was Superman. EJ was the dog. He was never hurt because he was made of Teflon. There was only one time I saw him down, and that was when he was a sophomore in college and missed one game because of an irregular heartbeat.

That was a quiet flight home from Kansas City. We didn't hear that country, Immokalee, Florida, laugh. We didn't see those gold teeth blinging. It was one of those things where everyone was thinking the same thing: "Damn, we lost one of our Three Amigos. Now what?"

—Reggie Wayne

I WAS leading the league in rushing in my third season—again.

In a game, you've got 60-some snaps, maybe 70. You're going to carry the ball 20 to 30 times. The quarterback is going to throw the ball 20 to 30 times, give or take. With all that being said, after that game is over, when do you start your recovery? When do you start getting yourself together? By the time Wednesday came, I wasn't one of those guys who was saying this hurts and that hurts. I would do all the things it would take to prevent injuries. I'm getting stronger as the game goes, that's my thing.

I always took care of myself. You have to really be in tune with your body. My routine consisted of, as soon as the game was over, I was in the locker room with the chiropractor. You get flipped around in the game. The chiropractor lines you up and puts you back in form. I didn't wait until the next day or Tuesday, which a lot of players did. I started the recovery process way before everybody else. I had to, because the next morning I was right back in there doing my squats and lifting weights.

We'd play a one o'clock game on Sunday. After the game, I'd go home with my buddies. We'd play basketball in the yard—right after the game! I didn't know anything different.

Early in my career, football was easy for me. Ask anybody. These are some old dudes out here I'm playing against. I'm not going to let this dude who's thirty-something years old keep up with me. That's your mindset, and that's your mentality.

In Week 6, against the Kansas City Chiefs, I got hurt on a toss play late in the fourth quarter. It was a fluke injury. We had to change our cleats because the field was bad at Arrowhead Stadium. The field was soft in one spot and hard in another, so we changed to longer cleats because of the softer side. It was a bad field, but in certain spots it was a good field. My foot got caught in the ground on the harder side of the turf when I got tackled. It was the wrong surface for the cleats that we changed to.

The Colts diagnosed the injury. I really didn't know. I tried to practice. I tried to do everything.

I didn't lean on the team. I didn't lean on anybody to tell me this is the person to go to, or go to the team doctor. I went back to my home base: Miami. I went to see Dr. John Uribe for a second opinion. Dr. Uribe was my team doctor at the University of Miami.

That's where I found out I had a torn ACL.

Once I got the injury confirmed, I took control. Your body is your business, and so I set my plan for recovery.

I broke everything down, learned everything I could about ACL injuries. Everybody that went through it, I asked questions or read up on them.

People can facilitate things or put you in position with people they know, but I always think it's best to take care of your body, take care of yourself—and that's what I did. I did what I had to do to get back on the field. To get back and help my team.

Thankfully, my team, the Colts, were going to do the right thing. I played for a good organization. That organization was about doing what's right. I was a player they just gave millions of dollars to, and they wanted to make sure I recovered quickly and safely.

Sometimes when people see that you're proactive, that you know exactly what you're doing or don't need your hand held, they usually get out of the way. It was a serious matter for me, it was a serious matter for them.

It goes back to the player. When a player grabs hold of a situation, that gives other people confidence. If you're kind of iffy, don't know what to do, well . . . that opens the door for somebody else to take over.

INDIANAPOLIS ENTERTAINMENT PROMOTER AMP HARRIS SAID EDGERRIN'S KNEE INJURY CHANGED HIS PERSPECTIVE ABOUT LIFE AND FOOTBALL

It was a box of emotions.

One, he realized that he wasn't invincible. I always told Edgerrin you're just a number in the professional sports world. When your number is up, it's onto the next one.

Edgerrin wasn't on the football field. Nobody was really talking about EJ. EJ was home by himself. He would never admit it, but I could see it on his face in his expressions. That was the first time he had a major injury. That was something he had to go through. Edgerrin was kind of in a state of depression. He didn't want a lot of people around. His family members wasn't here. I would go to his house and it would be just me and him, cracking jokes.

He invested in himself after the injury. He bought a machine that they use in hospitals. He bought one for his house. It was really a shock for him. The limo didn't matter anymore. He had a Rolls Royce. None of that stuff mattered.

During that time, you could see a transition in him dialing in on life after football. A lot of our conversations started to shift. It was hard for him because he didn't know what to expect. When he came back, he didn't know he was going to have the speed. He healed up pretty quickly. It was a culture shock for him. It was a mental thing he had to get over.

So many things go on in life. But when you're an athlete, you have to lock in on one thing. When you lock in as an athlete, you miss out on a lot of things in life. It's not so much an athlete being insecure, but it's unfamiliar territory. There's going to be hesitation because they're out of their element.

An athlete's thing is based around their sport. You talk about finances, that's not their thing. People look at athletes like they're Superman, but they forget that he's Superman to you because of what he's doing on the field. But in life, he doesn't have those experiences or he doesn't have the practice that everybody else has had in real-life situations.

Athletes are human, too. We're also Clark Kent.

For me, it was just a matter of what it's going to take to get this thing done.

During that time, the media tried to make a story out of my injury. But I didn't give them a chance. When I was one of the first NFL players to miss voluntary camp, the local media made a big thing out of it.

If the ACL's torn, let's repair it. If it's not torn, what's our next best option? That was my approach.

When you're going through something like a knee injury that can affect your livelihood as a running back, all you hear is negative stuff.

However, all you can really do is keep working.

Is there a way to get better? Is there a way to fix whatever the issue is?

All I need to know is: is it possible?

First of all, yeah, it's possible I can do this. When people say, "but," I stop them right there. Is it possible? If they say, "yes," then say no more.

The Colts preferred for me to be under their guidance so they could have their doctors perform the surgery. I was their investment, and they wanted me in the best hands possible.

When it came to doctors and my ACL surgery, the rules say you can choose your surgeon, you can choose your rehab.

I always knew my rights. I always knew the rules. Once I know the rules, the next question was, *Okay, what's best for me?*

In the NFL, everybody does what's best for them.

I always do what's best for me.

I didn't want to be up north. Why should I stay around the Colts facility when I have to train with the team trainer based upon the team's schedule? Why do that when I can go to Miami and have a schedule that works for me. That's tailored to me.

Some teams handle it certain ways. But when you have a true plan and it's legit . . . well, I didn't get any resistance. There were no issues with the Colts. They knew that they didn't need to monitor me 24/7. Even though I was more than a thousand miles away from the team facility, they knew I was doing what was necessary to get back on the field.

I'm a South Florida person. I had a good base in Miami. I wanted Dr. Uribe, who I'd known since college, to perform the surgery.

It all comes down to the athlete's preference.

Some people are just football players. I always thought of myself as more than a football player.

During that entire process, I took control of my life and took control of my rehab after the surgery. I tried to put everything in my favor.

When you rehab, you have to do things during certain hours to fit someone else's schedule. I always enjoyed working out in the middle of the night, two, three, or four in the morning. But I didn't have my own place to work out.

So I bought two buildings in Immokalee. One building was rundown, a crack house that wasn't being used. I turned one of the buildings into a place for kids in the neighborhood; we called it the Fun House. The other building I made into a weight room.

The thought behind it was that I needed to be able to work out whenever I wanted to. I didn't want to be on anybody else's clock. I didn't want to have to be here at this time and shut it down at that time. If I wanted to be a great football player, recover from a serious injury, then I had to be able to train no matter what.

I liked to go home to Immokalee, but I had nowhere to really train. That's what sparked it.

Every piece of equipment I needed, imma get it.

I got with the Colts' strength and conditioning coach and had him order everything I would need for my rehab. Every kind of weight you can think of. I was the only one who would use the equipment.

I would pull up there at two in the morning. I would get anybody out there on the street. I didn't care if they were doing drugs or whatever. "Wanna make a few dollars? All you got to do is spot me on the weights." After a while, they loved seeing me come around.

That created a little job for them. They looked forward to it. I would get my workout in. They would make a few dollars. I wouldn't let nobody else in when I was there. It was just something that I always did, workout while everybody else was chillin' or when everybody else was asleep.

It was my own personal cheat code.

I just wanted to get my work in. I got hurt and had to bounce all the way back. I had to show what it takes to get back.

I wasn't going to let an injury hold me back. There were no excuses. I had everything I needed.

I had to be in tip-top shape. I had to be physically able to play ball. If not, I served no purpose. Whatever it took for me to be successful, I was going to do it.

ANDREU SWASEY, THE UNIVERSITY OF MIAMI STRENGTH AND CONDITIONING COACH—WHO EDGERRIN HAND-PICKED TO OVERSEE HIS REHAB—ON THE WORK ETHIC HE PUT IN TO GET BACK ON THE FIELD

Everything was so calculated with him. First year in the NFL he hits all his incentives. Then he comes back and tells me it's too easy. I told him I don't want to hear about too easy. The only reason it's too easy is because you worked so hard and we're way ahead of the game. Some of the guys you're playing against are older; you're way younger and faster right now. But if you don't keep working, it's going to catch up to you.

He was killing it! He told me, 'Coach, I don't have to do too much. I'm going to play basketball, do my core work, and be good.'

So he gets injured.

He never had anything wrong with him, not even pulling a hamstring. Nothing. After the knee injury, he comes to me. We sit down in my office and close the door. We go over the whole plan.

He tells me, 'Bro, we've got to lay out everything. If I'm not here, if I'm at the house, I've got the same workout. I'm going to buy the equipment I need, the same weights that I've got over here.'

He made me go over the whole in-season program, the summer program, everything.

'I've got to get back from this knee injury,' he said. 'So tell me what I've got to do.'

He was very calculated. He laid out his calendar for the whole year and knew where he was going to be. I haven't had a player that calculated in all my years that detailed and organized.

The reason he was able to come back faster, if you always train hard like that, your body adjusts a little bit faster and better. None of this is possible if he doesn't have a work ethic.

(Continued on next page)

As a coach in this field, it's nothing more satisfying to see you're having an effect on somebody in a positive way where they trust you. For him to reach out to me in his time of need . . . 'I'm depending on you to get back to where I was. I've got millions of dollars. I can go to anybody, anywhere. I'm coming to you because I trust you to get me right and I know you can get me right.' It's pretty humbling to feel that somebody trusts you that much. I didn't want to let him down.

He trusts what he trusts. A lot of people make decisions based on other people making their decisions for them. Edgerrin isn't doing that. He's going to stick to what he feels is going to work, and he's going all-in. It may not be the coolest thing for everybody else, but this is what he's going to do.

The human body is not meant for playing football. But if you're going to do it, get something out of it because you don't come out of there without some scars and scratches. If you play the game the way it's supposed to be played, you won't come out of it normal. So make sure to come out of it with an abnormal amount of finances.

You have to live with those things. You have to live with everything that happens. But I don't have a problem with that. I can't complain because I took a business approach to the whole thing, making sure that me and my family would be set after my playing days were over.

I got hurt in late October and had my surgery in November. By the time we had minicamp, I was ready to go.

I was able to get back and run for 1,500 yards twice. That's a big deal.

The injury made me change my game, the way I looked at the game.

When I was younger, I could make any move, make defenders miss.

After the injury, and as I got older, I had to become more gritty, more strategic. I became a smarter runner. It made my game stronger.

You never know what could have been had I not gotten injured, but it may have been the best thing for my career. I was able to get more perspective and evolve my game in a way I may not have had to before the injury.

I had to tighten my game up. I had to become more of a student. I had to learn my body. You want to do this move, you want to make that move. But your body's not yet ready for that. So you just keep changing your game, the way you run and think on the field.

It made me a better player. Before the injury, I was just running.

It also helped me look at things differently off the field. You start paying attention to everything outside from football. You start understanding things you didn't think about before. Once I got hurt, I was driven to play this game.

> ### TONY DUNGY ON EDGERRIN'S ACL RECOVERY
> When I arrived in Indy in 2002, he had gotten hurt in 2001. So I never got to see the real Edgerrin James physically and on the field. I watched the first five or six games he played in 2001 before he got hurt . . . amazing!
>
> *(Continued on next page)*

He's talking about I know I can come back. I know every-body says fifteen months, eighteen months, but I'm going to be back this year. And I'm going to do everything I did before.

Then you saw how unbelievably hard this guy worked. That's the first thing that I noticed, the fact that he wanted to be good. He didn't want to let his teammates down. He wanted to be out there. Even under duress coming back from ACL surgery.

He had two years that I don't know any back has ever had, leading the league in rushing and catching the ball, being in a prolific offense like that. Had he not gotten hurt, it's easy to say and project, but he would have had a Barry Sanders-like career. Gaining 1,700, 1,800 yards, catching balls all over the place.

But then he gets hurt and he's not the same player, he doesn't have the same electric explosiveness and doesn't have the same speed, and he still puts up seven or eight years of Pro Bowl numbers, dominant numbers—1,400, 1,500 yards. Catching 40 balls a year.

Even without those first two years, you take the last years of his career and say my goodness. This is high productivity. But it's about 85 percent of what those first two years were. Those years after the injury, take that as a career, most backs would love to have that. He probably gained 10,000 yards and 75 touchdowns. It's crazy how good he was those first two years. **"**

I had incentives in my contract. That's when everything comes full circle. I'm playing for those incentives.

Every time we came off the field, one of the equipment guys would let me know how many yards I needed.

Every game.

Just know I'm going to do everything to win. I'm never going to cheat the game. I love the game. I played the game. But I'm always going to have my mind on, *Hey, I need to get this, I need to make that*, because you understand how much this game is numerically driven.

You have a bunch of stats, you get a lot of money.

You hit certain numbers, you get your incentives.

It's all about numbers.

I needed to be in the game all the time so I could get those yards so there ain't no bullshit at the end of the year.

When the team says we need to sit you down because we've got a playoff game next week and we don't want to risk anybody getting hurt, you tell them, "You remember I've got incentives, right? We need to get this stuff out the way before Week 16, because Week 17 we might not be playing." You have to think along those lines.

The Kansas City game was my 38th-straight start since I'd entered the league. I had never missed a game up to that point. I rushed 27 times for 102 yards against the Chiefs before getting hurt. That gave me 24 career 100-yard games in my first 38 games. I averaged more than 100 yards in our first six games that year. I was on pace to rush for more than 1,700 yards and lead the league in rushing for the third year in a row.

The only issue I had with my first contract was the year I got hurt.

I was playing for those incentives, but I was going to miss out on a lot of money because of my injury. If I didn't play, I wasn't going to reach my incentives and I wouldn't get paid.

I did everything the Colts asked me to do, but now I've got to leave a couple million dollars on the table because I got hurt?

The year I didn't get those incentives, I didn't get that money. That was an eye-opener.

I was like, "Hey, I proved myself." After proving myself, I shouldn't have to hit incentives.

I learned from the incentive thing. Once I got hurt, all the incentives went out the window.

I made sure not to go for that in my next contract.

It just so happened that my next contract was the franchise tag for one year. With the franchise tag, you're guaranteed to get what you're going to get. The franchise tag was $8 million.

The year after I played on the franchise tag with the Colts, I signed with Arizona for guaranteed money. No incentives.

I learned from my first contract. When I signed out of college, I wanted those incentives. It drove me. I wanted to prove myself. But after I got hurt, I realized that all those incentives were a headache. You've got to be watching the clock. Watching the game. When you're playing, you're asking, "How many yards do I need?" Instead of being dialed into the game, what the team needed, I had to be dialed into my numbers, what did I need.

My second contract was, "This is my money."

I probably would have led the league in rushing the year I got hurt—and I hadn't even gotten into a groove yet. I had a nice system. I had everything mapped out. I was in a good space as far as running the ball, playing the game. It's just one of those things that when it happens, it happens.

The good thing about the Colts was, after I put up a little bit of a fight, we had a conversation and they re-did a small part of my contract, which they didn't have to do. We ended up working something out.

Something was better than nothing.

FROM GOLD TEETH TO GOLD JACKET

PRO FOOTBALL HALL OF FAME VOTER MIKE CHAPPELL SAID EDGERRIN'S GREATNESS WAS DEFINED BY HIS PERFORMANCE AFTER ACL SURGERY

Before his ACL injury, Edgerrin was on pace to have a better year than he did the first two years when he won the rushing title. Before the injury, he had 3,900 yards and averaged 103 yards a game.

After the injury, he rushed for 8,900 yards, which was more than what at least 15 Hall of Fame running backs did. That's more than Terrell Davis. And this is post-ACL. People said Terrell Davis never came back after his knee injury. You can't compare knee injuries, but what he might have been.

Well, Edgerrin came back from a knee injury and rushed for almost 9,000 yards and twice rushed for 1,500 yards.

He wasn't the same player when he came back, he was different. But in 2004 and 2005, when he ran for 1,500 yards in both years, in my mind, if you didn't know he had the knee injury, you probably wouldn't know he had the knee injury, if that makes sense. You wouldn't think this is the running back that came back from the ACL.

13

BUSINESS, NEVER PERSONAL

Jim Irsay cried making that call. I'll never forget.
—Tony Dungy, on the Colts not re-signing Edgerrin

I LEARNED a lot about business playing for the Colts. I played with Peyton Manning, and Peyton ended up getting released in 2012. Peyton was the face of the league, but the Colts made a decision not to keep him because of business. Because of his neck injury. A lot of people complained, but the Colts had a chance to get a new quarterback, and took Andrew Luck with the first pick in the draft. People said it was wrong, but think about the business side of it. They got a top quarterback in the draft because of those hard decisions that you have to make.

I've got so much respect for the Colts. I love Jim Irsay, the owner, to death. They wanted to win. For me, leaving the Colts was about business. There were no hard feelings.

Everybody around there, that's my family. That organization has always been good to me. People tried to put things in my head, tried to make me go against them. But you can't make me go against an organization that's been nothing but good to me. I'm forever grateful to be able to have played for the Indianapolis Colts.

The more you look into it, the more you realize not to get caught up in that stuff.

When I say leaving the Colts was a business decision, all you have to do is look at the salary cap. Numerically, the only way I could have stayed with the Colts was if I took less money. But why should I take less? If you value yourself as a person, it has nothing to do with the organization. You hold yourself to a certain standard. When you have value—and you *know* you have value—you cannot water yourself down just to please somebody else because then you're doing yourself a disservice. All you can do is end up being mad. When I walk away from something, I ain't mad, I ain't trippin'. I'm doing what's in my best interest.

> ### TONY DUNGY ON THE COLTS NOT RE-SIGNING EDGERRIN
>
> That '05 team was great, and it would have been really fitting to win it with Edgerrin in '06. But we had to make a decision. Jim Irsay cried making that call. I'll never forget.
>
> Bill Polian said Edgerrin's going on the free agent market. We can sign him. We can do a deal with him before he hits free agency. But what he's going to demand and what he deserves and what he should get, is a huge deal. If we do it, at some point down the road, we're going to lose Dwight Freeney,
>
> *(Continued on next page)*

Dallas Clark, Reggie Wayne. We're going to lose more guys to the salary cap.

It was just one of those cruel, system-type things. But that's a decision we had to make.

When Bill Polian put it to me like that, I said that's what we have to do for the good of the team down the road.

It hurt me a lot, but it hurt Jim Irsay. Edgerrin was his guy. It hurt him tremendously, but he knew from the standpoint of going forward with the team, it was absolutely the best thing to do.

I can't say it was the right thing, but it was the right thing for the team in the long run. It was a very tough decision. "

If those are the rules, then those are the rules. The things I can't control, that's all a distraction to keep you from getting more money to position yourself and position your family because you're all riled up about something you can't change. Not saying you shouldn't be concerned, but don't let it stop you from getting some money. After all, you've still got to feed your family.

I could have accepted less money, but I'm not going to disrespect the position and I'm not going to disrespect all my hard work and just settle. Because the organization was doing business, I had to do business, too.

" ***COLTS OWNER JIM IRSAY SPOKE WITH EDGERRIN FACE-TO-FACE TO EXPLAIN HIS DECISION***

I was heartbroken when we had to part ways and Edgerrin went to Arizona.

We met in Miami. We had a long talk.

(Continued on next page)

189

> He said, 'I understand the business side of this thing.'
>
> It was just devastating because we had so many great players, having to deal with the salary cap and everything else.
>
> But it was just as rewarding to have him as the only player that I'll ever put a Super Bowl ring on who had left the team. He was so much there with us in the state of Florida when we won the Super Bowl.
>
> His presence, his dominance, his leadership . . . all the things he meant to us was so evident in us being able to accomplish that.
>
> To see him go on and have such a memorable career and pile up the numbers he piled up was incredible. Believe me, they would have been ridiculous without the knee injury.

When the Colts drafted Joseph Addai to play running back, I called and told him, "Whatever you need to know about this offense, I can help you." We talked about it. I never made business personal. The veterans helped me when I joined, so the least I could do was return the favor.

I knew my worth, and I knew they had a tight salary-cap situation. They've got to do what's best for them. I wasn't going to play for less than my worth. I can only play this game for so long. If it's not going to work in Indy, I'm going to make this move and get the kind of money I'm supposed to get.

You know when you grab a bag and go into the store and someone says, "Grab what you can?" Sometimes you have to look at this sport like, "Hey, football is not long-term. Grab what you can."

Not saying you have to chase the money, but you have to do what's best for you overall.

If you look back at the history of contracts, and what I signed for with Arizona, was that really a bad decision?

Okay, so I didn't win a Super Bowl. That's fine. But I did make it to the Super Bowl. You've got players that never made it to the Super Bowl. But because I left on good terms, and the organization knew I gave them everything I had, Jim Irsay gave me a Super Bowl ring after the team won SB XLI.

You can be manipulated into thinking that you've got to win a Super Bowl because all those people are telling you their dreams. But they're forgetting that when your career is over, this is all you've got.

You've got to make sure you take care of yourself along the way. I've always been a team player, but I make sure to take care of myself. Anybody that has a problem with that is not being truthful with themselves.

> ### COLTS RECEIVER REGGIE WAYNE SAID EDGERRIN PREDICTED HIS DEPARTURE A YEAR IN ADVANCE
>
> It was sad because we talked about this for a whole year. He warned me what was coming.
> He said, 'Bro, I'm going to be out of here.'
> I said no way.
> 'Nah, Bro. It's the Three Amigos. You, Marv and Peyton.'
> We debated it every day. We'd drive together to practice. EJ was like, 'I'm on borrowed time.'
> When it happened, I was already numb to it. Everybody else, it probably hit a little bit harder.
> He was the El Jefe. He was the bulletproof vest. He was the locker room guy. He was the on-the-field-guy.
>
> *(Continued on next page)*

A lot of stuff didn't pop off until he said, 'Let's do it.'

Like the damn cab ride.

Once again, learning from EJ.

Training camp's coming up at Rose-Hulman. It's 2002. We normally get there about a week before camp starts. We go to K-Mart, get all our stuff.

EJ never wanted to drive. He always wanted to be chauffeured, a passenger. This time, he had a suspended license, so he couldn't drive even if he wanted to.

He's like, 'Weez, what time you coming to get me?' I said, 'I thought I was getting in the car with you.' He said, 'I ain't driving.' I said, 'I ain't driving either.' EJ said, 'If you ain't driving and I ain't driving, I guess we'll get a cab.'

So we took a cab from Indianapolis to Terre Haute, Indiana. It costs $200. We were laughing and smiling the whole way.

EJ being EJ, he's plotting everything out. He tells me, 'You know when we get to camp and get out of this cab, the media's going to ask us questions.'

When he got out the cab, the first thing EJ told the reporters was, 'This is what you do when they take your license.'

He had that aura.

Irsay loved him. Bill Polian loved him. Tony Dungy loved him.

Joseph Addai, his first day, he walks into the facility. He introduced himself. To this day, he will tell you I shrugged him off. I really didn't show him much love. It's probably because they brought him in to replace EJ. He's got some big shoes to fill.

When EJ and Joe Addai met for the first time, it was nothing but love. I remember Joe talking about it: 'He was cool as hell.'

PART VI:

FOOTBALL IN THE DESERT (2006–2009)

14

NEW ATTITUDE

When EJ got there, he made it his business to include every-body and made sure that guys felt comfortable. You could see a difference in the team. You had guys playing for one another because guys felt included. It was offensive linemen hanging with defensive linemen, defensive linemen hanging with receivers. All that just because of EJ. It made everybody on that team closer, and you saw the results in how everyone played.

—Anquan Boldin, Edgerrin's teammate with the
Arizona Cardinals

IT was time for me to say, "What kind of money am I worth?" "What kind of money did I deserve?"

I'm not asking for something ridiculous. It just happened the organization where I had played my entire career, they were just unable to do it.

The Colts locker room, after you've been around for a long time, that locker room changes a lot. The organization went in a new direction.

I had to make the proper adjustments.

I was one of the top free agents. I did my homework. I only took one visit. I kind of already knew. In the middle of the night, I jumped up. As soon as twelve o'clock hit on the first day of free agency, we had a flight to Arizona. It was a beautiful thing for me to go out on a limb and do something different.

I can go to Arizona and also pick up a few coins.

Everybody talked bad about Arizona, but the Cardinals had all the pieces. They were getting a new stadium. They had a Black head coach, Denny Green, who was well respected. Coach Dungy came up under him. Denny was coach Dungy's mentor. I assumed they did things the same way. I got along so well with coach Dungy that I only assumed that Denny is a cool brother I'd probably be able to relate to. That was one of the main reasons I went there.

When you start looking at everything, I was like, "What about this doesn't make sense?"

I weighed my options. I had just left a great, established situation with the Colts. To me, Arizona looked like a potentially great situation.

The Cardinals had two great wide receivers in Anquan Boldin and Larry Fitzgerald. The Colts had two greats in Marvin Harrison and Reggie Wayne. The Colts had Peyton. Arizona had Kurt Warner. The Cardinals had a top-ranked defense. The only thing they didn't have was a running back.

I had recently changed agents. Drew Rosenhaus recruited me harder than anybody the first time. When it came time to let Rosenhaus know I was going with Leigh Steinberg and Jeff Moorad, he was disappointed but said good luck and that he'd stay in touch.

I was a Miami person, he was a Miami person. Anytime things were going on in Miami, he would still treat people with the same type of respect and energy from when he was recruiting them. That wasn't the case with a lot of agents.

I had a lot of respect for him after that because even though he didn't sign me, he never changed the way he was with me. When it came back around to selecting an agent, that's what made it a no-brainer to go with him.

Moorad became the part-owner of baseball's San Diego Padres, so he split with Steinberg. That's the only reason why I left. Otherwise, I would have stayed with them.

When it was time for my next contract, I told Rosenhaus, "Let's go get this money."

A lot of times when you meet a person, if they don't get their way, they treat you like shit. But when a person doesn't get their way and they say they understand and the opportunity comes up again, you remember when things didn't go in their favor and how they treated you. If they treat you right, they might have a little good in them.

Other agents and people in the media bad-mouthed me because I went against tradition the first time and didn't hire an agent until after I got drafted. They were saying things like, "This guy doesn't know what he's doing." You weren't going to hear one agent say, "That kid with the Colts negotiated his own deal. He did a great job." I understood where they were coming from. Nobody praised me because it didn't work in their favor.

I signed what I felt was a great deal with Arizona: four years, $30 million.

In life, if it works in somebody else's favor, they're going to devalue you. They're going to downplay it. But at the end of the day, you have to know your value. The fact is, I positioned myself pretty well. I knew I was the top free agent running back on the market. As such, I ended up getting what I was supposed to get.

One of the things I learned before I signed with the Cardinals was that their owner was trying to change the image of the organization.

As soon as I got there, I realized things were going to be different.

I always had a detailed training schedule. As soon as the season was over, I'd get the data for the first minicamp, the mandatory minicamp. The day before minicamp, I would write one, two, three . . . on the calendar. All the way back to the current date. I've got forty-plus days, fifty-plus days. It was written down right in front of me. I'm not going to do any running until this many days before I have to appear in front of the team. I'm creating my base. I stopped running and was just lifting and getting my base back.

But when I got to Arizona, that was the first time I got away from my training schedule.

It was totally different. At first, I was surrounded by people that didn't love the game.

It felt like a college team.

I was used to winning, but I found myself going to the Cardinals facility and going to sleep every day.

I found myself not being detailed with my training. I did the bare minimum because of the environment. I started telling myself, "This is not me."

The night before home games, you didn't have to stay at the team hotel; you could show up an hour before the game. I wasn't used to that. I always stayed at the team hotel with the Colts—but again, this was different.

I had to get myself back together. I started doing better with my training, and while I was over a thousand yards my first year with the team, I definitely did better my second year.

They never fixed the offensive line and I didn't have all the success that I wanted to have, but I did have back-to-back 1,000 yard seasons in a rough situation.

Once they put the right system in place, we turned that entire program around and ended up going to the playoffs, and going to the Super Bowl.

For me, it was something as simple as changing the color of our shoes.

I thought the white shoes they wore looked old and outdated. My new teammates wanted to wear black shoes.

I went to the owner's son, Michael Bidwill, and said we should wear black shoes. It will make the whole thing look fresh.

It was all about timing.

I was just utilizing the opportunity to voice my opinion as a leader and speak for the team, so I talked to Denny. Next thing you know, we got black shoes.

We still got our ass kicked, going 5–11. That first year was definitely rough.

But we turned it around the next year with the same team. Just a change in approach, a change in the way things were done. One of those changes was letting coach Green go.

Denny was a big reason why I signed with Arizona. But he wasn't there anymore. It's pretty rare you're going to have a situation like that, where he's gone one year after I got there.

Nobody wants to lose. One thing you learn about this business is nothing should shock you. What you do is you keep taking care of your business. This is somebody else's organization. I have nothing to do with those things.

It's definitely accurate to say that I wouldn't have gone to Arizona if I knew Denny would be gone after one year.

That second year, after they let coach Green go, we had a new head coach, Ken Whisenhunt, who came from Pittsburgh. He implemented some new things, and things took off from there.

I was a leader in Arizona, an established veteran with six thousand-plus-yard seasons under my belt. But with the change, the new coaches never knew how much influence I had. Even Mr. Bidwill told me he never knew I was that popular in the locker room. They never heard me talk. But I didn't need to talk to be heard. The whole locker room knew me, appreciated me, respected me.

I've always been a quiet leader. A lot of people just talk and get in front of people. I'm more personal with situations. I can take you to another level. I can help you. I can give you some good advice.

When you have a name or you have influence, people are somewhat intimidated. I get people to let their guard down because I'm not coming to you with bad intentions. Hey, it's cool. I'm cool. You're cool. Everything's cool. That's why so many people gravitate toward me. This dude has all this money, but he's real, he's genuine. He's down to earth.

When I went to Arizona, I was just being myself. I was always open, honest, and real with people. I was mature for my age, which goes back to my youth. It was just one of those things where experiences carry over from other places. You see young guys come in, you embrace them. You don't stand away from everybody and say, "Oh, I'm a superstar."

Guess what? I'm going to have fun with the young guys. The veterans, I'm going to have fun with them, too. I would have fun with anybody, the equipment people, you name it. I didn't care who it was. I'm here to do what I'm gonna do, but I'm gonna have fun doing it.

When you're a person that likes to have fun and likes to be doing things, people gravitate toward you.

You ask, "What y'all doing tonight?" Some people are looking for somebody to do something with.

"We're going to the pool hall," or "We're going to rent out the whole movie theater," or "let's go to the bowling alley." I was always doing cool stuff like that.

Somebody's got to step up and say it. And that somebody was me.

That's my comfort zone. It's not an act. You've got to remember I wasn't that far away from being just like everybody else. I appreciate genuine people.

It boils down to discipline. I never cared to have anything or want for anything. I'm used to not having. I'm content with not having. It goes back to that Jehovah's Witness upbringing.

I used to hang with the equipment people just like I did with the Colts. I had my own locker in the back of the equipment room. I had my own closet at the Cardinals facility. My first year in Arizona, I didn't buy a house. I stayed at the Ritz-Carlton, or I stayed with Antrel Rolle, my brother from The U. On weekends, when his parents would visit, I'd stay at the hotel. I was automatically booked in the Ritz-Carlton.

With the Colts, I had a closet in the back of the equipment room where I kept my clothes. When I'd go to work, that's what I was coming back to work wearing. But when I leave work, I leave work fresh because I got a bunch of fresh clothes in my locker room closet. The locker room became my second home. Me and the equipment managers . . . I always made sure they were straight.

And when I got to Arizona, I always had to hustle. I had a hustle for the team plane. I had a hustle for the locker room. I had a hustle for everything. In the preseason, you've got these star rookies coming from college. I'd go to the defensive players and ask: "How many tackles are you going to get in the game? Seven? Cool. I bet a hundred dollars that you don't get seven." Same thing with interceptions. I'd do that every week during the preseason with the rookies. They're still thinking it's college. This is the NFL.

Monday rolled around and I'd come in the locker room with my sheet of paper. I'd go down the list: "You only got one tackle. You said seven. You owe me a hundred dollars." I did that for anybody that walked in the building. I would ask the running backs what they were going to rush for. "At least 40 yards." Next, the receivers: "How many catches you good for?" "I'll get at least three." I would make money on that.

I was always figuring out ways to make extra money, but to also motivate my teammates. While I didn't mind the extra few bucks in my pocket, I was more than happy to pay out when they did their mark, or exceeded it. Them doing that was in the best interest of not only the club, but themselves. I'm good giving them some money if they show improvement.

When I was with the Colts, I did a best-dressed contest on the team plane. Everybody put up their per diem. We let one of the stewardesses pick the winner. When I got to the Cardinals, I did a raffle. Me and my fullback, Terrelle Smith, would collect everybody's per diem. Every player put their name on a sheet of paper. Whoever's name was called got all the money. I also put a little basketball hoop in the locker room. Who can shoot hoops? I had my dice. Who can shoot dice? I gave everybody an opportunity to win some extra money, all the while bringing the locker room a bit closer. Getting guys that may not have previously hung out to be competing in things other than football.

Everybody comes from places where they think they know everything and they are the man—until they run into The Man: me. Believe me, I know all the tricks. I saved all the money I won and bought a jeep. I still have that jeep. Probably cost me $30,000.

I had a lot on my mind in Arizona. I ran for 1,000 yards my first two seasons and went to the Super Bowl my third year there. But I clashed with Whisenhunt. At the time, during the 2008 season, my kids' mom was going through leukemia. Because of that, I was dealing with a lot of things off the field.

That's one thing I appreciated about coach Dungy. He was the best coach I ever had. He was a people person who understood family values. You didn't have to go into detail with him. The Cardinals, with the coach they had, were different.

After Week 6, we had a bye week. So I go to coach and I'm like, "I've got to take care of some family stuff." He told me, "If you're not back here tomorrow, you're going to be benched."

I had so much influence around there, and that's how they treat me? They didn't know how to go about dealing with somebody like myself. I had all this stuff going on with my kids' mom and my kids. I don't got time to play games. It's not like I was asking to go on vacation or something. I had real-life things to deal with. After that, it kind of went downhill from there.

Me and the GM, Rod Graves, we're still good to this day. He understood what was going on. I talked to Rod. I asked him to release me and let me go versus handling me like this. There wasn't much he could do, though he did the best he could. He had his hands tied with the whole situation.

That's the nature of the business. You can't put your job or all that on the line for a player. It has to be something that's really, really serious. I asked Rod, "Can you release me? Can you do that so I can move on?" And he couldn't. His hands were tied.

I understood. Me and Rod always remained solid.

I was already in a situation where I was good with football. But I'm still going to make sure that I'm prepared and ready. You could really just lose it and say, "I'm not into this." But I had been programmed for long seasons. I had routines that prepared me to go the distance.

The reality of it is there were a lot of good times out there. The team started jelling and making better decisions on the pass-run option. We hit our stride at the right time. You can insert one person and it can throw off the whole situation. But, instead, it enhanced the situation.

> ### *ANQUAN BOLDIN ON THE CARDINALS BENCHING EDGE DURING THE 2008 SEASON*
>
> When they tried to bench EJ, I got pissed off. I said it to the press. I said that in order for us to win, we're going to need EJ in the backfield because he was more than just a guy running the ball.
>
> Unfortunately, there's politics in the NFL. Coaches want to make guys who they draft look good. If those guys that they draft look good, it makes them look like they know what they're doing.
>
> A lot of coaches don't have a clue. I'm just being honest.
>
> My honesty got me traded a couple times.
>
> They understood how important EJ was to our offense, but they tried to go away from him.
>
> I knew that if we were going anywhere, especially talking about competing for a championship, EJ was that guy we would have to rely on. They tried to go away from him, but when we went on our Super Bowl run, we most definitely went back to EJ.

As things went on, it really didn't bother me because I had bigger, more important things on my mind. I really wasn't into football.

When you let people know they don't intimidate you, some have a problem with that. I've always positioned myself where I don't have to bow down to no man, and I never will.

You know what? Pay me my $5 million to chill. We're going out every night, hanging out, because I don't even care. I'm still going to work out, but now I'm going to hang out through the week. I ain't playing in the games. I haven't even been taping my ankles on game day.

I remember one game the coaches wanted to start acting like everything was cool again, so I would leave my helmet way on the other end of the bench. I'm not going to do nothing you can suspend me for, but I'm going to walk around real slow—even at practice.

When you become a head coach, you have to know how to deal with a player that has influence and has been in the league for a long time. He wasn't a bad dude. He just didn't know how to handle EJ. I got real influence around here. I've been in the league a long time. Communicate with me like a man versus pulling all these little moves.

It's no hard feelings with me. I got $5 million to chill.

I was having my best year with the Cardinals. But because I'm not going to kiss nobody's butt, things started going downhill . . . but then they came back around.

Next thing you know, when we're in the playoffs, they see I wasn't wrong, and they needed a spurt, they wanted to put me back in the starting lineup. We made our Super Bowl run. I knew I wasn't going to be there the next year. It was a lot of unnecessary stuff during that time, but it's no big deal because we got to where we wanted to get. We didn't finish the job, but we got there.

I led the team in rushing, but they sat me down for seven games. I could have rushed for 1,000 yards three years in a row—even without the best offensive line. I hate that I didn't get those yards. I went there knowing they didn't have the best running game. But I've got a chip on my shoulder. I'm from Florida. We think we can do everything. I got the most that I could out of that situation.

Not everyone's going to be perfect. You've got to find their strength and utilize it. I can't take a person and try to turn him into someone they're not. But if you find something they're really good at, play to their strengths. Let's put pride aside and do things that work for them. That's what started to happen with me and coach.

Life is an ongoing learning process. Some people are stubborn, some people are not. It's right there in front of you. You just have to get out of you own way.

The players know the coach is young and don't know shit. Sometimes they give people a position . . . but they just need to learn. Sometimes when you don't know what the hell you're doing, it shows. The good thing is you're able to recognize, "I might have misjudged this situation because this person was built for this team." No. It's not going to be said. There's too much pride involved. You don't have to say it. What's said is what was done. So much is said in what's not said.

For me, it was more like I knew this team wasn't terrible. I looked at the roster. I looked at the players. Then we get to the Super Bowl and it's like, "See, I knew what I was talking about." Deep down inside, as a player, I've been around certain things, and then when I got to the Cardinals I could see why they'd been losing. If we just get some structure and everybody buys into it, we've got a good team. I couldn't wait to say: "I told y'all I wasn't crazy." I was three years removed from leaving the Colts and going to one of the worst teams, and now we're in the Super Bowl. Some people never made it to the Super Bowl in their whole career. Some people never played in a playoff game. I was a major piece to that puzzle. That's what felt so good.

I made it to the Super Bowl the hard way. That's what's so good about my situation. I went out on a limb. I didn't go to the most popular team. That's part of my whole life. I do a lot of stuff the hard way. I did my first contract the hard way. When I rehabbed my knee, I did it the hard way. It may not be as easy as some people, but I've got that grit and grind in me that I'm gonna do it and be successful regardless.

HALL OF FAME QUARTERBACK KURT WARNER SAID EDGERRIN IMPLEMENTED A WINNING CULTURE IN ARIZONA

When I played in St. Louis, I was fortunate to be around a bunch of unselfish superstars. Guys that were all about the team. Yeah, they all wanted the ball, they all wanted to be highlighted and featured. But I was around some unbelievable men that said, at the end of the day, what's important is that we have success and I'll play whatever role I have to play.

In Arizona, we didn't have a lot of that.

Edge came in, not only with his reputation because of the kind of player he was and what he accomplished, but just his personality brought us together as a team. Especially at a time right now in our country with all the racial issues and divisiveness.

It was easy for him to talk to anybody, from Michael Bidwill on down. He connected with all of our players, brought our locker room closer together. I remember him bringing music into the locker room. Pushing the envelope in regards to where the organization was in terms of presenting its players with things to be successful. Things that connected with them. A TV in the locker room. He was part of that leadership group that had been someplace else and brought that attitude to the organization as a whole.

One of the things that I'm most proud of is we helped to change the perception both inside the building and outside the building of who the Arizona Cardinals were. Edge was a huge part of that. Even though he was there a short period of

(Continued on next page)

time, it was his leadership and his ability to bring guys together and his willingness to step in. A lot of guys come for a year or two and it's like, 'I can't really say anything, I'm only going to be here a short time.' He helped usher in what is this era of the Arizona Cardinals and people perceiving the organization completely differently because of willingness and perspective and really just the person he was.

What always stood out to me was that he never went backward.

Even though we didn't have a great offensive line, the guy never lost yards and he never put us in a worse situation than we were before.

He wasn't running for 1,500 yards. But when we handed him the ball and it was 1st-and-10, we were going to be at worst 2nd-and-8. He was going to move the pile forward and do something positive with the football.

We were a throwing team, and all of us as quarterbacks feel like if they give you the ball three times, I'll get you a first down. But what you always hated was 2nd-and-12, or 3rd-and-13.

That was the one thing I appreciated about Edge because we couldn't run the football. But we had to hand the ball off to keep people honest. Edge was able to keep us moving forward and always keep us in a manageable situation that allowed us to be successful and do a lot of good things with a very limited offense.

In the stat book it might look like 35 yards. But I knew those were positive yards and they were done in a manner that helped us throw the football. But more importantly, it kept us in good situations so we could continue to churn out first downs and score points and win football games.

We actually got the run game going in the playoffs. So much of that team was about our offense and what we had to

(Continued on next page)

do throwing the football. But a lot of that pressure was taken off in the playoffs because we started running the ball better. Edge was a big part of that; he was able to make some plays and guys started playing at a higher level. We became a more complete team in the playoffs. Our defense and Edge were a big part of why we were able to get all the way to the Super Bowl. **"**

15

CHANGING PRIORITIES

You can't say "My kids are important," and then remain selfish. Your actions have to back your words.

FOOTBALL is a young man's sport.

As you get to a certain level, when you're willing to do the things that it takes—or the things that it took for you to be the player that you were—I believe that you're doing the game a disservice. I also believe that you're doing yourself a disservice.

The roster spot that you occupy, that spot can be given to somebody that might actually need it. A kid who could change his whole family structure.

Why do I want to take that spot?

I may not be the player that I was, but I still have value. I didn't get a lot of wear and tear from my last year with Arizona because I sat a lot.

That's the football side of it.

But on the personal side, I was depending on people—every day—to take care of my responsibility. And my responsibility—the most important to me—is my kids.

As a ballplayer, one of the things that's always a struggle is finding time or being there for your family. The same with football, at home it comes with organization and understanding you have to have a strong team.

I brought my kids into this world, but now, because of their mother, Andia, getting sick from cancer, I had to lean on people. I needed people to do a little bit more for me.

You also realize the power of women and the things they have to do and endure with motherhood.

I take my hat off to women when it comes to raising children. It's a whole lot. You have to make a lot of sacrifices to make this thing work.

I was running a business from Arizona on the West Coast, then I ended up signing with Seattle. Every morning, I was on the phone. My last year in Arizona, every morning I was checking in.

I wasn't even thinking about football. That's what football turned into for me.

Some people love football that much, but that wasn't me. Growing up, I really liked basketball. In fact, I liked it more than football. However, I was just a lot better at football.

Football was what you were expected to do. August had been the start of football all my life. I was expected to play football. That's what you did. That's what I was mostly known for.

But, more and more, you start to ask yourself, "What's more important? Am I doing the right things for football? Am I really committed to the game?"

You start looking at your situation, you start looking at your purpose.

I move through my life through energy, through good vibes, through what I feel is right. Whether something feels right or not, that's the direction I'm headed. I'm headed in the direction that my body and everything is pushing me toward.

I started playing Pop Warner when I was eight, and was thirty after a decade in the NFL. As you can imagine, you're not the same player you once were. You have to really train to make sure you're able to play at a high level.

Though it may be different for some—those that still have the passion for the game—at some point you're just taking up a roster spot. And for what?

If you're going to be real, be real. Be real with yourself. Be real for your family.

I used to work out in the middle of the night. I used to have this chart that I followed faithfully. I still had the chart, but now there were some blanks. I'm still doing the workout, but the numbers aren't going up.

Then you start dreading working out. I'm just doing this because you think it's what you're supposed to do. Those are the little things that tell you: "Am I still doing what it takes? Do I still have that drive?"

That was part of my thing. Doing things that not everybody else is willing to do. What everybody's not willing to do? If that becomes your thing and then, all of a sudden, you stop? That told me I was no longer doing what it took.

I promised my momma that I was going to take care of her so she could live a good life. But now, I've taken years away from her, as I had to lean on her to help raise the kids that I brought into this world.

You can't say "My kids are important," and then remain selfish. Your actions have to back your words.

I understood what was important. No matter how much I enjoyed football or how much I set up to reach those goals, I knew that it was time to re-evaluate what those goals actually were. In doing so, I realized that, no, it's time.

The only thing was, dang, I sat back and thought, "If I don't clash with the coach, I have another 1,000-yard season."

But, you know what? I told myself I'm *supposed* to be in the Hall of Fame, I'm going to get in the Hall. I'm making the right decision. I've got to shut this down. The personal priorities outweighed my personal, on-field wants.

I understood the business side of football. The business side's motto is: as long as you can produce on the field, you have leverage. As you drop in leverage, you have to bring something more to the table.

I didn't play special teams. Imagine me running downfield to cover kicks? Let's be real. That's not happening.

I didn't want to become a senior citizen where I had to do all this extra stuff just to stay on the roster. I looked at that as taking steps back—and I wasn't taking steps back.

As I said, it's also bad for the next wave of players. There are only so many roster spots. You're taking a spot from someone else. When your time is up, tag the young kid and say, "You're it. I'm done."

Now, if you're still capable of playing at a high level, that's one thing. But if it's clear you're not capable of doing it anymore and giving the game what it deserves and giving yourself what you deserve, why not walk away?

I never wanted to hold a spot just because. And I'm never going to be in a situation where somebody was doing me a favor, and any day now they can release me.

No. I was cool with going home—on my terms.

I always made sure that I protected myself financially. Protect yourself financially so you're not dependent on football. But, unfortunately, that's not the case for everybody.

In order to enjoy life, you have to get out of your comfort zone. If football is the only comfort zone that you know, you're not going to get a chance to really explore and enjoy life.

I just looked at it as a phase in my life where I played the game, I enjoyed the game, but now that's complete. Now it's time for me to do something else.

Me, I got a chance to be a parent.

When I went to Seattle in 2009, I signed a $2 million deal. Thing was, I really didn't want to play ball anymore. It's something that athletes do. We're so caught up in the game, caught up in this is what we do, we forget that the end of the road is near.

I was still playing ball. All eyes are on you. But we weren't that good. I wasn't playing that much. The team wasn't doing what it was supposed to do. I was used to winning.

I only played seven games with Seattle in the 2009 season before being let go, but I was able to get all the money that I signed for.

After the Seattle experience, I had an opportunity the following season to play for another team. It felt good because I still had the opportunity to play, especially since they knew that if I didn't get a guaranteed contract, I wasn't coming out there.

It was one of those deals that if somebody got hurt, I would play a veteran, leadership role. I wouldn't have to do much in training camp. It was easy.

It took me about five seconds before I decided against it.

I called my agent Drew Rosenhaus a few minutes later and gave him my answer.

"I'm good. I don't want to play anymore."

My football career started and ended on August 1.

My first day in Pop Warner. My last day in the NFL.

To this day, I know I made the right decision because I'm in the Hall of Fame where I'm supposed to be.

I could have tried to get some more yards to solidify my status. I could have put in a little more time. But it was time to remove myself from the game and take care of my kids and be there for them.

That's one of my proudest moments, one of the proudest decisions I've ever made.

Now, I base my whole schedule, my everything, around my kids. They come first.

If I'm not going out to make money, I was somewhere next to those kids, or somewhere close by.

* * *

When Andia passed away from leukemia in 2009, we lived in Naples, Florida. My oldest daughter was twelve. Our plan was when she finished high school, we'd move the rest of the kids up to Orlando, and she'd go off to college, while my next oldest daughter would be beginning high school.

Everything was mapped out.

When you have kids, it's about holding yourself accountable, holding others accountable. For me, the joy comes from the fact that I'm able to position them to be successful. My oldest daughter stayed on campus four years. She did exactly what we set out to do: to give them a fair shot at doing everything. That's the beauty of it. Your kids hold you accountable. You have to live up to it. You can't be one of those guys that says things got rough. You've got to be willing to do whatever it takes for your kids.

My personal time is late night. When they're supposed to be asleep, I can do me. I still get to be a great father. I still get to be a good friend. I still get to rip and run the streets. I don't have to cheat myself. When you're trying to be a great parent, you cheat yourself. You have to take care of you. I make sure I take care of me.

I'm going to do my part as a parent. I enjoy my kids, but I also have a lot of help. I like to be hands on as much as I can. Once I come up with a way, I like to have it done my way. Then I put somebody in place to do it my way once I learn what's best for us.

I don't want my sons to learn anything from another kid or another man. I don't need them to look to somebody else. They've got a real daddy. I try to beat them to the punch to make them say "if my daddy said it, you better believe it's true."

I try to do that with all my kids.

I've got three daughters. The day your cycle comes, I don't want to hear it from nobody else. You come right to me. I know that's an uncomfortable situation, but I want you to know I'm right here. As soon as that happens, I'm going to give you my speech. You're growing into adulthood and becoming a woman. You're not a little girl anymore.

Throughout my life, I've always been extremely detail-oriented—and it's the same with them. I encourage my daughters to go to the doctor twice a year. I don't trust family, friends, the preacher—nobody. I'm letting them know I'm involved in their lives. But just in case you're slicker than me, I don't want my daughters to make a mistake. You hear about so many girls that a family member or somebody close had done something to them and threatened them. Anybody that's around, I'm letting you know that's how it is. I would hate to lose my whole career for doing something that I could have prevented or they just could have been aware of.

I'm on the go. I've got things going on. But I want to make sure my kids know that I'm right there for them.

They're going to make a better decision at sixteen than they would at fourteen. And they're going to make a better decision at eighteen than they would at sixteen. All I wanted to be able to do was say, "You're an adult now. Make good decisions."

I'm a real father. I make it real clear. Sometimes you have to talk rough, you have to talk real, but this is the world we're in.

I always tell my daughters, "I'm out here. I don't live the perfect way, but I see everything that's going on. I'm in the trenches." I try to make them aware of everything.

I think all men have empathy. We're all gangsters and we're all cutthroat until it's your daughter, until it's your aunt, until it's your momma.

I'm so about women indirectly because I am the circumstance of a woman that had to live that life and run that race. And then I had an unfortunate situation where I had to really step deeper into their shoes growing up. You start looking at things totally different: How can women prevent this? I'm still a man, but I still can come down to that level and realize, as a woman, you could prevent a lot of these problems. I always say, "God's gonna punish you for choosing the wrong man. You went after the wrong thing."

PART VII:
POOR MAN, RICH MAN

16

MANAGING YOUR MONEY

Nobody that never had money or doesn't have money can tell me that money ain't everything until they get some. Get some money first, and then you'll realize money's not everything.

Then, after you make your money and do what you need it to do, you realize it's all a game. It's really not that big of a deal. All it does is give me access to the world.

PEOPLE don't realize that money isn't everything . . . until you have money.

I know money isn't everything because I have money.

You don't know or realize what you really want until you take money out of the equation.

You don't know who you really are or what you really are until you take money out of the equation.

That's one thing I realized about having money. You see what type of person you really are, what you're really like, and things you really want to do because it's not influenced by money. It's really, truly motivated by what you want to do . . . and nothing else.

When I got my first checks from the Colts, everybody wanted everything from me right away. What's the rush? Let me first learn about money and get an understanding. I went years without money, so why should I be rushed into making decisions about money?

I always prayed to get some money just one time: if God gave me some money, I promised not to mess it up.

But when your prayer is answered, everybody's counting your pockets. People have all this advice for you. It's always a person who never had any money telling you what to do.

I was a kid when I came into all this money. I had just turned twenty-one when I signed my first pro contract. I didn't know much about finances and handling as much money as I had just come into.

Nobody respected that. They would say things like: "You got money. We need money. You're a kid. We've been working all our lives trying to get some money. Give me some money."

It tears a kid down. It actually runs the kid away. You can try to help so many people, but the money's going to run out. If you're coming from the situation I came from, if you divide your money into all those people, you ain't gonna have much left.

That's what a lot of people don't understand.

It looks like a lot of money because you're comparing it to a person that makes fifteen dollars an hour. But in the grand scheme of things, once you take all your money, take away taxes and divide it by all those people, you have zero chance of surviving.

You have to have an interest in yourself. You have to have an interest in your future. You have to have an interest in business. So many guys say they're cool with the money they make from football. But look at the history of that approach. It doesn't work. The money that you come into playing football, that's just temporary money. The real money comes later because you have to be able to have this money forever.

Take all the money you have and divide it by the rest of your life expectancy. Say a man is supposed to live to be seventy-five years old. Divide your money into that. That's how much you need to have available to spend each year.

As an example, let's say I've got ten million. Divide it by all those years and break it down with you and your family. Your family's still gonna be here. So, it only makes sense to get involved in your finances.

You have to learn how to get residual income; keep money coming in outside of football.

But how is the money going to come in? Your family doesn't give you time. With some in my family, they somewhat disappointed me. It kind of turns you away from them and you get isolated from them a lot.

That's where the problems come with athletes and their families and friends. You sign the contract, and they're right there. They're pulling up to your house.

You lose all the genuine parts of your relationship. You shouldn't be surprised that they're coming. But at the same time, you're put in a situation now where that kind of spearheads the conversation. The way you respond kind of dictates their reactions.

Before, you used to kick it, laugh, have fun. But now that you've got all this money, it's more of how they can get some from you, or how can you fix their problems. It takes away all that pure stuff and the relationships you had built.

Every issue, you're the first call they make. Every one of their problems is usually financially based. It gets to where it's not even cool to be around them anymore.

I feel for God because he's got everybody pulling at him. I'm not God, I can't fix all your problems.

That was one of the hardest things for me to deal with because I didn't change, but my role changed.

Now people have a problem with you because the relationship changes from the standpoint that they want you to give them something. You can't really be yourself anymore because you never had this type of relationship before. Now, all of a sudden, because I'm in this new situation, I'm supposed to fix all these problems and if I say no it's a problem. Or if I say I can't, it's a problem.

Who wants to get a phone call every day about somebody's problem? You can't be yourself anymore. That was one of the biggest challenges I had to face.

I started hearing, "I'm not going to be rolling with you anymore. You've got all this money and I'm broke."

When we would go to a restaurant, I'd hear, "He's got all the money. He's paying. It's on him. Matter of fact, I want to try all this food because it's new to me. I ain't going to be able to come here all the time."

I had to get strategic over the years with family members. I told everybody I would pay for the food but they had to pay for their own liquor. Man, the bills probably dropped 60 percent. Instead of a $2,000 tab, now I've got a $900 tab.

You pick and choose when to do things. It's a process because you're the first one in the family with money.

I wanted to buy my grandma a house. She said, "I don't need a house. I'm comfortable where I am." Then she told me something I would never forget: "Keep on giving and you're going to give your blessings away. You have to be aware of what you're doing."

I wrote that down: "You have to be aware of what you're doing."

My grandma's words were so strong: "Some people give so much, and now they don't have nothing. You were blessed. You didn't know how to handle or deal with the blessing that was given to you. You the answer to somebody's prayer and you missed it, or you let somebody trick you out of it."

I don't know why I was put in this position. Maybe because of my momma's prayers. My momma's a good person, a good woman. Always tried to do things the right way. Maybe I am that. I don't know. But I'm not about to give it all away.

My grandma's words gave me so much confidence. I wanted to give her anything she wanted because she did everything for me growing up. And she didn't want nothing from me.

And then you've got all these people who didn't do shit for me all my life coming at me for everything. But my grandma—who did everything for me—don't want a thing.

I don't have a problem telling someone no. It comes out of my mouth so easily and effortlessly. I also don't have a problem saying, "yeah." But I always put things in perspective. I spent so many hours, days, and years in that hot sun, I don't even know if I cut my life short from playing this game. You think I'm going to let somebody get my money after I did all that? Made all those sacrifices? Worked as hard as I did?

Now don't get me wrong, I don't mind helping people. I'm one of the biggest helpers around. But you're not going to pimp me, you're not going to beat me out of my hard-earned money. Because of this, I created rules over the years.

You can't borrow money from me twice. If a person called me with an issue, I was like, "I can help you this much, but you've got to get the rest on your own. Look in your phone. Make sure you reach out to all your contacts. These are the people you spend time with. Gather up as much money as you can from them and I'll come through on the back end. I need to know everything about the whole situation. Do you work? Why not?"

I made it real clear: "I'm a let you hold this money. I'm not *giving* you this money. If you don't give it back, you can never come back to me again . . . in life."

> **"**
>
> ### *JEFF JAMES ON THE ONE TIME HE ASKED HIS BROTHER FOR MONEY*
>
> When I was a freshman at Illinois State, EJ was already in the NFL. I'm struggling. My brother's this millionaire. I'm in Immokalee, so I catch a ride to see him at his house in Naples.
>
> 'EJ, I'm getting ready to go back to school. Can you help me out?'
>
> My brother's a millionaire. I'm thinking can't you just get me a flight?
>
> *(Continued on next page)*

He tells me to go in a room, look in the top drawer, and bring him that money. I go in the room, open the drawer, and there's a wad of 100s.

There had to be $5,000 or $10,000. All 100s.

I take him the wad of money. I'm thinking I'm about to get paid. He's about to set me straight.

I hand him the money and he starts flicking back the 100s. I'm counting . . . $1,000 . . . $2,000 . . . $3,000.

Then he pulls out a $100 bill . . . and gives it to me.

I looked at the money. Then I looked at him.

'Is that it?'

Literally, I was like, 'Is that it?'

'Yeah.'

'All right, then.'

I dapped him up. Told him I'd call when I get back.

I was mad because, here I am, anything EJ asked me to do, I do it for him.

So here I am trying to get back to school. I have no transportation. No money. I ended up hitchhiking. Called a couple friends on the route back to Illinois State.

When I got there, I called EJ to let him know I made it back.

'Jeff, you got a second?'

'Yeah.'

'I could have easily bought you a plane ticket, did all these different modes of transportation to get you back to school. But the reason why I didn't, I wanted you to learn how to use your resources and not just depend on one resource.

'Right now, I'm your only resource. I want you to learn to use multiple resources and not just depend on that one ace in the hole.'

EJ didn't want his kid brother to be like those other dudes. He didn't want me to be comfortable just being around him all the time. He wanted me to develop my own resources.

From that moment forward, I stopped depending on people to do what I can do for myself.

You're surrounded by people that don't have. You have to be a strong-minded person to be able to say "I'm still going back to the hood. This is what I will do, this is what I won't do." I'm not going to pay people to hang with me. I don't pay for my friends. Believe it or not, a lot of players end up paying people to hang with them.

I understand why the athlete does certain things. I also understand why people look at an athlete a certain way. I look at it both ways. I see where an athlete is coming from. And I see where a person from back home is coming from. Some athletes balance it better than others.

A lot of guys go through depression, because you actually lose your family, lose your friends. This guy don't talk to his momma no more. And this guy and his brother haven't talked in years. They see you with all this money, and you can't fix their problems.

I've seen so many dudes running and hiding. They won't come around. I've talked to some of them and they ask me, "How do you do it when you go back home?" You have to actually coach some players. It's not as easy as people think. Now you're the richest person in that town. Now the whole town depends on you. That's a lot to ask of one person. And, often, that person is just outta school. He may not even be old enough to drink, yet he's got everyone's problems on his shoulders.

Statistically, time is not on an athlete's side. They need to make sure that they make their money, make sound financial decisions, and prepare themselves for life after the game—because it could end in the blink of an eye.

I had the mindset of, "I'm going to do everything to learn about money." I'm going to walk away from this game with some money because you knew going in that if you played football long enough, something's not going to be normal. The human body wasn't meant to play football, but I can't tell somebody I want you to feel sorry for me. That's why when I played the game, I played with a purpose. It's no surprise that I made a lot of money because I came into the game to make money. I'm going to do everything to win, but, hey, I want some money, too. Not everyone has that mindset.

All the buddies that you went to school with and played youth football and high school football with, they didn't get to extend their careers like I did. I enjoyed the fact that I played in the NFL, but now that the game left me with broken bones and a bankroll, you take the good with the bad.

I look at my kids and what I was able to do for them. Whatever happens, happens. I know that I was able to impact them, I was able to position them and they're going to have wonderful lives. There's always going to be some type of sacrifice made by some people. You can't have your cake and eat it too. The older players in the NFL who played before us made it better for players of my era. Back then, when players came to the sideline after getting shaken up, they were told, "Okay. You're good." And you'd get back out there. I came up in an era when they were just getting into taking care of players and having concussion protocols.

As long as I'm here and I'm sane and everything's intact, I'm going to make the most of it. Now if it comes to a day where I'm affected by the injuries I suffered when I played, man, I ain't trippin' because of what I was able to do.

* * *

I really didn't realize how much money I had. I just knew that it was a lot.

What money gives you is freedom. It gave me the ability to do things for my momma. She took care of me. It was time for me to pay her back and make things easier so she wouldn't have to work another day in her life.

For my kids and my family, I wanted to make sure that I positioned them to be themselves, to be free. You're not free until you take money out of the equation.

I'm a free man. Really, really free. Not just talking about being free, but actually *being* free.

It's hard to be free in this world. Even if you make millions of dollars, it's difficult. Being free has to be part of who you are, as in, "This is how I live."

I don't come from a negative position. I come from a real position. I can say whatever I see. At the end of the day, we can agree to disagree and move on.

Yes, money makes people laugh. Money makes people turn the other cheek. Money moves things. But it takes more than money to be free. Having money helps, but it isn't the answer.

I don't think people really want to get up in the morning and go to work. I don't think people want to sit in traffic. Nobody likes to be told what to do. But after a while, you start accepting and start making those adjustments—all because of money.

But how can you want something and you don't really know about it? How can you want it, how can you obtain it, if you don't study and understand money?

People don't like to talk about money, but everybody wants it, everybody needs it, and it's everybody's problem.

People talk about money, but they talk about it in a different way or in a different tone. Or they try to make it to where it's an embarrassment: "Everything ain't about money."

I agree. It's really not. But you don't know it until you get some.

Nobody that never had money or doesn't have money can tell me that money ain't everything until they get some. Get some money first, and then you'll realize money's not everything.

Then, after you make your money and do what you need it to do, you realize it's all a game. It's really not that big of a deal. All it does is give me access to the world.

Look at the things that people have access to in certain areas. It's convenient. It's always in an area where you can walk to it, or get right to it. It stays in that area because those are the people that stay right there.

My kids started going to school in Naples, Florida. That's one of the richest cities per capita in the United States. You don't realize how much more money people that live in places like Naples have, how these people are living, until you pick up your kid at school and you have to wait in that long line.

You go to a Black school and you go damn near right to the front of the line and pick your kid up. You go to a white school and it's the opposite.

Why are these people not at work? What do they do?

They make you think, "Dang, they got it that good?"

But you start to understand the significance of having money and being able to take care of your kids and pick your kids up from school every day and understand that these people are able to put in time that Black people don't have. I didn't realize that until my kids went to school in Naples.

Where I grew up, you didn't get picked up from school; you walked home or got on the bus.

You start seeing all these little things that are different, that people in places like Naples do things different. They live different.

Parents whose kids go to Black schools have to work. That's where the generational wealth in all those situations comes into play. That's why certain people are farther ahead. They're able to spend more time with their kids, put them in educational institutions that can help them in the future versus being dependent on somebody else to lead their kids.

I always wanted to make sure I was hands-on with my kids, make sure they're aware of everything I learned. I'm going to try to expedite their learning curve.

Let the chips fall where they may, but I like our chances.

17

COMMON SENSE
DOLLARS AND CENTS

*Other guys wanted to be accepted. They needed to be vali-
dated. They spent a lot of money trying to camouflage their
color with green. I guess in their mind, society didn't see the
Black person because of their money. You had a lot of guys
who did that. It was their way of feeling accepted.*

—Rod Mack, Edgerrin's business manager

WE—ATHLETES—ARE impatient.

We're impatient because we get everything we want,
when we want it.

Everything goes fast.

Who's the fastest? Who can do this first? Who can be the first
one to get this car, or buy this mansion?

Everything in our world is speed.

Speed, speed, speed.

Business doesn't work like that. The con man's game is speed. The con man says, "You've got thirty minutes to make this decision. Make this decision right now or somebody else is going to buy it."

I grew up around the con. I know 'em.

Speed is your worst enemy in business. When you make that decision, you don't have time to send it to an attorney. Speed is the enemy in business when you don't know what you're doing.

The real thing is: How can we be world-class athletes and all of a sudden understand the stock market? It's impossible.

When you're twenty-one years old with millions of dollars in your bank account, everybody looks up to you. You become a genius every time you open your mouth. For you to have all this money and everybody around you laughs, you're not going to tell them that you don't know something. It misleads you into thinking you're smart. You're not smart. You've just got a bunch of people kissing your ass. You get caught up in being this smart guy who says, "I got this guy, he handles my finances," even though you're not educated on it. That's why he's trusting someone else with his money.

You're introduced to that someone who's really smart, a white dude who's a financial planner. Sometimes you get Black dudes, but it's usually white dudes. You don't know who he is, but he knows who you are. He's real articulate and he might be using words you don't understand. You don't want people to know you don't really know what you're talking about, so you start agreeing to stuff because you don't want to be shown up. You don't want people to know that you don't know.

I would just tell them I don't know what you're talking about. I'm not interested right now. I wasn't afraid to say I don't know. It didn't matter when they said, "You can make this much money on your investment." I told them all I wanted to do was play football.

The perception that people have about athletes is totally wrong. I always defend the players, my peers. They're not actually so much wrong as in what they were trying to do. It's more that the system they work under is broken.

After all, nobody would make a bad decision if they knew it was a bad decision.

Everybody thinks that athletes are out there blowing money. Most of the time they just had bad advice, bad guidance, or maybe some bad luck. To lose money, you have to be trying to do something with it to make it better. They were trying to do the right thing.

Now, I'm not speaking for the guys that just blatantly mess up their money. Most guys have good intentions. They invest their money. They put so much away. They have their play money. They tell you, "I have my money invested in this." The problem is they don't know what they have their money invested in. They end up getting people that they don't know to watch over their money. Their interest and your interest goes in two different directions. They're not going to say what's best for you. They're going to look at what's best for them.

The statistics never say former football players are doing better financially than in previous years. That 70 to 80 percent of our players were bankrupt or struggling financially two years after retirement, but the numbers are now down to 50 or 60 percent. After all these years, you still see the same thing happening over and over.

These things should have been addressed a long time ago, but you can't blame the NFL. The league needs to govern the situation better; programs have already been put in place to help teach the players on how to properly handle their finances, but it's going to take more than that. The statistics aren't changing. But how can you address it when the things that will fix it are going to cause other people financial losses? I'm talking about agents and financial planners who push each other's agenda and drive their personal business. But at the end of the day, who steps up for the player? Who steps up and says, "You're only twenty-one years old. You don't need to have all this money. You need some deferred money." Something needs to be done.

To keep hearing that same narrative repeating itself, to keep throwing those same numbers out there, year after year, people keep rolling their eyes and saying: "Another athlete messed up his money." It's time to present a different perspective.

When you say NFL player, you're talking about a guy that probably made $600,000, $700,000. Salaries are getting higher, but the percentage of guys that actually make big money isn't high. There's only a few players on every team making all the money.

Now take a guy making $600,000. That isn't a lot of money in the football world. There's a lot of successful dudes in the league and a lot of dudes that are actually okay and not broke, but everybody doesn't make millions of dollars.

Think about how many guys play one year or two years before they're out of the league. If the average lifespan of a ballplayer is three and a half years, and the guy never catches on to what's going on, how is he going to leave the game with any money?

If you're coming into the league at twenty-two or twenty-three, the first two years you don't know shit. You don't know that, on top of paying taxes in the state where you live, you have to pay taxes in every city where you play a game because that's where you make your money.

When you finally get yourself together and figure out how the system works, there's no more money coming in because you're out of the league. It's too late.

While all this is going on, the kid is told he needs a financial advisor. But how does he know which financial advisor to choose? He's still a kid, barely out of college. All he knows is football. The people he has to learn about money from are strangers. Somebody comes and teaches you about bonds, teaches you about mutual funds, teaches you about annuities, but that stuff goes right over your head. To be good at sports, you've got to commit to it. You don't have time for anything else because your whole life is pretty much football—and, most likely, it has been since you were a kid.

A lot of times when you come into money, no matter how much it is, you just don't know. I only did what I was willing to do in my comfort zone. I've always been about my family, my circle. My circle has always been close. I like the same people around me that have always been around me.

When things are moving fast, you have to slow down and see what's happening, what's really taking place. I would ask: "Why are all these new people talking to me about money?" I grew up without money and needed money. Where were they then? Why me all of a sudden? I know some people that really need money. Go holler at them. No, they wanna holler at me. It started making sense. It ain't that they want to help me get some money. They want me because I have money.

I'm not quick to invest my money. I'm not interested in something that takes risks. I'm only going to do business with people that have their own skin in the game. You want somebody to at least put in the same amount of money you're willing to put in.

I came up under a street mentality. I just want my money up under the rug, so to speak.

FORENSIC ACCOUNTANT CHARLES BENNETT SAID EDGERRIN'S DISCIPLINE IS THE SECRET TO HIS FINANCIAL SUCCESS

EJ came up with his investment strategy, which I recommend to every player, quite honestly. EJ was invested in municipal bonds. He owns his own municipal bonds. It's all double tax-free if you live in a tax-free state. EJ's in Florida—no state tax.

Basically, all his income was tax-free while he was making those mega salaries in the NFL. All of his money was growing tax-free. Once he paid taxes on it, he was investing it tax-free for all those years. Then when he retired, he saved all his money, so he's getting an annuity tax-free.

This is EJ's story: You ain't gotta invest your money. You don't need a financial planner. Save your money in municipal bonds. It's tax exempt. And if you diversify the portfolio, your risk is minimized. You don't lose money on municipal bonds. You buy them. They pay the interest. And then you cash them in.

My uncles did everything. The drug game. I'm very familiar with all that stuff. The mentality is: "I just don't want to lose my money."

My mindset is, if I put $100 over there, that $100 better stay over there. I don't need it to be $105. I don't need it to be $110. It just better not be $99. I always treated it just like a street hustle.

I didn't say, "I've got to invest and I need to make this return." Man, fuck a return on my money. Just don't lose my money."

That's what I told Ron Mack, my teammate at the University of Miami who became my financial advisor: "I'm gonna make the money. I need to make sure my money is somewhere it's not going to be lost. I'll learn more about investing later."

Nobody outside my circle really understood that concept. My concept is put my money up under the rug, under the mattress. Put it wherever you want to put it. Just make sure it's protected.

Everybody else was looking at it like, "You need to get this return on your investment." Not me.

Anybody that gets taken for money, especially when it comes to athletes, it's not the dudes in the hood or the people in their circle. Advisors and financial managers run you away from the hood.

It's the "buddy system" in place.

Who ripped off all those athletes of their money? Not the dudes in the hood they told you to stay away from. Those aren't the people that gypped all those brothers of millions of dollars. It's always the new people. It's always that other guy you were told was okay to be around.

Go through the history of athletes that lost their money. Look at how they lost it.

Look at Tim Duncan. Did everything the right way. Clean cut. Articulate. Doesn't mean he's untouchable. Nobody's untouchable.

This is my thing about forging signatures. I look at my money every week. I talk to the people I need to talk to. I tell them, "Nothing moves unless I go through these steps. I don't care who calls. Who says what." I don't cash out. I tell them, "This is the only account that money moves out of whenever I have to move money. When I talk to you, this is the only account that I'm talking about." When you start narrowing things down, I don't see where somebody can come in and sign or forge because I deal with those people directly. No money moves unless I say so.

Yeah, sometimes dudes from the hood can get on your nerves. They're genuinely good people you know well. Dudes in the hood can be aggravating sometimes, but they want peanuts compared to what those other people want. Those new people are going to empty your bank account.

Do you really think a financial planner is going to tell you to make a safe investment if it means they don't make a big commission? During the conversations you have with them, they always highlight the things that are in their best interests. For me, that was an immediate turn off. You're a multimillionaire athlete making money playing a game. You think he's going to help you save your money if it means he only gets a small commission? When he can tell you this other deal is better for both of you if it hits, and even if it doesn't hit you're still a multimillionaire? Why would those people tell you what's best for you if they're not benefiting financially?

When I started learning about bonds, I would ask them what's the safest investment you can make. They're not really high on doing that because they don't get that much of a commission on those transactions.

Then you start understanding why they're saying what they're saying. Is it in my best interest, or is it in their best interest?

Their interest is to get your money and bring it to their firm. They make their money off the type of investments they put you in. When you understand what's in it for the other guy, you ask yourself how can a financial planner who makes $100,000 a year tell you what to do with your millions of dollars? No way would I let you touch more money than you've ever seen or dealt with.

I'm not your traditional athlete. People that actually have money and are into their money like I am, no way am I going to let somebody else control my money knowing there are better options out there.

FINANCIAL BUSINESS MANAGER ROD MACK ON EDGERRIN'S INVESTMENT STRATEGY

I hosted Edgerrin on his recruiting visit to the University of Miami. Butch Davis did a good job of putting people together who were very similar. We were very similar in a lot of ways. We hit it right off. At that time, it was like a big brother, little brother type of relationship.

I was his first financial advisor. He was my first athlete client. Everything he did, and the structure that he put together and the philosophy he had, was something that we created very early on. It came from me pretty much knowing his personality, the kind of person he was.

He grew up in a Habitat for Humanity house. I remember on draft day right after he was picked by the Colts him saying I'm never going to mess this up where I have to live in those conditions again.

I was a double major in college, finance and business management. I think the blessing for me is that I got hurt and realized that football wasn't going to be my future. Working in the financial industry was pretty cool because most people weren't hiring young Black boys from the hood, to be honest with you. I came into the business cold calling and spending time on Wall Street before returning to south Florida.

Edgerrin didn't even want to cash his game checks at first. It stuck out in my head that he said he'd rather not lose money than make money.

(Continued on next page)

FROM GOLD TEETH TO GOLD JACKET

He started interviewing financial advisors. I said let me put something together for you. He knew I studied finance and business.

We were college teammates. He was in the NFL. Every financial advisor in the country was coming at him, but they didn't understand him. His look, a guy with gold teeth and dreads, everybody knew who he was so he was approached everywhere he went. They offered him all types of complicated investment strategies but it was definitely something he was not comfortable with.

I had an advantage because I knew his personality.

Safety and preservation of his money was more important than growing it at the time. I introduced him to a municipal bond portfolio which was all triple-A rated bonds. He was never going to lose because it was guaranteed, he was going to be very disciplined and not touch the money.

We put that plan together in the 2000–2001 season and it's been more than twenty years now. We started with $3 million and built it from there.

That's been the foundation of his financial strategy to this day going forward.

He was the highest-paid player in the NFL. He made $20 million in his first two years. Nobody had ever made that much money that early in their career. And he had a twenty-two-year-old Black financial advisor new to an industry that didn't have a lot of people of color.

Edgerrin's money is impressive because he didn't spend it. He let it grow first. After he let it grow, he put himself in a position where he could spend it, or he could live off the interest.

A lot of guys, as crazy as it may seem, they're spending their money to fit in at places where we never fit in before. Ain't no way to do that but to show off our money. A lot of us who

(Continued on next page)

244

never came from nothing, we never had white people come to seek our attention. We've never been the person who they make feel like they're sitting at the head of the table. When guys feel like they're getting attention from white people, they automatically feel like they're important because white people are giving them attention and seeking them out and making them feel like they're smart and funny. They think that validates them when they don't come from nothing.

I'll never forget when EJ was going into free agency after playing for the Colts. Everybody was clamoring for him. This was after he left Leigh Steinberg and Jeff Moorad and hadn't signed yet with Drew Rosenhaus. We were leaving Joe's Stone Crab when an agent showed up. He was begging to talk to EJ. EJ wanted to leave. We were in an SUV. He said, 'No, man, I've got my people with me. You can't fit in the car.' The agent said, 'I want to talk to you.' EJ said you can sit in the back and you've got until we get to the next place we're going if you want to talk to me. The guy jumped in the back and rode scrunched up trying to talk to EJ.

Other guys wanted to be accepted. They needed to be validated. They spent a lot of money trying to camouflage their color with green. I guess in their mind, society didn't see the Black person because of their money. You had a lot of guys who did that. It was their way of feeling accepted.

18

FINANCIAL LITERACY 101

Edge figured out how to keep everything. So if it was a hustle for Edge, he figured out how to never put his money at risk. He's playing with house money. But that's because he was never in a rush. He always understood: 'Y'all need me. I don't need y'all. I'm okay with this $1 million that I have already. But if I don't give you this $1 million, then you're not okay.' For us, it was this $1 million that I have, that I know you need, you know what, give me a couple extra percentage points and here you go. You could promise whatever. That don't mean you have to deliver. Edge's got collateral on his $1 million. We put our money up and waited for a future promise.

—Clinton Portis, former NFL running back and
friend of Edgerrin

NOBODY likes a know-it-all.

Everybody wants to figure things out on their own. I respect that, but sometimes you have to realize that part of the reason I've been financially successful for more than two decades is because I don't trust people, I don't have strangers in my life, I'm not afraid to pick up a book, and I'm not afraid to just do nothing.

You can't be so antsy that you always want to do something.

A lot of times you find people who just want to do things, who always want to be moving. Sometimes people think movement and productivity are one and the same, when they're really not. You can't be moving just to move. You have to move with a purpose.

Most people don't move with a purpose. They're just moving and then something bad happens and they're willing to accept the loss.

I'm not willing to accept a loss.

It means a lot when I make a decision. My decision means more than a lot of peoples' decisions.

It's personal with me and Clinton Portis.

We both attended The U. We hang out with our families, we travel together all the time. I guide him like a big brother. We played the same position, and we both were successful early in our NFL careers. It's so many things.

I'm somebody that Clinton will open up to. Especially when he was going through all that stuff.

I knew a lot about what was happening with Clinton. I was aware of his situation. He would always come to me. His thing is he wishes he would have done things different.

You want to figure out things on your own, but you keep hearing, "You need to talk to EJ."

You're dealing with athletes. You're dealing with egos. They don't like that. They're getting sick of hearing my name.

Clinton's situation is exactly like other situations. His intentions were great. But he wasn't involved. He wasn't hands-on. It's not like he wasn't investing his money—he *was* investing his money. That's what people don't understand. He set aside so much money to play and party, and he put up so much money to invest and bring him more money.

So, what the hell happened?

The problem is he picked the wrong people and he wasn't involved.

The majority of people that lost money this way, they had the right intentions. But just because you have the right intention, it goes deeper than that. And I don't think a lot of players go deeper than that.

At the end of the day, you've got know what you're doing.

I'm serious about my money. This is all the money I've got. I'm hands-on. My due diligence goes to another level that everyone else's won't. I'll put in hours upon hours and then come back and say this doesn't make sense. A whole month is gone and I don't have to get anything out of it. It's like the river in poker. You go all the way to the last card dealt and throw your hand in. Some people say they came this far, I might as well try it. And they end up losing anyway.

The only person you can con is a person who's greedy. You can't con a man who don't want nothing. It's the man who wants something and he wants it fast and he wants it now. That's the easiest person to trick.

A lot of guys invested money with Portis in those deals. You're investing your money and being misled and told it's going to bring you x plus x dollars per month. Now, the money you have over here to play with, you're really going to play with it because you're expecting what these people said to come true.

I've always been honest and upfront with Portis. I said, "If you don't see me doing it and I know about it, you better read the signs."

When I see an athlete who's doing well financially, I tell them, "Enjoy what you have because you earned it, but be smart. There are consequences for everything you do. If you want that Rolex, go get that Rolex. But know what you're getting into. I'd rather see you go broke knowing you're going broke rather than going broke not knowing it."

> ### FRED TAYLOR, ON HOW EDGE MANAGED HIS MONEY
>
> I started paying attention to how EJ moved from being on top of his money; he called his own shots and didn't let the financial guy or whomever dictate how he would move. And then a few bad things happened in our circle where our (financial) guy manipulated a lot of us and we got into investments that could have been decent investments. A few things that could have been decent deals but politics and the law got in the way. EJ was the guy who had his money in the right place. He was into a lot of funds and his investments looked good from the outside. You say, 'OK . . . I've got to pay attention to that.'

When I bought a Lamborghini, I knew it was stupid. But I put the stupid money to the side. A person can't come to me and say, "That was dumb." "Yo, I already know it was dumb. But it was something I just wanted to do."

Well, I had a Lamborghini . . . and sold it for way less than I bought it for. But you know what? I took my Super Bowl money and bought it because if I ever made it to the Super Bowl I was going to do something like that because it's so hard to get there.

A lot of times we think we're doing things that are smart and they're really dumb. Thing is, we don't have nobody to tell us it's dumb—especially when you're surrounded by "yes" men. But as long as you're willing to accept that, have at it.

My business partner told me people don't realize I've got all the same toys these other guys got. Thing is, I just got them in a different way. I've got a Rolls Royce. I had a Lamborghini. I bought a Bentley, but I didn't buy that Bentley until I did a card signing. I did a card signing for $250,000, and I bought the Bentley for $222,000. You can say, "Edge is stupid the way he's spending his money." I'll take that. But you have no idea that I did a card signing and put this deal on the side and said, "That's the Bentley money right there."

Just look at my first car. I saved up the entire summer, skipped meals, all to buy that car. And when I did it, I knew it was what I wanted to do. I didn't just see it and buy it on the spot. I spent the entire summer thinking about it. Planning for it. And I got it.

If I want something, it has to make sense. It would be nice to have, but I'm not trippin'.

It's not what you do, it's how you do it.

If you wanna buy a house, don't buy a $5 million house that's way out there in a new development that has no comps and has no chance of getting your money back or gaining any value. And don't buy a house that was fixed up to fit the previous owners' taste. They put in a million dollars' worth of stuff they like and tell you it's worth this much because of those additions. That's not how you buy a house.

When you talk about housing or even real estate, people don't realize your personal home, if you do it right, well, that's a way to build your net worth.

But you can't be like, "I'm gonna live here forever."

You have to look at it like, "I'm gonna live here three to five years, let this house build so much equity, and then I'll take the $200,000 house and sell it for $600,000." Now I do the same thing again with another house. Next thing you know, you've made a million dollars without even trying by being your own personal tenant.

When some people—successful people—move into a new property, they settle in and live their normal lifestyle, but they'll use it as a stepping-stone. Not everyone understands that part. They settle in and plan to live there forever when they could actually say, "This is an investment."

> **JAMES CRAWFORD (EDGE'S BUSINESS PARTNER) ON HIS APTITUDE FOR BUSINESS**
>
> Me and Edgerrin have been talking about business for more than fifteen years. We had conversations about different projects I was working on in real estate and multiple clubs that

(Continued on next page)

I own. Every time he does a business venture, he has a certain number of people he calls to get their opinion about what he's doing.

What athletes normally do is something that Edgerrin doesn't do. They link up with somebody who has an idea. I always tell Edgerrin if you and I do business, I'm not looking over your money. I don't want to see you broke because you're my friend. But my interest is because my money is in there. Your money's not more important to me than my money. The benefit you're going to get from me looking over your money is it's in the same place my money's at. With that concept, what me and Edgerrin always discuss is I'm only going to do things with people that have their own skin in the game. I told him years ago you want somebody to at least put the same amount of money you put in.

Athletes get misled. The first thing a financial advisor tells you is "Why would you pay for the whole house when you can put 20 percent down and use the other 80 percent to invest?" That's one of the biggest tricks or gimmicks there is.

If the financial advisor tells you to buy the house, there's no money for him to invest. So he's not going to tell you that. It only makes sense if you have true legitimate investments. There's no way you can invest and get 20 or 30 percent on your money. You're paying more on the interest in your mortgage than what you're getting on the investment.

If you're committed to this piece of real estate, if you've got the money, then buy it. Once you buy it, it's yours. Now if you gain any equity, you get true equity. If you're able to sell it for $300,000 more than you paid for it, that's a true $300,000.

When you're paying a mortgage, those are fake numbers. Say I bought it for $299,000 and sold it for $399,000. You've been paying a mortgage for five years. When you add interest and everything else, you really didn't make $100,000. But it looks good and it sounds good. But when you get to the bottom line or the true numbers, that's not what it is. If you can, it makes more sense to purchase.

A lot of the properties I have, I saw an opportunity. I have a five-acre spot in Orlando, where we host our camp every summer. I bought that when it was a narrow piece of property. I saw it online. I needed a big spot in Orlando. I needed it to be in the thick of things. It was priced at $1.4 million. And then it went down to $1.2 million. I started hearing the owners wanted to try to develop it so they could put twelve to twenty homes on it, three or four homes per acre. It's five acres but one and a half acres into the water.

It didn't make sense for the owners to go through all the stuff with the city, but this narrow piece of property was perfect for me. I ended up buying the place for $925,000. Then I went to the Florida Turnpike Authority office located on an adjoining property next door and asked if I could buy more land. I bought fifty more feet, so the property got a little bit wider.

When I bought the property, I saw a great deal. That's what I was looking for. It's our playground. And it's right in the heart of Orlando. There's a house there. A weight room. I keep adding on. I put a basketball court out there. It's all because I saw something that everybody else couldn't see. This is the family hub.

Me and Rohan Marley are real close. We both played at The U. He was telling me about having a family house. That really kind of sparked the idea. Growing up in Immokalee, you had grandma's house. That's where everybody went. I moved the family to Orlando. I wanted to create a "grandma's house," a hub where everybody could come. Family, friends, and it's big enough for everybody.

Everybody thinks we live there. The kids go there after school. The tutors come there. They eat there, somebody comes and cooks for them. Then they have their home. Everybody has their different places they go to, but that's the central location for the family. I was able to create that one mile from Universal Studios; when we go to Universal to go to the movies. The movie starts at eight. We don't leave until ten, fifteen minutes before. It's basically two miles or less from us. That's how good of a property it is. It's right around the corner on the cusp on the high end near Tiger Woods's and Shaquille O'Neal's spots. The next tier of homes is right there near the Windermere area. Shaq and them gotta ride by our house to get to their house.

That was part of my thought process, that this was an excellent buy. Nobody can build next to me at all because it belongs to the Florida Turnpike Authority. I tried to buy more land; they're just not selling it to me right now.

I learned how to purchase things. I look at my purpose first. The previous owners were looking at it for the chance to build a place, develop it, and put properties on it. I still have that option. I just don't want to. But if I ever want to make some money, that's another opportunity.

*CLINTON PORTIS SAID EDGERRIN NIXED AN
INVESTMENT OPPORTUNITY THAT RESULTED IN
PORTIS LOSING IN EXCESS OF SEVEN FIGURES*

We come into so much money at a young age. People try to convince you to take shots, instead of convincing you that you've already made it. You've already made it when you go from $1,000 in your bank account in college and paying bills until three, four years later you have $1 million in your bank account. That's the greatest flip of all time.

Instead of people saying, 'Damn, boy, you hit the jackpot, you just won the lottery,' it's like, 'You can get more.'

And for a young mindset, you're trying to get more, you're trying to do that again. You're looking for investments. You're looking for ideas that you know nothing about, but you just know you're supposed to be doing it, you're supposed to be taking a shot.

It's someone you're familiar with or someone who was recommended to you. In my case, it was someone I felt like I was familiar with. Not knowing that he didn't have the power that I gave him. He didn't have the power that I thought he had. He wasn't the boss; he wasn't the final decision maker. He was still taking my money to someone else to make that move. Although I had a relationship with him, he's still depending on someone else. And that someone else outthunk the both of us.

They come with the most elaborate schemes and ideas and promises. No one gives you the downside of the investment. They give you the positive side, they give you what you really want to hear, which is the no-risk, the return, the future finances that are going to be provided if this hits. But by the time this doesn't work, you're off the phone, the conversation is over. They leave you with the good news instead of saying it's a possibility that we lose this money.

They don't tell you it's all gone until there's zero left.

(Continued on next page)

The scheme is so elaborate. Your financial advisor comes to you and says: 'You give me $1 million. I'm going to invest in the low-risk and at the end of the year I'm going to give you back $1.1 million guaranteed. But we're not taking a risk, so it's impossible to lose. I'm going to make you 10 percent on your money. You get to live off $100,000 next year, but you still have $1 million.'

For Edge to be involved in something, it's gotta be a clear-cut win. He's not taking chances. Everything that he makes a move on, he's already won. He's going to end up in the investment that you put $200,000 in today, and next week you already have your $200,000 back. If you don't get anything else, you already got your money back. You get to sleep at night.

Edge figured out how to keep everything. So if it was a hustle for Edge, he figured out how to never put his money at risk. He's playing with house money. But that's because he was never in a rush. He always understood: 'Y'all need me. I don't need y'all. I'm okay with this $1 million that I have already. But if I don't give you this $1 million, then you're not okay.' For us, it was this $1 million that I have, that I know you need, you know what, give me a couple extra percentage points and here you go. You could promise whatever. That don't mean you have to deliver. Edge's got collateral on his $1 million. We put our money up and waited for a future promise.

So then when you come out with a story line like mine that this was about to be my reaction when I know this ain't okay, because if I took something from you, then I'm going to prison. You're going to bury me if this is me taking from you, but if you're taking from me, it's okay. But, in reality, at no point did I think that I was crazy. At no point did I go back and retract my statement: 'You know what? I shouldn't have been thinking that way.' I was right for thinking the way I was thinking. The best thing to happen was that I didn't react and I didn't do it, but I damn sure wasn't wrong for thinking about doing it.

There will never be any consequences for what they did. The money is being dispersed among them, not us. They took $1 million from me. They took $1 million from Santana [Moss]. They took $1 million from Fred [Taylor]. They took $1 million from Jevon [Kearse]. They took $1 million from Ray [Lewis]. And now we've got to fight to get it back? So while we're going through hell trying to figure out where our money went, you go from one company to the next, same title, same position, insurance pays your portion, you're getting the same money and us, on the flip side, we're the laughingstocks. Everybody says: 'Another dumbass athlete.' Our boys from the hood were never that expensive. ”

19

OWNING THE DIRT

I want to continue to lead by example. Buy property. Buy things that Black people actually frequent and get us to support them.

MARVIN Harrison was always buying houses.

Marv was always doing different things. He was already in the housing game. Marv would do houses. He would do cars.

It all started with our conversations. In the locker room, you have a lot of down time. The trainer's room kind of becomes the place where we hang and socialize. They had tables; you could go in there and sleep.

Marv was one of my good friends. We would talk about what we had and what we were doing; all the different moves we were making. Every day during special teams period, me and Marv would have a spot and sit during practice and talk. That was over our whole career. I knew in the beginning that Marv was doing those things. He has a bunch of properties now. He has a club.

I started asking questions. Once I got interested, I started buying books about real estate. I realized this was something I could really do, but I couldn't teach myself. If I had a question, I now had somebody I could go to who I could relate to.

What I did all stems from that.

Marv grew up in Philadelphia. That's where he did his real estate and other business.

If you're gonna make a mistake, make a mistake at home.

That's the logic I followed. "If you wanna learn something, learn it at home."

In the beginning, the risk was minimal. I knew I wasn't going to make a lot of money there, but I'm not going to lose a lot of money, either. Worst case, if I buy a property and it's not making sense for me to make money on, I'd just tell a family member, "Hey, go live there," so you don't really lose.

I went to a real life real estate class without having to sit down in a classroom. As you start making more and more moves, it gets easier and easier.

You have to be disciplined. And then you have to understand you can't buy a piece of property that's not worth what you're paying for it.

You don't need a lot of money, but you do need a lot of patience to make sure that you find the right deal, because there's going to be a thousand of them out there.

There's no ceiling in real estate. You can start as low as you want, and you can go as high as you want. I already made money playing football, so I didn't have to do million-dollar deals.

The money I made from card signings or any other outside income I had coming in, I would put that to the side and buy a property. That's how I started building.

You start with one property; that one gets you two. That two gets you three. That three gets you five. That five gets you seven. Then, all of a sudden, you look up and you have twelve houses. It's a snowball effect. Once you get them it becomes easier to get more. You can easily buy forty homes all in one lump sum. I was playing the percentages and learning along the way.

The law of attraction started putting opportunities in front of me, so to speak.

I was able to buy the building I grew up in. My grandparents were going to lose the property. My granddad had passed when I was young. I spent a lot of time on the couch in that house. Everything came full circle.

So I got to the pros and they're gonna lose the house. One of my uncles came into some money and saved the house, and I was able to buy it from him and keep it. I bought it at the number it was worth. It wasn't like I got this big discount because it was family.

It's a sixteen-unit building. Sixteen times $500 a month. Thirteen or fourteen of the units were always rented out.

I bought the building. I learned a lot about deeds, titles, and how easy you can lose money in real estate. I learned about tax liens. It's so much more than people realize. You can be a victim or you can be somebody that capitalizes on it. If people are not paying their taxes, there's people out there paying those taxes and getting a percentage of that money.

The more I got into it, the more I liked it. It was like a little game for me to play. I'd look for an opportunity and buy another property.

I would give each of my daughters a building. I told them, "This is yours. You do the paperwork, you collect the money, you get paid this much." That was my way of teaching them.

My daughter—who's in law school—started when she was twelve years old. When she left to go to college, I told her to teach her sister to do the monthly rentals. She did the teaching so I didn't have to. I'd put the system in place and they took it from there.

I was doing well in real estate, so it was time to look at where else I could expand and add to my portfolio.

In 2009, I ended up going to Seattle for two million dollars. I said that money is going to jump-start everything because I really didn't think I was going to play there. I made sure I did a contract that guaranteed that I got the money, because I wasn't going out there just to go out there. I wasn't really trippin' about playing ball. It was a matter of when I was done with football, I was going to work for myself because I always wanted to do business.

But after my kids' mom passed away from leukemia, I knew I was done playing ball. And I was cool with it because I had already prepared for my life after football. I knew it would involve real estate, but I didn't know exactly what it would be. Every time a piece of property became available, I'd make a purchase. I was focused on business and my kids. I had money. I had a system in place and was bringing in a certain amount of money a year. All I had to do was maintain. Knowing I've got seven figures coming in every year, I can do what I'm doing right now for the rest of my life with no worries.

But then you start getting into a routine. This is not really cutting it for me. I'm too young. I've got all this money, but I have all this energy and I love business. I really can't do too much for people outside of helping them when I can, because they'll run through your money.

I want to be able to help people. I want to be able to employ people. Now that I was home, more people started coming around: "Hey, man, can you give me a job?" People getting out of prison were looking me up for a job.

I don't have a "job." I have money coming in, but that's for me and my family and my close ones. I can help somebody out from time to time, but to actually employ somebody, it just wasn't there.

I was sitting around, not really doing anything. I was finding myself so bored with being retired. All my friends were playing ball and anybody that was my age was working, so I found myself standing on the corner, hanging around the crew that ain't really doing nothing.

The kids are good, I got everything in place. But I needed to do more. I *wanted* to do more. I had all this energy. I had all the time in the world. I needed to be doing something.

I had my real estate, but real estate is slow. Real estate moves at its own pace. A good deal comes along, you jump on it.

I made a decision that I like the nightlife; the service-type atmosphere where people can have fun. I'm a night person. I always wanted to own a gentleman's club. It was a place where we always hung out. It was my style.

I don't know too many athletes that haven't been to a gentleman's club. As an athlete, it's not as much about the girls. It's more of a meeting spot. It turns into the hangout where you say, "We'll meet here." We're not going to meet at Starbucks. We're going to meet at the cool spot. Everybody comes and listens to music. Then you're in Miami. When people think of Miami, they think of fun.

People like to hang out, and they really like to enjoy themselves. That's what it all boils down to. Socializing and kicking it with everyday people, that's what our culture does. You've got some people that can't go to a gentlemen's club because they're too commercial. I have some people say, "Edge, I would love to come by. But you know I can't be seen in there." I say, "Man, I understand." So they've got to sneak in. But they still go. People can say what they want, but people are going to keep going and they're not doing anything wrong.

You're not going to stop men from going to see women. You're not going to stop women from wanting to be in places where men are. People drink when they go to the club. People dance when they go to the club. People want to enjoy themselves. That will never change.

That's what attracted me to this business.

However, the opportunity to buy a club came out of nowhere.

I usually wait on real estate opportunities, but I had to be aggressive with this one. If you know what you're doing, this opportunity was a no-brainer. I ran the club through my channels and hoped everybody approved.

It was a great real estate deal. It was in an area that was going to go through gentrification in a few years, but not everybody saw it. It was prime real estate.

Everybody else that was bidding didn't know the value of the club, because they were just looking at the real estate. They didn't know the value of the business.

I did my homework. I talked to anybody that knew about what I was trying to get into. I went to all the previous people that owned the place, people that paid rent on the property. I had one of those meetings with myself and I said, *Edge, if you want to have something in this world, you have to be aggressive. You can't sit back. Are you ready to take things to another level?*

I'm going to buy the club, but there are certain people that are very important to me. The last person I need to talk to before making a decision is Charles Bennett, my accountant. I value his opinion. If he says, "Edge, don't do it," I won't do it.

Charles got straight to the point.

"Edge, you know we've been doing well. But you deserve a fuck-up. You understand what goes on with this business, but you've got to do it the right way. You know how much money you put into it. But we're not going to put you at risk. If you're going to do it, you've got to get the best attorneys, make sure you're protected."

So I hired one of the best lawyers in Miami. I wanted to make sure I was doing everything right. I could have cut so many corners, but part of my agreement with Charles was that I do everything the right way.

I wanted to learn everything about the business inside and out. I went to every club I knew. I started going to gentlemen's clubs in different cities. I went to Magic City in Atlanta and talked to Magic, the owner. I went to different clubs in Atlanta. I went to every club in Miami. Even the little holes in the wall. White clubs. Black clubs. I went to bartending class.

A few months after I bought the property, I received an offer that was much more than what I paid. It gave me confidence that people were interested and I got with the city of Miami and looked at the future plans. I spent extra money to make sure I'm doing things for the future versus the right now. That was part of the reason I made the deal. I knew things were taking place in the area.

Everything that I learned about real estate over the years kicked in at a crucial time. I felt good that I had a place that I know I can sell for way more than I bought it for.

As an African American who grew up in South Florida, it was important for me to own a gentleman's club in a prominent city like Miami that is frequented by African Americans. Somebody else always owns them.

This was my chance to do it for our culture. I always wanted to be an example. When they talk about gentrification, they talk about rich people moving into urban areas. However, in most cases, it's people running us out. This was my opportunity to make sure that we could call this our own and prevent outsiders from taking it away from us.

Nationwide, if you look at all the clubs and nightclubs—especially in major cities—there are very few African Americans that actually own the dirt. Some of them may own the business, some of them may own the lease, but I'm talking about actually owning the dirt. It was important for me to own the dirt. That's a big deal.

What piece of property out there nationally is Black-owned and frequented by other cultures? You don't really see it that much anymore. But then you ask what type of businesses are frequented by Blacks that are owned by other cultures? Those places will pop up all over the country. There's nothing wrong with that, but we should own some businesses, too.

As a people, history's kind of repeating itself.

We say that we want these things. Certain people are making certain moves. But I don't think enough people are making the proper moves to actually get things done. The information is not being withheld. The opportunities are not being denied.

It's just a matter of figuring it out, understanding, and actually pulling the trigger and doing it.

I want to continue to lead by example. Buy property. Buy things that Black people actually frequent and get us to support them.

For us as a culture, to get respect, it's important to have property that's attractive to others. Or it's that area where we want to come, or we have to come to. We have to go to a lot of different areas to get the things we want and need. That's a fact. If we want to go shopping, we have to go over there. But we don't own anything over there. We should take advantage of those opportunities to own things that other people need and want.

We're supporting everybody, but it seems nobody's supporting us. That needs to change.

It's not anybody else's fault. We have to create that. And, if you look at sports, you're able to see that it's indeed possible.

Clinton Portis once told me he had a chance to buy a club. I said, "No, CP. That's not what's up." He's looking at me like, "You bought a club. Why don't it make sense for me?" I said, "I bought the property that just so happened to have a club on it. The real estate is what I bought. These people are trying to sell you a business. They're not selling you the real estate. You're going to be a tenant. You're going to be forced to run a business and still have to pay a landlord. I bought a piece of real estate. The club is on it."

The real estate is what I bought. Next thing you know, I'm offered three times what I paid. It's very important to own anything. Everything in the world revolves around real estate. If you want to separate classes of people, it's usually through real estate. As far as gentrification, that's about money. It's money coming in, people seeing an opportunity, and then capitalizing off said opportunity. It just so happens that the people that get hurt, or the people who are often forced to move, are the people who don't have money.

Any business should be glad to be able to help people, help a community. I turned that business into a positive thing versus the negative that it was. We cleaned up the area. We made it look better. We've got a spot people can come to. That place is like Cheers: everybody knows your name.

The club business that I have is based upon so many factors. We have a food truck outside. We have a person that comes and washes cars. We have janitors. We have bartenders. We have bouncers. We have security people. They all have an opportunity to make money and help their families. We have so many people that we're able to employ. Girls dancing in the club is just a small part of the equation.

We can talk as much as you want about it, but the core of that business is real estate.

I don't care how anybody tries to spin it. We can tiptoe around it or whatever. The club is the least of my concerns. I mean, if it was a bar, or a concert hall, or a restaurant, I'm in it for the dirt.

I like to beat people to the punch. If there's an elephant in the room, I want to address it. But if I address it the way that it needs to be addressed, I don't have to worry.

One thing that's always been an advantage for me was I never ducked nothing. I'm honest with myself. I don't have to hide that I'm going to the gentlemen's club. I love the environment. I love the freedom. You see guys tiptoe into the club. That's not my style. You've got all this money, and you've got to duck and hide. Everybody has different takes, but mine don't change.

This is where all the fellows are going to be. I've talked to so many young fellows in the NFL right at the club. Guide them. Exchange information.

It's when the person tries to portray something else or you let that person get to you. Nobody's going to get to me. I don't care what it is, I'm always going to find the positive.

FORMER NFL PLAYERS ASSOCIATION MARKETING EXECUTIVE ANGELA MANOLAKAS MET EDGERRIN HIS ROOKIE SEASON

I always remembered him being kind and honest in a different way. Not just the people he was dealing with, but himself. He understood who he was as a man and what his goals were in life. He's really a good person and I don't think people understand that because of the way society views professional athletes. I really feel he was overlooked a good part of his career. He doesn't need other peoples' accolades to define him. He is very comfortable with who he is as a person and as a family man.

When you think about the clubs that he has, you really think about people who are not reputable—the stereotype for that kind of business. With Edgerrin, it's a business. It's not about the type of club it is. It's bringing in money. Those businesses make a lot of money. That's what he was looking for. It's not about people liking him. It's about him providing for his family. The best way he knows how. I have a lot of respect for him.

As women, we have the right to choose how we want to live our lives. If I choose to go and dance at a club and make some money, for whatever the reason is—something like he did with

(Continued on next page)

the NFL; he put his body at risk, they all do—it's my decision. As long as he's providing a safe, working environment for the dancers, and I have to believe that he is, and he's not putting up with shenanigans because that's going to hurt his reputation.

Look at the brilliant business side of EJ and find out a little bit more about the business side of it, not the fact that there are women taking off their clothes.

He's not forcing women to do that. He's offering the opportunity for them to do it.

I used to think differently when I was younger. Now it's like: 'Why not?'

I didn't go to his club when I was in Miami. I don't have any desire to go to clubs like that. But I respect him for doing it. He takes over a business that literally rains money. If anything, I just smile and go: 'Only EJ.'

20

MORE POWER TO THE PLAYERS

Take a person that comes from nothing—like I did—and ask them what they're going to do with their money when they get some. They may say they're going to invest. What are they going to invest in? They don't know. They may say they're going to sign with a financial advisor or an agent to represent them to secure those marketing deals.

And there you go. They're in the same boat as everybody else. They don't know. All they're doing is saying the right thing. This is where it gets confusing, because they have to go to school to learn about this. Ain't no way they're going to give the same energy to school, sports, and finances.

THE Fair Pay to Play Act opens up a whole new horizon for kids at all levels—college, high school, and middle school. The NIL (Name, Image, and Likeness) affects entire families: parents, coaches, teachers, and counselors.

I'm 50/50 about the whole thing.

Main reason: Who's going to truly benefit?

Companies, business owners, and corporate sponsors that sign athletes to marketing deals will benefit because it will increase their profits. Some college athletes will stay in school longer and benefit from marketing opportunities they didn't have before.

But are athletes going to be okay? I can't say I'm sold on that.

Honestly? I'm not sure athletes are going to benefit in the long run. It's not a bad thing, but if used wrong, it could be like water: it could quench your thirst, or it could drown you.

I'm glad that amateur athletes are finally getting the chance to make money. But everybody's not going to get paid. A lot of players aren't going to make money. The ones that do make the real money are the ones that look like they're pro material. A couple of them might steal a few dollars, but you know who has the potential to go pro and who doesn't. Most of the money is going to trickle down to a few players on select teams.

Schools are always going to protect themselves. I'm not so sure about athletes.

Now, I'm not telling athletes don't do it. But understand what you're doing. Understand you need to be financially educated. I don't want to see college kids get taken advantage of, where they agree to do something and sign some papers and now they're dealing with attorneys.

The NIL is confusing to me. I don't know what the rules are. Who's going to educate kids about this stuff? They're already signing marketing deals before taking their first college class.

I understand how money works. I was a first-round draft pick who signed a record rookie contract. I earned millions of dollars, saved all my NFL money, invested wisely and patiently.

How many parents or family members or teachers or coaches can pass that kind of information on to their kids?

Who's helping kids understand the paperwork they're signing? Can the deal they sign extend beyond college? Everybody wants students to get paid, but more structure is needed as to how these deals work. It's a slippery slope.

What about taxes? Tax evasion? Agents? Financial advisors? You're talking about college students and money? All I'm saying is to be careful.

After all, what's the difference between a college junior, a college senior, and a pro rookie? They're all around the same age. I saw rookies mess up their money when I played. If rookies are messing up their money, what do you think a kid fresh out of high school is going to do? They're going to buy stuff with all their new money. They're going to buy cars. Buy houses. Buy things they don't have the money for.

Take a person that comes from nothing—like I did—and ask them what they're going to do with their money when they get some. They may say they're going to invest. What are they going to invest in? They don't know. They may say they're going to sign with a financial advisor or an agent to represent them to secure those marketing deals.

And there you go. They're in the same boat as everybody else. They don't know. All they're doing is saying the right thing. This is where it gets confusing, because they have to go to school to learn about this. Ain't no way they're going to give the same energy to school, sports, and finances.

That's where I think the problem is going to come from: kids who don't have somebody to advise them or govern them. They don't know what they're signing. And for some of these kids, it's going to be the last real money they get.

These kids need people that really have their best interest at heart. People may come around and do all these things that seem wonderful, but to them it's just business.

You're going to see eighteen- and nineteen-year-olds getting money they never got before. Say it's the top football recruit in the country and a big booster wants the kid to go to Ohio State or Michigan. The booster is going to sign the kid to a marketing deal and that's where he's going to school.

And it's all legal.

What about that big-time recruit from a single-parent home? A vulnerable kid whose family doesn't have any money. This school over here is guaranteeing all this money. It may not be the best school for the kid in the long run, but it will help his family now. If a booster goes to his mom and says, "I can get your son a quarter of a million dollars if he signs this marketing deal," what do you think she is going to push him to do?

You're going to have high school and college coaches getting kickbacks from companies to get their player to sign with them. And how about the kid who was a top recruit entering college, but loses his starting job and enters the transfer portal? A business owner whispers in the kid's ear, "Come over to our school. I got you." So the kid transfers based on nothing more than a conversation. It's going to get crazy.

The NCAA messed up by restricting opportunities for student-athletes to work and make money. Now they can potentially make millions. I think the NCAA is going to sit back and say, "We told y'all. Look at this clusterfuck."

I think it's going to ruin some kids for the simple fact that we don't know if signing these marketing deals are going to make them work as hard.

They're going to have distractions. Money comes with distractions.

If they're getting money in college, do they still have that desire to work at their craft? What if they don't become that player and go for the money? Sometimes it's going to be a distraction from actually playing ball. I can even see some kids losing their scholarships over this.

Obviously, if you're in college, somebody saw something in you because you're playing D-I ball. But nothing's better than pro ball. The pros are getting millions. College kids aren't, and won't be, getting money like that. I wouldn't want my child to be so focused on that little money in college that it distracts them from getting the big money in the pros. If you have the potential to go pro, don't let your mind get clouded. Keep your eyes on the prize.

But that can be difficult if you don't have any. As a father and former athlete, I've been looking at it from that standpoint, because I have two sons who play sports at a high level. Kids of former athletes are going to have an instant advantage.

You're going to start seeing father-son marketing duos. Next-generation marketing. Famous athletes being connected to their sons who play sports. LeBron James is a leader for doing everything with his kids. My son's AAU basketball team played against LeBron's son's team. The gym was packed. They had to stop people from coming in.

When you have that boost from a former athlete as a parent, you get two-for-one. You get the connection. My oldest son Eden plays football. He plays running back. What does everybody know me for? Playing football. Playing running back. My son Edgerrin Jr. plays basketball. I'm hooking him up with the right basketball people because of the people I know. That's just the nature of it. Advertising. Let my son play for the Colts one day. Huge. The comparisons start coming, and it's already built in. So is the built-in pressure to play in their famous father's footsteps.

If my boys get to be good enough, we've got the future covered because we're already talking about those unique challenges they face. We constantly talk about financial independence. My kids already have a business mindset. They're in a pretty good situation where if anybody approaches them with a business proposition, they know they have to come to me.

Over time, parents need to look at it from the standpoint of "there's no right way or wrong way to make this work." Look at yourself and look at your kids and ask, "Step by step, what's best for us in our house? How good are my kids?"

Kids whose fathers are former athletes usually have a smoother path when it comes to all the outside dealings and all the outside people that get next to them, because they're not first-generation millionaires or the first one in their family to have money. It's already been figured out for them, and their kids usually follow suit. Peyton Manning. Grant Hill. The Currys. They all had fathers that played in the pros. You don't hear about them getting messed up with the wrong people or somebody taking advantage of their situation because they have parents who were there, or they have people who have been there, done that, who know how the game's played.

From that standpoint, if I ever get superstar kids I'll make sure they're guided on the right path from the beginning. A lot of stuff I had to figure out on my own. For them, it wouldn't be so much figuring out. More like, "Let me make sure the business side is taken care of; you take care of your body and doing the things it takes to be successful." If they have what it takes, you can extend their career in so many aspects because they'll be able to put in more time just working on their craft versus figuring things out and taking care of the family.

I always had a plan for my son if he decided to play football. I made it very clear to him. The day he doesn't listen is the day I quit. I'm only going to do this one time. From youth football, I kept it fun for him. I coached him for a year and went over the basics. When he got into high school, I turned it up. I had a clear agenda. I laid out a schedule for him all the way to college. I didn't allow him to lift weights until a certain time. His high school coach knew about it. I made sure everybody was aware of what I was doing.

Football is a game that comes from within. You can have skills, but you have to want it deep down inside. Football is tough, plain and simple. It's not YMCA ball where everybody participates. It's a real game. You have to take it seriously. What you put into it is what you get out of it. You don't just get fast. You don't just get tough. You don't just get strong. You build upon these things year in and year out. I taught him how to lift weights. I told my son he has to be able to work out by himself because you can't depend on a work out partner. You can't depend on a coach. I told him I didn't have anybody to work out with me when I was his age, so I wasn't going to train him to where he required somebody to work him out. He knows how to do it by himself. I saved all my workouts from all my years of training and brought them out when he was going into tenth grade. He believes everything I told him because he saw his squats go up almost two hundred pounds. A lot of kids want somebody to wait on them hand and foot. I'm not going to do that because you don't make it that way.

Look at the Black athlete's story.

They usually come from a single-parent home. They didn't have this. They didn't have that. They wanted to do this for their mother. It's the same story over and over again.

They have this internal thing that you really can't measure. I look back at myself coming up. I had that same storyline. You've got to look at it from that perspective. You've got to really want it. My son's coming up in a household where it ain't, "I want to do this for my mom." His storyline's different from mine. My son has to find something that's going to drive him. I'm going to give him all the tools, everything that he needs to be successful. But he's going to have to put it together. He's going to have to actually bake this cake. He's got to find the reason why he's doing this.

When it comes to playing running back, I took the mystery out of it for him. That's where the parenting comes in. I can't make him as hungry as I was because I came from nothing. But I can have him better prepared. I can have him more knowledgeable. I can eliminate the false steps. As far as having that dog in you, that fight in you, that's something he has to develop. There's no way you can duplicate it. When it really means something to a person—for me, it was "I don't want to go back to this"—then it truly means something.

It's one thing to have the advantages, but you have to be talented. He's naturally talented. That heart, that determination, running with a purpose. I didn't have an out. I didn't come from a good situation. That's the thing I can't give him.

The thing I've done from the beginning is surround my boys with those kids that were me growing up. I made sure they were surrounded by kids that, it means something to them. It automatically raises your level of play. We're not playing kiddie ball. We're in an inner-city park. I train inner-city kids, and my kids were right in the thick of things. You better be ready to play with these kids because, if you can't, then you don't have a chance. The thing I respect about my boys is I always tell them, "You don't have to do this." That tells me they've got something in them. Their something might be a different something, but they have the will to want and both have that winning mentality. They're not going to lay down. They embrace it. When they run into kids that come from different circumstances, they always stand up and stand out.

Both of my sons wanted to play sports. The basketball player used to play football. He was really good at it. But we shut football down for basketball. Basketball's not a sport you can just pick up and play unless you're physically gifted. You have to put in a lot of work to be a good basketball player. He hasn't missed a day of training. It's like eating to him.

To me, the running back has an easier path than the basketball player because I gave him everything I've got. Plus, he's really good. But I told him there's more to it than just playing football. He's Edgerrin James's son. People are going to test him. They're going to try to hit him in the mouth and see how he responds. I told him he doesn't have to try to be like me: "I'm going to put everything in you to be better than me. That's my goal. That's my job. I'm going to make sure that you have every advantage at an early age. Everything I know, I'm going to make sure that you know."

That's the difference between some players and others. Some of them just know a little earlier and the game comes easier and slows down for them. I make sure my son watches film. When you watch film, you're looking at the game through a different lens, a professional lens: "This is what you look for, this is what's going to happen. Now just play ball." The game is so simple when you look at it from that perspective.

Now imagine knowing this at a young age.

As far as football IQ, he has that. As far as the training, he has that. As far as genetics, he has that, too.

As soon as I saw my son run with the football, I got in touch with (former NFL running back) Fred Taylor and told him, "You've got to teach my son. You've got to talk to him." If he runs like Fred, and Fred can give him tips and I can give him the gritty running back game that I had, he's going to be unstoppable. He runs smooth like Fred T. Fred T is one of the baddest running backs the league has ever seen. He could have been top four all-time if he didn't have injuries, because he was able to hit the big runs. Fred T is one of my favorite backs. He had the total package. He was smooth. He had size. He had speed. I had grit. If I teach my son the gritty part, and he already naturally runs like somebody that has home run speed and he's smooth, that's going to be pretty tough to beat. The gritty part is the hard part. Always falling forward. Getting the yards that weren't there. The forward lean. Using the stiff arm and all those other things to steal a few yards that other runners probably wouldn't have gotten.

FORMER INDIANAPOLIS COLTS RUNNING BACKS COACH GENE HUEY COACHED EDGERRIN'S OLDEST SON LIKE AN NFL PLAYER

I retired from coaching in 2010 after forty-two years. Twenty-three years in college at Ohio State, Nebraska, Arizona State, New Mexico, and Washington. Nineteen years in the NFL, all with the Colts. That was enough for me.

Everything about coaching Edgerrin was a joy. He had power when he needed it. Speed when he had to step away from people. Elusive. Just the overall strength and power that he had. He always had his feet under him, had his legs under him. Tremendous balance.

He knew how to compete. He knew how to be mentally and physically prepared to compete. He does it with his kids. I witnessed it. He asked me to come down to Florida and work with Eden. I was more than happy to do it.

Edgerrin wanted to focus on Eden catching passes. He said, "I want to do five hundred balls a day." I hadn't thrown a football in years. We're down there in Orlando at the place they call The Property. It was so exciting to be there and watch. To see Edgerrin bring those young kids in there starting around eight years old playing football and basketball. On the periphery, you'd see young females with soccer balls. His brother Jeff was working there. Other friends were also working the camp. Edgerrin Jr. was there working on his basketball skills. Edgerrin would bring Eden and work with him on ball exchanges. Everything was seemingly done on sand. Uphill. I thought: What a workout. I sat there quietly watching Edgerrin instruct kids and his own sons and daughters.

I would take Eden after Edgerrin had finished with him in the morning. And then he and I would do ball drills. I threw 250 balls in one practice then another 250 balls later in the day. My

(Continued on next page)

arm is like a rag doll the second day. Edgerrin shortened the length of the drills, but I got through it.

It was a pleasure to work with Eden because he worked hard. He worked hard in the weight room. He'd come out of the weight room and do ball drills. He worked hard the entire time to exhaustion, every day. It was a joy to work with him and teach him some of what I knew and did in drills over the years. He's a nice young talent who will only get better.

When Edgerrin's sitting there talking to his kids and what he expected and what they needed to do to get better, he's not only talking to them, he's talking to the personal trainer and personal coach about what his expectations are. He understands what it takes to reach greatness. He's trying to impart that to his kids and anybody else who will listen.

PART VIII:
HELLO HALL OF FAME

21

NUMBER 336

Peyton and I had worked in the past on trying to come up with supporting voices among the voters. He's always been in Edgerrin's corner. He sent me the letter and I made sure all the voters got it.

I referred to it in my presentation. Everybody who does these presentations, every year you talk to teammates. And, of course, teammates are going to say he's a great player. You're always going to get people endorsing their teammate.

Peyton was different. His voice carries a little more weight.
—Mike Chappell, Pro Football Hall of Fame voter

YOU don't realize how big the Pro Football Hall of Fame is until you actually become a Hall of Famer.

No matter where you go, you're tied to it forever. I'm number 336. There's 190-something living Hall of Famers. You start looking at this fraternity and realize this is a big deal and how tough it is to get here. That's what stands out to me about being a Hall of Famer. It's bigger than you can possibly imagine. It's bigger than you anticipated. This made me so happy because I could feel it.

The reflection part is an ongoing thing. It didn't just happen right then. I just let those things come up and then I think about them. I sit back and think about the work I put in. Dang, I put in some work! You start thinking about all the things you've accomplished. I'm supposed to be here. I know I went through a lot to get here, but that all becomes irrelevant. All of a sudden you get to this special place you've been trying to get to and you've got to backtrack. Myself personally, I'm going to walk my steps and go back to Immokalee and spend a day there and walk where I used to walk. There's old things that I've done, but they're new to myself and the people around me. I want to tell my story and bring up stuff I may have forgotten. It's been twenty-something years, but who remembers twenty years?

Every year before I made the Hall of Fame, I tried to make sure that I protected those close to me. I didn't want them to be disappointed if I didn't get in. I was also protecting myself; I didn't want to have a bad taste in my mouth.

Before I got in, all I heard was, "Man, you're supposed to be in there."

Then, all of a sudden, you realize that you really are in the Hall of Fame.

Before it was like, "Maybe next year."

Now I'm in the Hall of Fame. For real.

The first thing I did when I found out was call my mom and told her," We did it!"

Mom was at our place in Orlando. She laughed. She just burst out.

They've been pulling so hard for me. I have a poker face, you don't know what you're going to get from me. They were really, really happy for me.

I didn't take the easiest route, even with the way I exited the game. I didn't do things the politically correct way. I didn't take people's advice and go on Radio Row the week leading up to Super Bowl LIV in Miami and be in front of everybody.

All I did was stay true to myself. This was before it settled in how big of a deal it really was.

It was just time.

Everything fell in line. When your time comes, your time comes.

In certain Hall of Fame classes, certain players are positioned better than you are, and it just so happens it's in the same year. It wasn't a matter of am I going to get in, but a matter of when.

You see everything taking place to where all signs kind of point to, where if there's any year you have to bet that you're going to get in, this is probably the year.

The year before I was elected, I had a great experience just to actually see my college teammate, Ed Reed, go in. I had a coach Tony Dungy get in. I had my former Colts teammate Marvin Harrison get in. But, with Ed, this was my college teammate getting in. We both went to The U, ended up going to the NFL, and took a similar path to get to the Hall of Fame. Watching him get elected with the 2019 class kind of prepared me for what to expect when I would get in.

A lot of people tried to beef up my chances of getting in the Hall of Fame while I was there supporting Ed. I knew what I was there for. I wasn't up there to politicize for myself. It was only about coming up to support my buddy.

I tried to put everything in perspective. I saw people get in with less credentials than me. You tell yourself that, maybe, they had just been a little more popular.

Then you tell yourself, "If it happens, great. But it's not something that defines me."

You tell yourself that, deep down, you want to be in there because you earned the right to be there.

I'll be honest. It's cool when you see the way the process takes place, the way it shapes up. Then you start to wonder. Is it a numbers thing? If it's not a numbers thing, then what is it?

I couldn't say what's right or what's wrong. I didn't understand the voting process and really don't know how things were gonna go. So, hey, let that work itself out on its own. But when the time comes, I'll be ready. More than ready.

I never entertained things that I couldn't control or things where I couldn't affect the outcome.

I'm a solutions person. You can go cry, whine. Guess what? In time, everybody stops crying, everybody stops whining.

After a while, they're going to run out of people who play running back. There won't be any more names to call. There won't be anybody left to pass me up.

The NFL has gone to a passing game. So you have more value because nobody's going to be getting those 10,000, 11,000 rushing yards no more.

It's the passing game and two running back sets. Eventually, they're going to call my name.

And they did.

I love numbers. They often tell the story. So let's not overanalyze.

Every year there's going to be seven guys going in the Hall, including five modern-day players. Every year, there's going to be a couple first-ballot guys. It's going to go position, position, position. You look for your name on that list. At some point your name is gonna come up.

The other thing that stood out for me is that when you get in a room with famous football players at the induction ceremony, you start seeing how not everyone has been fortunate enough to position themselves financially, for one reason or another.

I think former players should be better compensated for what they gave to the game. I think a lot of the things that they're saying are true. Thankfully, I was able to put myself in a situation where I didn't need financial assistance after my career, but not everyone is as fortunate—especially those that played before my time.

You hear so much of that from some of these conversations.

You're at the highest of the high. You're at the top of the chain when it comes to saying, "I played this game." But you're still in the same position as the player that just got their first contract. That shouldn't be the case.

The Hall of Fame is a meeting spot for a lot of players that were former teammates of the guys being inducted. But even when you sit at the table and have conversations with players, when you talk about needing to change the narrative, the system didn't work or the system failed us, it sits right in front of you, loud and clear, because these aren't young people. They no longer play the game. And the conversations become repetitive because you hear, "If I would have known this . . ." It's like a broken record.

Do I think the NFL, NBA, MLB, and all the major sports leagues should make sure their players are good financially? Yeah, because it protects their future. You're talking about a billion-dollar industry. These people should be taken care of for the rest of their lives. That's how you can make the game so much better. But that's not what you're hearing. Money becomes an issue.

It's heartbreaking when you see a person who was the face of a franchise and an all-time great, and all of a sudden people look down on him. From a business standpoint, it's only smart to make sure we take care of our people so that we're all making money.

But do they have to? No, they don't.

But it goes back to youth. All you know is playing ball. And you never really got a chance to learn things. That's one thing I was thinking about the Hall. A lot of times to be great, you have to put your all into it. And you see some people are not there in the financial aspect maybe because they put too much into becoming great on the field.

The same thing happened when I was in Vegas with a bunch of my football buddies. You should have heard the conversations: "Man, I'm just trying to get my permanent and total disability from the league." Anytime you get around a group of former players, you know what they're going to talk about: "You need to reach out to this guy. He can help you." They're pushing you to this guy that can help you get your total and permanent disability, but you're going to give him a percentage of your money. You can't escape the same thing you were doing from day one. When you enter the league, they push you to somebody. When you exit, they push you to somebody. It doesn't change.

From birth to once you become an athlete, it's the same pattern. You get treated different than everyone else. Once you're no longer an athlete, you've got to go sit in that chair in the hospital, or that doctor's office, and you've got to wait. You didn't have to do that when you were playing. You didn't have to wait. You were seen on the spot. That affects some people—especially those that have things going on in their head. If you played ball a long time, something ain't going to be normal physically. When the guy used to go to the doctor, it was pretty easy. Now, do you know what he has to do to get his insurance? He has to pay for his medical bills, get a receipt, and call the league to get a reimbursement. You have to do that every single time. For thirty years, you've been doing things a certain way. It was easy. Just sign right here. All of a sudden, everything is complicated. For a lot of players, that's a difficult transition.

When I played ball, I took pride in doing all three phases, even though I know you're not going to get as much credit for pass protection. Maybe if I focused on running and receiving, I would actually be better statistically and be higher on the all-time rushing list. In hindsight, I could have put all my energy into being a ballplayer and not focused on positioning myself financially and been a way better ballplayer.

I may not have gotten the credit in the beginning, but when it all comes together, they say, "I want a career like that guy. He's in the Hall of Fame. And he has his money right. And he's taking care of his responsibilities."

When I played football, I was never one of the most popular ones. That was part of my strategy: to stay out of the spotlight. I didn't jump in front of every mic. I didn't go to every interview. I just came to play.

When it comes to the Pro Football Hall of Fame, that's the big stage. The Who's Who. The Big Kahuna. When it came to that moment, there's no way I would have felt good about passing up the opportunity. I couldn't have done that and felt good about myself.

My speech was a reflection of me. It was appropriate.

It was also very special for the simple fact that only my oldest child saw me play, and she was pretty young at the time. This brings it all full circle. My boys might have another level of respect for me now because their dad really did what he said he did. On the highest of the highest level. Now my boys can see I'm not just all talk. They're not just hearing it from me. They're hearing it from people around the country.

REGGIE WAYNE WAS A SOUNDING BOARD FOR EDGERRIN DURING THE HALL OF FAME VOTING PROCESS

I am so excited for EJ.

Every year, I would get a phone call. He would call and throw me an alley-oop about the Hall of Fame. And I'd dunk it.

I would tell him, 'This is your year. You're getting in this year. Let's see who's up. Let's look at the numbers.'

And then all of a sudden, he would block my alley-oop. He would say, 'I don't care about that. It is what it is.'

(Continued on next page)

His biggest thing was, which is now my biggest thing as a Hall of Fame eligible, 'In due time. I'm going to get in eventually.'

He downplayed it. When I say downplayed it, 'Oh, my God. It's okay to get excited at least once in your life.' I told him, 'They can't keep doing this to you. This is your year.'

It was his year because the Super Bowl was in Miami. If you looked back on the last few Super Bowls, it's at least one guy that made the Hall of Fame that had something to do with the last couple Super Bowls. In 2019, it was Champ Bailey. Champ Bailey played at Georgia. That Super Bowl was in Atlanta. The Super Bowl before that was in Minneapolis. The Philadelphia Eagles played the New England Patriots. Brian Dawkins played for the Eagles. He was up for the Hall of Fame and got in. You kind of saw a trend .

I'm like, 'Bro, the Super Bowl is in Miami. It's your time.'

So he makes the Hall of Fame. This is the happiest I've seen him. He changed his profile picture on his Instagram account to the Hall of Fame. The same dude that downplayed it, he got that call. It's like he hit the lottery. Deion Sanders said it best. He said, 'I have a jacket that you can't buy.' That's what EJ is feeling. He's an example of making the Hall of Fame and doing it his way.

Many people had never heard me talk before my Hall of Fame speech. I wanted to make sure that, when I did, it was worth it. I wanted to make sure I delivered my speech the right way.

If I would have gotten in the Hall of Fame earlier, I probably would have had the shortest speech in NFL history. That's what everybody thought about me anyway. I was still in the stay-in-my-own-little-lane, leading-by-example mode, but you start realizing that's not enough. You can lead by example all day, but what example are you leading by? I had to make sure

I was ready. As you grow, you get better at what you do. I'm a better businessman now. I'm a better father now. I'm better at everything right now because life is a natural progression.

On Thursday night, two days before the inductions, they lined up all the inductees at the Hall of Fame Game where our speeches would take place. While I'm standing there with everybody else, I'm saying my speech in my head. It felt like I had been there before. It felt like back when I was playing football and preparing for a game. In my mind, I had already been there. I was ready.

I just wanted to make sure I had some good, strong punchlines and presented it the right way.

I didn't tell everybody else what to do in my speech, but, instead, to do what you feel is real. I wasn't trying to get a certain type of reaction. I wanted to make sure that moment was a reflection of me, and that I could stand by every word. I made sure I memorized the entire thing. I wanted people to hear every word. I said what I meant. It came out just like it was supposed to.

If you only knew how many times I listened to and rehearsed that speech. I don't know if I got to a thousand, but it was pretty close.

People ask why I selected Jim Irsay to be my presenter.

There are certain people you come across throughout your life that are real. From the day that I met this guy, he was always straight up. It just made sense. He was the only person I wanted to be my presenter.

Throughout my time in Indy, he was always legit, always cool. He had my grandma on the sideline in a wheelchair—during the game! He would do things that other people probably wouldn't do. But he would do it effortlessly.

When it was time for me to sign my franchise tag with the Colts, he called and talked to me directly. No beating around the bush. He wasn't trying to pitch me on something. When it was time for us to go our separate ways, when I left to play for Arizona, I was still part of the Colts because that's the team that birthed me.

To this day, our relationship remains the same as it did on day one. You know the term, real recognizes real? It has nothing to do with your upbringing or financial status. It's more like, "This dude is real, down to earth." You can just feel it. I've always felt it.

My biggest concern with my speech was how much time I was going to have. I was more concerned with the time constraints than anything else. When I recorded my speech, it was seven minutes and thirty-two seconds, seven minutes and thirty-four seconds. I wanted to make sure I didn't talk too long.

When I looked out in the crowd, I saw my mom, I saw my family, I saw my boys from The U. I've got my Hurricanes on the stage to my right (Michael Irvin, Ray Lewis, and Warren Sapp). I've got my Hurricanes to my left (Ed Reed). It gave me the confidence to say, "I'm not worried about the time anymore."

At Miami, there used to be this thing in the locker room where the guys made this noise. When you heard that noise, something was about to go down. I haven't seen those guys collectively in years. You would hear it before we had a wrestling match in the locker room or when you were getting ready to go into the game. When I heard them go, "WHAAAATTT . . . WHAAATTT . . . " it all came back to me. It's a feeling that you can't really describe, but you knew anytime you heard that it wasn't just to be making noise. I heard them and I said, "I see y'all."

I don't think anybody should be offended by a speech. My speech wasn't directed to anybody in particular. Or this race or that race. It's about what's real. I consider myself real. And I carry myself real. We need to make sure we're doing real things and standing up for real situations because a lot of things are uncalled for.

I really think a lot of times when we look at things from a social injustice standpoint, it's just a natural reaction. Like the way a white police officer interacts differently with a Black person and a white person. I've seen videos where a white person might take a white policeman's gun and nothing happens to him. When I look at that I say, "That policeman sees himself in that person." When I see white policemen do something like that, it's because they see themselves in people who look like them. When you see yourself that way, it's like, " I can't hurt my people. It would be like hurting myself."

But when white policemen see us, when they see a Black person, some of them see the enemy, or they see what they have been taught about Black people. With us, they react. That's what it comes down to. It's a reaction because this is what some of them were taught.

My speech was a reflection of those things. It was a reflection of, "This is why I am who I am. I'm woke. I'm aware." When it came to this moment, there's no way I would have felt good about passing up the opportunity to help. I think, overall, I was able to stand up there as a proud Black man and didn't offend anybody, but touched everybody.

The response of the crowd told me I was going in the right direction.

Maybe, just maybe, if that guy on the other side sees somebody that looks like myself, maybe now he thinks of me like: "You know what? He might not be what I have been taught." Maybe that could save somebody from addressing things a certain way. A lot of business opportunities have come and will continue to come because I think people have a different perspective of me now since the speech.

Mostly, I think it's because people didn't really know me. The Black community, that's who I relate to. The energy and response from our people was great. No negativity at all. To be able to touch people means more than anything because I'm here with a purpose. I try to make sure I live in my purpose, but not to where I'm a slave to it.

The narrative is being changed because a lot more guys have confidence. A lot more guys are understanding their platform. I think a lot more people are fed up because fair is fair.

When you become an athlete and you get put in a certain category, or a certain position or a certain situation, we get treated a little bit different or somebody may view us a little bit different because of who we are. But what about our families, our brothers, our cousins, our sisters, that aren't getting the same treatment?

We've got to make sure that we become the voice. We've seen that once you've become the voice, it actually serves a purpose. These voices are important. If you don't do it, you're kind of accepting everything that's going on around you.

I think every African American has to take that approach—anytime you have the opportunity. I'll never have this stage again. Nothing I'll ever do will ever give me the stage I have right now. It's not so much using the stage. It's doing what's right for our people. If people in my position remain quiet or act like it doesn't exist, we're not helping.

I'm not one of these guys that goes around bashing people or tearing people apart. But I'm aware. And this is the moment I step up there and say, "This is my take on it. Take it however you want to take it."

When I went to Utah to get my Hall of Fame bust made, I wanted to make sure it was done right. When you're going through that process, you have to sit there for hours. It's a full-day thing. You just sit there. I wanted to make sure they did the best they could with my dreads. When somebody comes to the Hall of Fame, they're going to know it's me. For me, it was important to say, "Those dreads, that's our culture. That's us."

I took pride in the fact I'm the first person in the Pro Football Hall of Fame with dreads. It means a lot to me. You go to the football field, that's all you see—especially in South Florida. All the kids rocking dreads. All the kids being themselves. And now, to actually have that in the Hall of Fame, forever and ever, that's something if people don't understand now, they'll understand later.

A kid from South Florida, with dreads and gold teeth, now forever immortalized in Canton.

PRO FOOTBALL HALL OF FAME VOTER JARRETT BELL COMPARED EDGERRIN'S RUNNING STYLE AND PRODUCTIVITY TO EDGERRIN'S CHILDHOOD HERO, WALTER PAYTON

I've always been a supporter of his. The takeaway from my perspective, in terms of five years versus two years or one year, reflects the competition out there. Everybody can't be a first-ballot Hall of Famer.

I love that part of the process when the voters discuss the finalists, pro or con. Sometimes it gets real heated with certain candidates. Edgerrin didn't really have any controversy that you could say kept him out or delayed him getting in. In his case, it was more or less a matter of who stacked up in each of those individual years.

One of the great things about Edgerrin is he had the knee injury and came back and really got it back on track and kept going.

Even his first two years when he rushed for all those yards, he was never this game-breaking guy. He rushed for 1,500 yards four times, but it wasn't like he was ripping off 80-yard runs like Adrian Peterson.

Edgerrin was probably a lot like Walter Payton when it comes to productivity and style. I've always had a lot of respect for the physicality, what it takes to play the game. In Edgerrin's case, to be injured and come back the way he did was pretty special.

HALL OF FAME SPEECH

August 7, 2021
Canton, Ohio

All praise goes to the Man up top.

This is such a special moment for me, my family, and those close to me.

So many individuals played a part in me joining this exclusive Pro Football Hall of Fame fraternity. I may miss a few names, but if you know, you know!

I wanna thank my Hall of Fame presenter, Mr. Jim Irsay, whom I consider to be a friend. Always been cool, down to earth, and accepted Edge for being Edge.

Standing on this stage, I see many of the faces that have traveled every step of the way with me, on this incredible journey.

To my Momma . . .

We're here . . . No blueprint, no manual, and most importantly, no man.

I'm your man. Ever since you told me I was the man of the house, I took that role seriously. Momma you did the best you could raising your five boys (Bird, Dederrian, Me, Jeff, and GMan). As a matter of fact, you did such a great job raising us, God gave you the assignment two times. When God took Andia, you stepped in without hesitation to help raise our kids and I can't thank you enough.

To my children . . .

You all make me proud to be your Dad. Watching and helping y'all pursue your dreams is a beautiful thing.

QuiQui, my first born, future lawyer, and business partner.

Eyahna, my singer; with such a beautiful voice.

Emani, my plastic surgeon; you're gonna help so many women feel better about themselves.

Miss Deborah . . . Thank you for giving me a beautiful daughter and being the selfless person that you are.

Eden, my running back; keep working hard and blazing your own trail. And always take care of your mother; she did a wonderful job raising you.

Jizzle, my basketball player; keep working hard, kid. It always pays off.

Euro, my youngest, my hero. Keep living the life I wish I could have lived at a young age. Stress free, without a care in the world.

Maine Maine, keep being my main man.

Family is important to me. I come from a big family. I don't wanna leave anybody out. But y'all know how much y'all mean to me. Shout out to all my family in attendance, and those that couldn't make it.

For me, it all started in Immokalee, Florida. I learned the virtues of hard work growing up in Immokalee. Those qualities remain with me today. Immokalee High School is where I made a name for myself in football, and where I became a man at a young age. I realized I could support my family through football. It took hard work, dedication, and sacrifices to achieve my goal. Thank you to my coaches at Immokalee High. Thank you Audrey Moss for giving me that extra push down the stretch to get into the University of Miami.

The U has always been a second home to me. The city of Miami has always showed me nothing but love. Thank you head coach Butch Davis for believing in me and holding that scholarship. Don Soldinger, my position coach, you motivated me to be the best, I was always confident, but it was at the U where I realized how good of a football player I really was. I mean, some of the best football players in the country played at the U . . . shout out to my teammates in attendance.

Also shout out to Dr. Ed, Pierre Rutledge, Gene Mato, Charles Bennett, and the rest of my team behind the scenes. After all these years, we're still rolling.

The Indianapolis Colts made me the fourth pick in the 1999 NFL Draft. I'll always be grateful to fellow Hall of Famer Bill Polian for shocking the world and putting his faith in me. I played on some great teams in Indy. Played with some great teammates. Peyton Manning, we couldn't have been more different as people, but when it came to football, the way we worked, we connected like brothers. Marvin Harrison, every day we'd meet up during special teams period and talk post-football life. Reggie Wayne, my homeboy from the U to the Shoe. Dwight Freeney. Cato June. My O-line. Tarik Glenn. Jeff Saturday. Ryan Diem. Adam Meadows and Marcus Pollard, to name a few.

It was also dope to play for fellow Hall of Famer Tony Dungy. A great coach, but an even better man who related to his players on a personal and professional level. Gene Huey, my Colts running backs coach and personal friend. Always on point and never missed a detail. Shout out to all my Colts teammates and members of the organization in attendance.

I'll always cherish my years with the Colts. I was born and raised in South Florida, so coming to the Midwest was a whole different experience for me. To the city of Indianapolis: Thanks for embracing me. Leaving Indy was tough, but you know me: Edge has always been about his business.

Special thanks to Cardinals owner Michael Bidwill, general manager Rod Graves, and the late Dennis Green. My time in Arizona was short, but sweet. I made enough memories and friendships to last a lifetime. We took the Cardinals to the Super Bowl. I played with some great players, like Hall of Fame quarterback Kurt Warner and future Hall of Famers Larry Fitzgerald and Anquan Boldin. Along with Antrel Rolle, Terrelle Smith, Leonard Pope, Reggie Wells, and so many other talented players.

Throughout my career, I took pride in representing my culture, my people, and keeping it real. And I did it all while doing my job. In the real world, we need to think about these things and protect the people we're supposed to protect. As a running back, I had to block and protect the quarterback. Just imagine if I don't protect him from the pass rush.

In society, we have witnessed a lot of people turning the other cheek. Since we're in the football world, imagine if I turn the other cheek and don't protect my quarterback. I played with two Hall of Famers. And I played against my brothers, people I went to school with. What if I intentionally miss my blocking assignment and one of my boys does damage to my QB? What happens to my team if I don't do my job and protect him? Now think about what happens to our culture, and to our families, when we don't get the protection we're supposed to. It tears us down. It kills our confidence. It divides us.

Do your job. That's what I did. I put my body on the line and protected my quarterback. We have a lot of things going on in this country. It's only right that we keep the light shining on these issues. Just do your job. If everybody did their job, the world would be a better place.

For some reason, I've always had to deal with perception. Perception, though, isn't always reality. It definitely wasn't my reality. People looked at my gold teeth and dreads and were shocked and surprised I'd never been under arrest, or spent time in jail.

So many people told me that you can't have dreads and gold teeth and be accepted in the NFL. But I never listened. I always knew who I was—a great football player, a great father, a proud Black man, a lion, and this was my mane. Which many of those doubters would later discover, once they got to know the real me.

Times have changed. Look around the league, look at some of the young stars. As a matter of fact ... look at my Pro Football Hall of Fame bust, rocking the same dreads they said I shouldn't.

My closing message: Proudly represent the real you. Follow your dreams, aim high, and create the life you want to live.

And to all those who have been judged prematurely—because of their appearance, the way they speak, where they come from, and, in the minds of many, should be locked up in prison . . .

I represent us.

I'm forever immortalized, locked up in the Canton Correctional Institution. Inmate number 336 in the Pro Football Hall of Fame.

My career started with gold teeth and ended with a gold jacket.

ACKNOWLEDGMENTS

When it comes to creating a book, there's a lot of people that take a role to really help make it what it is. I appreciate Edgerrin for opening his life and his home to me, speaking to me about anything and everything so that his story can be portrayed in his voice.

I was fortunate to be able to interview numerous people, including Edge's family, friends, associates, teammates, coaches, and several Hall of Famers. While there were many, to name a few: Peyton Manning, Jim Irsay, Tony Dungy, Bill Polian, Reggie Wayne, Cato June, Jeff Saturday, Dwight Freeney, Gene Huey, Kurt Warner, Anquan Boldin, Larry Fitzgerald, Antrel Rolle, Terrelle Smith, Ricky Williams, Clinton Portis, Santana Moss, Rod Mack, Don Soldinger, Andreu Swasey, Julie James, Ed German, Jeff James, Pierre Rutledge, Charles Bennett, Audrey Moss, Leigh Steinberg, Gene Mato, Robert Bailey, Angela Manolakas, Amp Harris, Mike Chappell, Jarrett Bell, Mike Silver, Vernon Cheek, Luther Campbell, Fred Taylor, plus many, many more. All of your contributions, big and small, are greatly appreciated.

I lovingly acknowledge my mother and father, my wife, Yulanda, and my children, Courtney Rose, Myles, and Langston. You're my inspiration.